Inflation Under Different External Regimes

The case of Uruguay

EDUARDO GIORGI

Edited by ARNE BIGSTEN

Department of Economics
University of Göteborg
Sweden

Avebury

Aldershot · Brookfield USA · Hong Kong · Singapore · Sydney

Published by
Avebury
Gower Publishing Company Limited
Gower House
Croft Road
Aldershot
Hants GU11 3HR
England

Gower Publishing Company
Old Post Road
Brookfield
Vermont 05036
USA

ISBN 1 85628 150 7

Printed and Bound in Great Britain by
Athenaeum Press Ltd., Newcastle upon Tyne.

INFLATION UNDER DIFFERENT EXTERNAL REGIMES

For
Alicia and Geronimo

Contents

Preface

Eduardo Giorgi was in the 1970s forced to leave his native Uruguay. Eventually he came to our department to study economics, which he did very successfully. On choosing a topic for his thesis it was natural for him to relate to his own country and the debate on stabilization policy which had been raging for a long time. After the fall of the military government it became possible for Eduardo to return to Uruguay with his family. There, he continued his work at CIEDUR and presented papers at the annual meetings of Banco Central. I took part in the last one of these in December, 1988. The paper presented there was essentially the final major chapter of his thesis, and we discussed then its final outline and decided that it would be ready to defend in Göteborg during 1989.

I then returned to Sweden, while Eduardo left for a two week holiday. During the first day of his return to work, he got a serious heart attack, which put him into a coma out of which he never woke. I will never forget the shock and grief I felt when I received the news. A finer and gentler man than Eduardo I have never known. After a long period in exile and having overcome serious health problems he had finally been able to settle down to a good life with his wife Alicia and his son Geronimo. Then, suddenly, he was gone. It is an enormous loss to me personally as well as to all his friends here in Sweden, but the blow was of course hardest for Alicia and Geronimo. This book is dedicated to them, and I only hope that they can look forward, while keeping fond memories of Eduardo.

This 'thesis' is the result of the work Eduardo had done within our project 'Macro—Economic Balance Under Different Trade and Foreign Exchange Regimes. The Case of Uruguay' financed by SAREC. I have revised the papers produced by Eduardo and put them together into this monograph. I am thankful for very useful comments from Renato Aguilar, Dick Durevall, Steve Mugerwa, Martin Rama, Boo Sjöö, Clas Wihlborg and other colleagues. Translation into English has been done by Rhoda Ndagire and Pablo M. de Torres Carballal. The final editing of the manuscript has been done by Eva—Lena Neth Johansson.

Finally, I hope that this book will make Alicia and Geronimo even prouder.

Göteborg, 15 November, 1990

Arne Bigsten
Department of Economics
University of Göteborg, Sweden

1 Introduction

1.1 Purpose of the study

The purpose of this study is to analyze the causes of inflation in Uruguay during the period 1956 to 1987. Particular attention will be given to the relationship between inflation and the regimes for external trade and monetary transactions. We compare the system of extensive trade barriers and currency regulations of the 1950s and 1960s with the period of liberalization, of capital and trade flows, of the 1970s and 1980s. We also compare the system of fixed exchange rates with those of the crawling peg and the clean float. Monetarist, structuralist and disequilibrium approaches will be used to formulate empirically testable models and to interpret our data.

1.2 The inflation debate in Latin America

With increases in the rate of inflation in many countries of the region, primarily those which had pursued an import substitution industrialization strategy, among others Brazil, Argentina, Chile, and Uruguay, the inflation debate in Latin America was intensified during the post war years. Inflation often became explosive and chronic, with rates reaching 80–100 per cent after the mid 1950s (Little, 1982). This was different from earlier phases of rapid inflation, which had been short–lived and associated with specific events such as war.

The debate in the 1950s and 1960s could be divided into two basic approaches with regard to the root causes of inflation: the monetarist and the structuralist views. The monetarist view, or that of its predecessor, the excess demand approach, lay behind the stabilization programmes advocated by the IMF, which were applied in several Latin American countries at the end of the 1950s (Chile 1956–58, Argentina 1959–62, Uruguay 1959–62).

Monetarists saw inflation as a purely monetary phenomenon (Friedman, 1968), caused by imbalances in the money market. When money supply increases faster than money demand there is an undesired increase in the cash balances held by the public.

1

This generates an excess demand for goods, which pushes up prices. Adjustment programmes based on this view contain short term measures such as control of money supply and reduction of the budget deficit. These measures are often reinforced by others such as devaluation of the currency, removal of price controls, and the elimination of subsidies.

The structuralist view of inflation (Kirkpatrick and Nixson, 1976; Little, 1982; Thorp, 1970) is associated with the names of many distinguished Latin American economists, such as Olivera, Prebisch and Pinto all at one time working at the Economic Commission for Latin America. For them the basic causes of inflation were of a non—monetary character and were assumed to be deeply embedded in the economic structures of the Latin American countries. These structural features included market segmentation, immobility of factors of production, sectoral imbalances between supply and demand etc. Owing to bottlenecks caused by the distortions, supply tended to lag behind demand in certain key areas of these economies, leading to price increases. Moreover, if prices were inflexible downwards, due, as claimed, to structural factors, relative price changes had to lead to increases in the general price level. Money supply played a passive role in this approach adjusting to conditions created by the structural imbalances.

A third approach to inflation, which is usually presented as an ingredient in the structuralist school, is the income share approach (Thorp, 1970). Here inflation is said to be the result of struggles between different social groups to preserve or increase their shares of national income. Such a conflict can arise from events which disrupt the existing equilibrium or alter expectations about the 'normal' development of incomes, for example a long—lasting stagnation. However, the income share approach is more an explanation of the spread and persistence of inflation than of its original causes.

The debate between monetarists and structuralists was in actual fact not only concerned with the immediate causes of inflation, since the structuralists did not deny the existence of a link between money supply and the price level. The debate was rather concerned with the basic causes of inflation and its economic and political remedies. The main points of the debate can be summarized as follows:

(a) Endogeneity or exogeneity of money supply. While the structuralists argued that money supply adjusts more or less passively to the decisive inflationary pressure deriving from the economic structure, for monetarists, money supply played the decisive role in the process of inflation.

(b) Flexibility of the price structure. For the monetarists the price system is sufficiently flexible to enable changes in relative prices to take place without disturbing the macro economic equilibrium in any significant way. The structuralists viewed the prices as inflexible downwards. Under such conditions every important change in the relative prices affects the general price level and disturbs the macro economic equilibrium.

(c) Orientation of stabilization policy. The monetarists concentrated on short term measures meant to bring about a rapid move towards equilibrium. These were based on the control of money supply and that of aggregate demand. Structuralists argued that such measures could only reduce inflation temporarily, and at the expense of grave disturbances on the real side of the economy. Instead they argued for a gradual stabilization programme, which had as its goal the change of the economic structure in the long run.

The inflation debate in Latin America was revived by the new monetarist stabilization measures of the early 1970s, primarily in the South Cone (Argentina, Chile and Uruguay). The new stabilization policy (Foxley, 1981) had some characteristics, however, which distinguished it from earlier attempts in the 1950s and 1960s. These traits were primarily the following:

a) A more developed theoretical basis, namely the monetary approach to the balance of payments developed during the 1960s and 1970s;

2

b)   Possibilities of instituting stabilization programmes in a more profound and consistent way. The stabilization programmes were often run by military governments, which suppressed all political opposition.

c)   The stabilization policy was pursued within the framework of a more comprehensive and long term programme, which aimed at a general liberalization of the economy.

It was failure of these stabilization attempts at the end of the 1970s, and in the early 1980s, which brought inflation back to centre stage. Old debates were revived along with new contributions. Among these were some inspired by old structuralist ideas, for example neostructuralism (Taylor, 1981, 1983), which emphasized new aspects of the economic structure in LDCs. It was argued that weak or segmented money markets made interest payments a large share of total production outlays. By increasing the interest rate, monetary contraction becomes an important cause of inflation. This meant that the link between money supply and inflation could become the opposite of what is assumed in orthodox theory, at least in the short run.[1]

1.3   The debate on inflation and the external sector in Uruguay

Since the early 1960s, the relationship between the regime for foreign trade, on the one hand, and macro economic balance, on the other, has been at the centre of the debate on economic policy in Uruguay. (Instituto de Economia, 1971a,b). The economic stagnation, which started in the 1950s, was reflected in permanent internal and external macro economic imbalances. Inflation and unemployment increased, while the seemingly permanent trade deficit depleted reserves and increased foreign debt.

Since then, suggestions for the reform of the external sector have taken a prominent place in the search for solutions to the economic crisis. Also here we have two main schools, one neoclassical and the other structuralist, with partly different interpretations of the causes and cures of the economic crisis.

According to the neoclassical view, the external regime was one of the main causes of the stagnation. Protectionism and foreign exchange regulations contributed to both the internal and external imbalances. This school saw the economic stagnation as a direct consequence of the development strategy pursued since the 1930s, that is the import substitution strategy (Anichini et al., 1978). Controls and restrictions of commodity and capital markets were seen as some of the main causes of stagnation and external deficits. Trade restrictions distorted domestic prices, discriminated against exports and protected inefficient home market industries, which were strongly dependent on imported inputs. This pattern of development created bottlenecks and permanent trade deficits. The regulation of currency and capital transactions meant that there was no functioning capital market, and this affected production negatively (Faroppa et al., 1974; Banco Central, 1984).

The main remedy proposed by this school was liberalization of the economy. It was considered essential to liberalize external relationships, for the country to exploit its comparative advantages and benefit from use of international capital markets.

Although the effects of trade restrictions and monopolies on inflation were conceded, inflation was mainly seen as a monetary phenomenon (Faroppa et al., 1974; Banco Central, 1984; Protasi, Graziani, 1984). In a closed economy, inflation may be seen as a direct consequence of the the way the government handles money supply and in particular its budget deficit. In an open economy with a fixed exchange rate, domestic inflation may be seen as a function of the international inflation, but monetary policy still plays an important role. Its effects are now reflected in the balance of payments (Banco Central, 1984).

Unemployment, according to this school, results from the monopolization of the labour market with trade unions setting wages above their equilibrium values. It was thus argued that an incomes policy was necessary to lower wages to their equilibrium levels.

3

The 'structuralist' interpretation of the economic crisis, put less weight on the role of the external regime. Stagnation was seen mainly as a result of the economic structure created by dependent development (Instituto de Economia, 1971a; Astori, 1981; Astori et al., 1982; Macadar,1982). Although the import substitution strategy allowed some growth and diversification of the economy, it could not eliminate the structural constraints on development. Instead production stagnated, unemployment increased as well as the external imbalance. According to this view a liberalization of the economy could not solve the structural problem, but could instead make the economy even more dependent. It was, thus, argued that the economic structure, including external relations, had to be changed.

This school saw inflation as a result of economic stagnation i.e. a result of the struggle between different social groups for income shares in a stagnating economy (Instituto de Economia, 1971a,b; Astori, 1981; Macadar, 1982; Astori et al., 1982; Notaro, 1984). Short term policy measures like variations in money supply, exchange rates etc. are, according to this perspective, only the mechanisms that spread the effects of the structural tensions (Instituto de Economia, 1971a, 1973; Astori, 1981; Notaro, 1984).[2]

1.4 Theoretical framework

In the monetarist or neoclassical approach (see chapters 3 and 4), the basic conception of the economy is that prices are fully flexible and there is a built–in tendency for the economy to regain balance after an internal or external shock.

In a closed economy, the variations in the price level according to this view depend on imbalances in the money market and, with a stable money demand function, on variations in money supply (Friedman, 1970). It is the handling of money supply by the government, and in particular the financing of the government deficit through the Central Bank, which is the cause of inflation.

Cyclical variations in production and unemployment are seen as transitory phenomena, which depend on temporary divergences between expected and actual price changes. The economy tends to full employment, and unemployment thus depends primarily on structural and frictional factors which affect the supply side of the economy (Friedman, 1968, 1970, 1971; Frisch, 1977; Laidler, 1975). In such an economy state interventions tend to be destabilizing, while the market forces tend to move the economy towards equilibrium.

In a pure monetarist model of a small open economy there will be full employment, and prices will be determined by world market prices. In such an economy, with a fixed exchange rate, the relationship between inflation and money supply still holds but the causality is reversed. It is the international inflation which, via variations in foreign reserves, adjust money supply to money demand. That is, the public may adjust money balances through changes in reserves so that the former becomes endogenous and outside the control of the monetary authorities (Dornbusch, 1973; Frenkel and Johnson, 1976; Swoboda, 1976; Frenkel and Mussa, 1985). The handling by the authorities of the monetary variables now affects the external balance.

As a long term model such a framework can also be applied in a less than fully open economy. In the short run, however, the closed economy model may be considered valid. In an economy where free international capital movements are not allowed, the adjustment of the money stock to the international rate of inflation may still be brought about in the long run through the balance of trade (Frenkel and Johnson, 1976; Kenen, 1985).

With a floating exchange rate the money supply again becomes exogenous and the monetary authorities regain control of it, and monetary policy is once again effective.

Structuralist approaches emphasize structural imbalances and factors which hinder market clearance (see chapter 5). With a rigid price system the structural bottlenecks and imbalances in certain economic sectors are long–lasting and affect the macro economic equilibrium.

The Latin American structuralist school has pointed at structural problems that are typical for the Latin American economies, and which create certain long term macro economic imbalances. Among these are the difficulties of adjusting to changes in the world market (Rodriguez, 1981), strong fluctuations in export incomes, and a large and backward traditional agricultural sector coexisting with a modern sector using imported technology, which is not adjusted to domestic conditions (Prebisch, 1961; Pinto, 1963; Rodriguez, 1981).

These structural imbalances are, according to this view, the basic cause of inflation. These factors cause certain relative prices to increase (of imports and agricultural goods), which, with a rigid price system, also implies that the general price level increases (Olivera, 1960; Prebisch, 1961; Pinto, 1963). Sociopolitical factors, like the distributional conflicts, spread these basic impulses.

Another interesting structural model of inflation in a small open economy is the so called Scandinavian model (Edgren et al., 1970; Kierzkowski, 1976; Aukrust, 1977). In this model the economy is divided into two sectors – the tradable and the non–tradable sectors – which are characterized by different rates of productivity increase. With a solidaristic wage policy encompassing both sectors, one could get a domestic rate of inflation which differs from world inflation. The extent of this depends on the relative size of the sectors and the productivity differences.

We will also consider a short term macro economic model, which takes certain structural characteristics of LDCs into account (Taylor, 1981, 1983). With a cost determined price level and with an inflationary process already in motion, one gets a positive relationship between the price level and the nominal rate of interest. With a weak capital market one gets a negative relation between the nominal rate of interest and the supply of funds. The result of these specific conditions is a short term, negative relationship between price level and output. This implies that the short term effects of certain policy measures like contractionary monetary and fiscal policy and devaluation may become stagflationary (Taylor, 1981).

The structuralist approach implies, contrary to the neoclassical monetarist model, macro economic conditions with lasting disequilibrium. In a macro economic model where general excess demand or supply may exist the price response is such that transactions take place under non–market clearing conditions. This implies that: 1) the short side of the market – supply or demand – actually determines the traded quantity, and 2) that agents take account of the fact that their plans may not be fulfilled when they act on other markets. Under these conditions a supply shock, for example a sudden shift in export demand, may have a cumulative effect on output which results in lasting mass unemployment (Barro and Grossman, 1971, 1976; Steigum, 1980).

1.5　　　Method

We analyze the relationship between macro economic equilibrium and external regimes in two dimensions.

Firstly, we deduce, using the different theoretical models discussed above, reduced forms for the rate of inflation and the balance of payments. We then formulate the relationships between these indicators and exogenous variables in an empirically testable form.

Secondly, we investigate how these relationships vary with respect to given external regimes. This is done by estimating the reduced forms which, from theoretical considerations, are deemed valid for periods with different external regimes. In this way one can investigate the extent to which the relationships between internal and external equilibrium and its determinants are altered by changes in the external regime.

Although we mainly use reduced forms in our empirical analysis, simultaneous models are used in some cases to investigate the relations between different indicators of macro economic balance and other relevant variables. This concerns, for example,

5

the simultaneous determination of inflation, balance of payments and exchange rate under certain exchange rate regimes (Blejer and Leiderman, 1981).

For the analysis of the relationship between external regime and economic policy we estimate models for different periods, which are characterized by different external regimes, and compare the qualitative and quantitative effects of different kinds of fiscal and monetary stabilization measures (Dornbusch, 1973, 1980; Taylor, 1981, 1983; Marston, 1985; Kamas, 1986).

Notes

1. See also Notaro (1984).
2. Other analyses of the relationship between eonomic policy and macroeconomic quilibrium which are worth mentioning are Torres (1979), which describes stabilization policies from the mid 1950s to the mid 1970s, and Notaro (1984), which is an analysis of stabilization measures in Uruguay during the last two decades with special emphasis on the effects on relative prices and income distribution. Among empirical studies we would also like to mention the econometric analyses of inflation in Noguez (1979), Protasi and Graziani (1984) and Graziani (1985). Finally, there is an inflation model constructed by the Department of Statistics in Montevideo in 1970. This model was used to simulate the effects of different political alternatives. It considers particularly demand pull and cost push factors.

2 Economic change and economic policy in Uruguay 1955–1987

2.1 Some facts about inflation and economic development 1955–1987

As shown in table 2.1 the rate of inflation in Uruguay was clearly on the increase in the early 1950s. It accelerated at the end of the decade and, even further, during the second half of the 1960s. During the rest of the sample period, it was on average around 60 per cent with large annual variations.

Inflation was not the only sign of the crisis of the Uruguayan economy since the mid 1950s. One can also point at the following problems:

(a) Stagnation of production. As shown in table 2.2 the rate of GDP growth fell to less than one per cent per year during the period 1956–85, after having been as high as 3.5 per cent per year during the period 1946–55.

(b) High and rising unemployment. From the mid 1960s to the mid 1970s unemployment was around 8 per cent (see table 2.3). After this unemployment increased which, irrespective of cyclical variations, brought it to a level of around 13–14 per cent at the end of the period.

(c) Balance of payments disequilibrium (see table 2.4). The deficit in the balance of trade has been a permanent feature since the mid 1950s and was increasing during the period of study. This, together with the extensive capital flight during the latter part of the period, meant that the foreign exchange reserves declined and the country's foreign debt increased rapidly.

(d) Uruguay has had significant budget deficits since the early 1960s and in spite of strong annual fluctuations one can note an increasing trend in the fiscal gap during the 25 years that followed. In the period 1963–69 the budget deficit was around 2 per cent of GDP, in 1970–79 around 2.5 per cent of GDP and 1980–84 around 3.5 per cent of GDP.

(e) The real wages increased during the 1940s, but stagnated during the 1950s and 1960s, and finally fell by about half between the early 1970s and the mid 1980s (see table 2.5).[1]

Table 2.1
Annual growth of the Consumer Price Index (%)

Year	CPI	Year	CPI	Year	CPI
1940–50	5.1	1966	49.4	1978	6.8
1951–55	11.9	1967	136.0	1979	83.1
1956	6.1	1968	66.3	1980	42.8
1957	18.3	1969	14.5	1981	29.4
1958	19.6	1970	21.0	1982	20.5
1959	48.7	1971	35.6	1983	51.5
1960	36.2	1972	94.7	1984	66.1
1961	10.3	1973	77.6	1985	83.0
1962	11.2	1974	107.2	1986	76.4
1963	43.6	1975	66.8	1987	63.5
1964	35.4	1976	40.0		
1965	88.0	1977	57.2		

Sources: Direccion General de Estatisdicas y Censos, Banco Central Del Uruguay, International Financial Statistics, 1989

Table 2.2
Annual growth rate in real GDP (%)

Year	GDP	Year	GDP	Year	GDP
1946–55	3.5	1966	2.5	1977	1.2
1956	1.7	1967	− 4.9	1978	5.3
1957	1.0	1968	1.3	1979	6.2
1958	− 3.6	1969	6.5	1980	6.0
1959	− 2.8	1970	5.0	1981	1.9
1960	3.6	1971	− 0.9	1982	−9.3
1961	3.0	1972	− 3.6	1983	−5.9
1962	− 2.2	1973	0.8	1984	−1.5
1963	− 1.0	1974	3.1	1985	0.3
1964	3.3	1975	4.4	1986	7.5
1965	0.8	1976	4.0	1987	5.9

Sources: Direccion General de Estatisdicas y Censos, Banco Central del Uruguay, International Financial Statistics, 1989

8

Table 2.3
Unemployment (annual percentage averages)

Year	Unempl	Year	Unempl
1965(2nd half)	8.5	1977	11.8
1966	7.4	1978	10.1
1967(1st half)	6.6	1979	8.4
1968(2nd half)	8.4	1980	7.4
1969*	9.0	1981	6.6
1970	7.5	1982	11.9
1971	7.6	1983	15.4
1972(1st half)	7.7	1984	14.0
1973(1st half)	8.9	1985	13.1
1974(2nd half)	8.1	1986	10.7
1975*	10.0	1987	9.3
1976	12.9		

* − estimates

Sources: Direccion General de Estatisdicas y Censos, Banco Central del Uruguay, International Financial Statistics, 1989

Table 2.4
Balance of trade of Uruguay

Year	Million USD	Exp/GDP(%)	Imp/GDP(%)
1956	− 7	15.8	15.3
1957	−117	9.3	17.2
1958	12	17.4	16.0
1959	− 65	12.3	19.7
1960	88	10.7	18.1
1961	− 36	11.1	13.4
1962	− 77	9.0	13.5
1963	− 12	10.8	11.6
1964	− 19	9.1	10.1
1965	40	11.1	8.7
1966	22	12.1	10.7
1967	− 13	9.6	10.3
1968	22	11.3	9.9
1969	3	9.9	9.7
1970	2	9.7	9.6
1971	− 23	7.3	8.1
1972	2	9.2	9.1
1973	37	10.9	9.6
1974	−105	10.1	12.8
1975	−173	10.6	15.4
1976	− 41	14.4	15.5
1977	−122	14.3	17.1
1978	− 71	13.4	14.8
1979	−418	10.8	16.5
1980	−622	10.4	16.6
1981	−426	10.7	14.5
1982	− 87	11.1	12.0
1983	258	19.5	14.7
1984	157	17.8	14.8
1985	201	17.5	13.6
1986	218	17.0	13.6
1987	47	15.9	15.2

Source: IFS, Supplement on Trade, IMF, 1988

Table 2.5
Real wage (Index 1968=100)

Year	Real wage	Year	Real wage
1955	112.8	1972	95.9
1956	116.5	1973	94.3
1957	120.1	1974	93.5
1958	117.0	1975	85.2
1959	106.5	1976	80.2
1960	108.6	1977	70.7
1961	116.4	1978	68.2
1962	121.5	1979	62.6
1963	111.5	1980	62.4
1964	107.0	1981	67.1
1965	100.7	1982	66.8
1966	112.0	1983	53.0
1967	105.2	1984	48.1
1968	100.0	1985	55.7
1969	111.5	1986	63.6
1970	110.0	1987	65.4
1971	115.7		

Note: 1955–62 concerns only the private sector in Montevideo.

Source: Instituto de Economía (Universidad de la República), Banco Central del Uruguay.

With regard to inflation it is impossible to note any specific trend since the acceleration in the late 1960s. There were, however, large fluctuations caused by the different endeavours to stabilize the economy. These attempts were particularly extensive during the period 1968–71, when a general wage and price freeze was instituted, and in the late 1970s a stabilization policy, which aimed at the convergence of the domestic rate of inflation with the international rate, was introduced. It was based on exchange rate pre–announcements.

The development of production shows two clear subperiods. Between 1955 and 1973, there were relatively small and short cyclical fluctuations around the long term trend. Since 1974, there have been longer and more marked cycles, with a long period of relatively rapid economic growth between 1974 and 1981 followed by a strong recession in 1982–85.

A similar pattern can be observed regarding the rate of unemployment. After having been around 8 per cent between 1965 and 1974 it shows large variations. First, there was an increase in 1975–76, followed by a decline in 1977–81 and finally a marked increase to levels around 15 per cent during the recession years 1982–85.

Imbalances in the external payments also indicate a clear change in pattern after the mid 1970s. Between 1955 and 1973 stagnation in exports was the most prominent trait (0.4 per cent annual growth in exports). Between 1974 and 1981 there was a substantial expansion of exports with an annual growth rate of over 20 per cent, but the expansion of imports was even faster. Net foreign debt (gross debt minus foreign exchange reserves) decreased until 1980, whereas it experienced an explosive growth between 1980 and 1985.

The changes described above may be attributed to important shifts in economic policy which took place in the mid 1970s and which implied a transformation from a protected economy with extensive controls of the capital and foreign exchange markets, to a more liberal and open economy.

11

2.2 Economic policy 1955–1987

In this section we will summarize the most important changes in economic policy during the period of study with special reference to measures against inflation.

With regard to economic policy we can distinguish between two main periods, 1955–74 and 1975–87. Within each of these two periods we can differentiate between different subperiods considering among other things, stabilization policy.

2.2.1   1955–74: Crisis of the import substitution strategy

The period from the mid 1950s to the mid 1970s was characterized by a crisis for the traditional inward looking development strategy (Instituto de Economía, 1971a; Astori, 1981; Astori et al., 1982). Although liberalization attempts were already being made during this period, there was no major change in the overall policy. High tariffs and quantitative restrictions on foreign trade as well as comprehensive restrictions on capital and currency markets were in place throughout this period.

Exchange rate policies became the battle field for different interest groups during this period. It was mainly a struggle between exporters on one hand and importers and industrialists producing for the domestic market on the other. The former, who faced falling international prices for their products, desired a higher exchange rate, while this implied higher import costs for the latter. Every devaluation was followed by increases in domestic prices on industrial products and other products using imports as inputs. Eventually the wage earners also demanded higher wages and in the long run the price structure remained practically unchanged.

Between 1955–74, the inflation rate soared reaching a peak of 180 per cent for the twelve month period ending in June 1968, just before the freeze. The official explanation was that it was caused by excessive demand. This was assumed to be caused by very high wages, which affected domestic costs as well as the budget deficit and the expansion of credit to the private sector. The recipe to deal with inflation was to control wages, reduce the budget deficit and pursue a more restrictive credit and monetary policy.

In spite of the attempts that were made to apply such a policy in the late 1950s, the political and social power relations remained a permanent constraint to the accomplishment of a stabilization programme in a monetaristic spirit (Instituto de Economia, 1971a,b; Torres, 1979). It was not until 1968 that systematic efforts to fight inflation were embarked on.

1968–71: The first systematic stabilization attempt. In June 1968 a general price and wage freeze was declared at the same time that a more strict monetary policy was instituted. The freeze was introduced at a time when the government felt that relative prices were at appropriate levels. The level of wages and interest rates was unusually low, while the exchange rate was high.

During the years 1969–70 it was possible to reduce inflation to 20 per cent by the price control measures, but in 1971 inflation started to accelerate again and in 1972 the package collapsed and prices increased by more than 90 per cent. Two factors contributed to this (Instituto de Economía, 1971b; Notaro, 1984). The attempt to keep the exchange rate constant implied that the currency became grossly overvalued, which negatively affected the external balance and together with the existing negative real rate of interest led to extensive capital flight. Moreover, since 1971 was a year of elections, there were political pressures which led to a relaxation in the wage freeze.

1972–74: Transition to a new economic policy. The economic policy measures of 1972 can be viewed as a transition to the policy that was instituted in the mid 1970s and was pursued with some variations into the 1980s. The aim of the policy was to liberalize the economy and to open it to the world market. The primary goal was to change domestic prices in order to improve international competitiveness, which in turn would put a stop to the long term stagnation in production (Astori, 1981; Macadar, 1982; Notaro, 1984). The aim was to reduce real wages and increase profitability in export production and, in particular, labour intensive sectors. Price stability was not a primary goal at this time. Rather inflation became a means — together with wage controls — to bring about the desired change in relative prices. The rate of inflation was particularly high between 1972–74 and real wages fell by 20 per cent.

2.2.2   1975–87: Opening up and liberalization of the economy

1975–78: Export promotion and restructuring of domestic relative prices. In the mid 1970s and after the military government had taken power, the above goals were integrated into a comprehensive economic policy which was consistently applied (Astori, 1981; Astori et al.; 1982, Macadar, 1982; Notaro, 1984). Although the liberalization and opening up of the economy were the primary goals, the government still chose to institute regulations and controls to bring about the desired price conditions.

The liberalization of domestic prices was continued (price controls on most commodities had been retained after 1967 although application was rather lax), but at the same time state control of wages was retained. The quantitative restrictions on foreign trade were abolished in order to bring about a gradual reduction in tariffs. At the same time an export promotion policy was built up to subsidize exports of non–traditional industrial products.

It was in the financial area that liberalization was most successful (Macadar, 1982; Notaro, 1984). Practically all restrictions on international capital movements and currency transactions were abolished. The nominal rate of interest was raised strongly in order to abolish the control of interest rates completely.

In the foreign exchange area a system of two different exchange markets, one for the financial and the other for commercial transactions was retained. In the first market the exchange rate was determined by supply and demand, while the Central Bank acted in the market to reduce short term fluctuations in the rate (managed float). Here the buying and selling of currency was practically free of all controls and restrictions. In the other market a crawling peg system for determining the exchange rate for foreign trade was pursued. The exchange rate was to follow the development of domestic and foreign prices in such a way that the gap between the financial and commercial rate eventually would disappear. In practice, however, this implied that a relatively high exchange rate was retained for commercial transactions.

The exchange rate was considered as a variable that had to follow the development of domestic and international prices. It was not considered to be an autonomous cause of inflation pressure, but was seen as a variable which adjusted to the domestic rate of inflation.

The primary goal of economic policy was to strengthen the price structure. This was considered beneficial to the expansion of production and exports. Price stability per se once again became of secondary importance. The policy was aimed at using inflation as a means to bring about and keep the desired relative price structure.

During the period 1975–78 real wages fell by another 27 per cent, while inflation remained at a relatively high level (53 per cent per year).

1979–82: Stabilization attempts in a liberal spirit. In 1979, a new phase in the economic policy was embarked on. It was characterized by a deepening liberalization of the economy. Price stabilization was now the primary goal for economic policy (Macadar, 1982; Notaro, 1984). The aim of the policy was to make the domestic rate of inflation converge to the international rate.

By end of 1976 a single market for foreign exchange had started, and this was legally adopted in March 1979. The authorities determined the rate. Changes in the exchange rate were periodic and became programmed and announced in advance from the end of 1978. The regime was meant to constitute a transition to a completely

13

fixed exchange rate. Other measures which were to contribute to price stability were an acceleration of the programme to abolish tariff protection and large reduction in the export subsidies. Extensive reduction of the remaining controls on domestic prices was also embarked on. All controls of the interest rate were abolished. The wages continued to be under state control and real wages continued to fall in 1979.

The exchange rate played a different role in the economic policy pursued after 1979. It was no longer considered to be an adjustment variable but a parameter to which all prices should adjust. The most important price in this adjustment process was the interest rate which was to regulate international capital movements and thereby currency reserves and money supply. With free capital movements it was expected that the domestic interest rate would adjust to the international one and domestic inflation to world inflation.

The actual development, however, turned out to be quite different. Free capital movements did not bring about equality between the domestic interest rate and the international rate. The high domestic interest rate caused capital to flow in and the reserves to increase thereby giving rise to increased money supply. However, the domestic rate of inflation diverged increasingly from the rate of depreciation and the currency became overvalued. Falling demand and high interest rates brought investment to a standstill from about 1983. The recession affected the budget deficit by reducing revenues. When the recession was already underway in 1982, capital started to flow out which, together with the large budget deficit, led to a drastic reduction of the foreign exchange reserves. In November 1982, the situation became untenable and reversion was made to the system of floating exchange rates, which still exists today.

The stabilization policy which was pursued during 1979–82 was to depend on a flexibility in prices and interest rates which did not exist. The attempt to bring down inflation during 1981–82 succeeded, but at the expense of large disruptions in the price structure. The financial agents however benefited, but also at the expense of producers and this contributed to a recession which caused the collapse of the whole policy.

1982–87: Transition to a new attempt at export–led development. The period 1983–84 was characterized by a transition from military to civilian rule, the latter taking place in March 1985. As expected there were no drastic changes in policy during the last few years of the dictatorship.

The civilian government, which took power in 1985, continued to pursue the same long term goals of liberalization and export–led development, although the political conditions for the realization of those goals had changed considerably. The previous tripartite committee's determination of wages was resumed. The guidelines applied in 1985–87 contemplate three wage adjustments per year in line with either past, or the past and forecast, inflation plus a certain percentage destined to restore the purchasing power of real wages. Between 1985 and 1987 there was a significant increase in real wages.

2.3 Different external regimes during the period 1955–1987

During the period under study there were substantial changes in the external regime with regard to foreign trade, exchange rates and capital transactions. In general terms, these changes may be described as a shift from a system with extensive controls and restrictions to a system, particularly after 1974, characterized by considerable reductions in trade barriers and practically total liberalization of capital transactions. It was the neoclassical interpretation which inspired the attempts at restructuring the external relationships and the search for macro economic equilibrium (Foxley, 1981). The result of the new economic policy was initially a greater dynamism in production and exports, but from the early 1980s the country became trapped in a deep depression, where the imbalances which had characterized

14

the economy in earlier decades came to the fore with even greater strength. There was high inflation, high unemployment and an enormous increase of the foreign debt. Uruguay had a debt of 5,400 million dollars in June 1987, a figure which was equivalent to 5 years of exports, and an annual debt service of 777 million dollars in 1986. However, the deep economic recession and the change of government in 1985 meant only modest changes in the liberal policy pursued since 1979 (Facultad de Ciencias Económicas y de Administración, 1977; Astori, 1981; Macadar, 1982; Notaro, 1984).

There were many changes in exchange rate policy in the period. Several different regimes for the determination of the exchange rate were tried, especially during the years 1956 to 1972. There were shifts between unified and multiple rates and between floating and fixed rates from the end of the period with multiple fixed rates in 1960 until 1972. From March 1972, a regime with a floating exchange rate was used for financial transactions and a crawling peg was used for commercial transactions. Particularly after 1974 the commercial rate was allowed to adjust to inflation to catch up with the financial rate. Then there was a switch to a unified crawling peg rate, whose changes were later programmed and pre–announced by the government one year in advance. This system was regarded as a transition to a system of fixed rates. Finally in December 1982, there was a switch over to a system of floating rates with occasional interventions in the market by the Central Bank during 1983–85 and more systematic intervention during 1986–87.

With the exception of a short period in the early 1960s, international capital movements were strictly regulated up to 1974. It was not until September 1974 that currency transactions were liberalized and capital could flow in and out of the country without government control.

The traditional system of extensive restrictions of foreign trade remained more or less intact until the mid 1970s. In 1975 all import quotas and quantitative restrictions were abolished, at the same time gradual tariff reductions were started. On the other hand, from 1972 until the end of the 1970s a system of export promotion was in place with subsidies for export of industrial goods and non–traditional agricultural commodities. Finally, after November 1978 there was an acceleration in the process of liberalization of foreign trade with a large reduction of tariffs and industrial subsidies (Anichini et al.; 1977, Astori, 1981; Astori et al., 1982; Macadar, 1982; Notaro, 1984; Sagari, Ramos, 1984).

In summary, the liberalization of the economy which had been advocated by the IMF and other international bodies since the 1950s finally took shape in the mid 1970s. A military government with unlimited power could do away with the system of protection and open up the economy. In 1979 the policy was extended further, but this experiment was followed by a deep recession in 1981. The new civilian government, which took power in 1985, has introduced only small changes to this economic policy

Let us conclude this chapter by listing the characteristics of the different economic policy periods:

1955–74:	The crisis period of import substitution.
	Fixed exchange rate.
	High tariffs, quantitative restrictions on imports.
	Comprehensive restriction on capital and currency markets.
1955–68:	Inconsistent stabilization attempts.
1968–71:	The first systematic stabilization attempt.
	Price and wage freeze, stricter monetary policy.
1972–74:	Transition to a new economic policy.
	Opening up of the economy, changed relative prices.
	More emphasis on international competitiveness
	than on inflation control.
1975–87:	The opening up and liberalization of the economy
1975–78:	Export promotion and restructuring of domestic relative prices.

15

Liberalization of domestic prices, but state wage control.
Abolition of quantitative restrictions on trade, and
introduction of export subsidies for non–traditional exports.
Financial liberalization and free capital movements.
Increased nominal interest rates.
Two markets for foreign currency – a managed float
for financial transactions and a crawling peg for
commodity transactions.
Price stability was of secondary importance.

1979–82: Extended liberalization.
Price stability the primary aim.
A unified exchange rate, programmed, monthly devaluations.
Reduced export subsidies, reduced price control,
and abolishment of interest rate control,
but wage controls remain.

1983–85: Floating currency.
Liberalization and export orientation.

1985–87: Civilian government takes over.
Few changes in policy orientation.

Notes

1. Martin Rama argues that the time series for real wages used in this study is
    not the best one, since it is based on minimum legal increases for many years
    (particularly in the 1970s) instead of actual increases. According to an
    alternative series compiled by him the decline in real wages between 1968 and
    1984 is reduced to about 33 per cent.

3 A monetarist model of inflation with exogenous money supply

3.1   Introduction

In this chapter we shall deal with the monetarist theory of inflation, that is, the dominating theoretical view in mainstream economics. We focus on the basic monetarist model with exogenous money supply. This model was originally developed for a closed economy.

This model is most relevant for the period before 1975, when the extensive controls of foreign trade and international capital movements made it possible to view the Uruguayan economy as a closed one. The liberalization of international trade and financial transactions in the mid 1970s plus the use of a fixed exchange rate implies that a model with endogenous money supply is more suitable for that period. Such a model will be considered in chapter 4.

The endogeneity of money supply, which reverses the chain of causation in the classical monetarist model, has, however, a completely different character than the one suggested in the non–monetarist models, for example the structuralist models, where it is assumed that inflationary pressure is created by structural factors. According to the monetarist view, the endogeneity of money supply is either due to the behaviour of monetary authorities (for example when the government in an inflationary situation, tries to maintain a certain level of real expenditures) or to the integration of the country in question into a large monetary entity (the case of a small, open economy with a fixed exchange rate).

3.2   The monetarist theory of inflation

3.2.1   *Main features of the monetarist approach*

In this section we summarize the most important concepts in the monetarist theory of inflation (see e.g. Friedman, 1970, 1971, 1972; Laidler, 1975; Frisch, 1977; Gordon, 1976, 1981; Santomero, Seater, 1978).

The monetarist approach to inflation is based on a general equilibrium model, where all economic agents are on their notional supply and demand curves. These curves shift in the short run depending on expectations of the agents about the behaviour of the relevant variables. Though these expectations may temporarily diverge from their actual values, they in the long run adjust to the actual values. Long run equilibrium in the monetarist model is defined as 'equality between expected and actual values'. This definition implies that disequilibrium in the monetarist world has nothing to do with quantitative restrictions and the activity of agents off their notional curves, that is activity on effective supply and demand curves. According to the monetarist approach, 'disequilibrium' is a state where the short run supply and demand curves, which are based on incomplete information and erroneous expectations, diverge from the long run curves based on complete information (see Gordon, 1981, p. 504; Santomero, Seater, 1978, p. 524).

Within the general equilibrium model, the quantity theory of money is the cornerstone for the principle of the long term neutrality of money. In the long run, all changes in real income depend on real factors only. The monetary factors, however, are decisive in the determination of nominal income. 'We have regarded the quantity of money plus other variables (including real income itself) that affects k as essentially "all that matters" for the long run determination of nominal income. The price level is the joint outcome of the monetary forces determining the nominal income and the real forces determining real income' (Friedman, 1970, p. 217).

This result — that inflation in the long run depends on the growth of money supply and the growth of real income is not dependent on an absolutely fixed k in the equation $M/P = kY$, but it requires that k is a stable function of different variables which in turn are relatively stable in the long run. In other words, a stable money demand function is necessary.

Although strict proportionality between the growth of the stock of money per produced unit and inflation does not have to exist (because of long term swings in k), growth in the supply of money becomes the main factor in determining the rate of inflation. With a stable money demand function the change in the money stock primarily depends on the development of money supply, which plays the main role in the determination of changes in the price level. Changes in nominal income are divided into changes in the price level, real production and velocity. In the short run, changes in nominal income depend on, among other things, an interest rate inelastic money demand function, and mostly on changes in money supply.

The short run distribution of changes in nominal income between changes in the price level and changes in output depends primarily on the expectations of the economic agents about the development of the price level and the income. Different micro models have been developed to analyse the short run dynamics of changes in the price level and output. For Phelps (1979) and Laidler (1975), the short run changes in output depend on faulty prognoses of price setting firms and employees regarding the demand for their products. These errors are due to confusion between variations in aggregate demand and demand for their own product. Friedman, on the other hand, argues that employers and workers have different views about the real wage level, which leads to short run variations in output. While the employers form their view about the real wage level from the actual rate of inflation, workers base their prognoses on the expected rate of inflation from past history. Changes in the rate of inflation lead to a divergence between their expectations and reality, and result in a short run aggregate supply curve, which is a function of the divergence between the actual rate of inflation and the expectations of the workers, namely

$$y_t = f(\pi_t - \pi_t^*) \qquad (3.1)$$

where y_t is the variation of output around the long term trend, π_t is the actual rate of inflation and π_t^* is the expected rate of inflation.

With endogenous expectations which gradually adjust to the actual values, changes in output caused by changes in money supply become purely temporary. When equilibrium has been restored, the aggregate supply function again becomes a function of a correctly perceived real wage. Unemployment returns to its natural level which only depends on real factors such as frictional unemployment, structural unemployment etc. This level is the natural rate of unemployment (NUR). NUR is the equilibrium unemployment rate with a certain set of real factors and it is consistent with any rate of inflation, if that rate is correctly anticipated. This means that any rate of inflation can be consistent with a steady state and that the long term Phillips curve is vertical. In the long run, the activity level is completely independent of inflation.

The explanation that cyclical output variations are caused by incomplete information on the side of economic agents has important implications for the short term theory of inflation. It is only the monetary surprises which cause variations in output. In other words, only changes in the rate of growth of the money stock can create a divergence between π_t and π_t^* in (3.1), having real effects (the acceleration theorem).

With endogenously formed expectations, changes in the growth of the money stock can only lead to temporary divergences between π_t and π_t^*. Then the changes in output and unemployment are just temporary (the transitority theorem). The only way to bring unemployment permanently below the NUR is by permanently accelerating inflation. It follows that real wages must show an anticyclical pattern.

The acceleration and transitority theorems gives the theoretical basis of the implication of short term fluctuations for the output and price levels, thereby giving important insights into the theory of short term inflation. Another important aspect of the monetary approach to inflation in the short run is the hypothesis about the cyclical pattern of velocity. In the short run, argues Friedman, changes in the nominal income depend on the divergence between the nominal money supply and demand. An increase in the growth of money supply beyond the expected growth in nominal income makes the nominal balances with agents larger than desired thereby causing variations in velocity as the agents try to get rid of these surpluses. Monetary surprises thus cause variations in velocity which strengthen these effects on the output and price level. 'If the rate of change of money exceeds the rate of change of nominal income, so will (it) also exceed the rate of change of money — velocity is increasing in a "boom"; conversely, for a "contraction" or "recession" ...' (Friedman, 1971, p. 332). (The theorem of procyclical variations in velocity).

In the long run, when expectations have adjusted to the actual development and equilibrium prevails, changes in the money stock can only affect the price level. Changes in the the real product now completely depend on real factors which influence the supply side of the economy (The theorem of the neutrality of money and the NUR hypothesis).

Accordingly, the expectations of the agents play a prominent role in the monetarist view of inflation. As mentioned earlier, divergences between the expected and actual values determine the division of changes in the nominal income between output and price level variations. The endogenous character of the expectations formation process explains the transition from short term disequilibrium situations to the long term equilibrium state.

The expectations formation process has two main formulations within the monetarist theory:

a)   Adaptive expectations. In this case expectations are formed through a gradual correction of previous divergences between the expected and actual values. The critique of the adaptive model is that it is an ad hoc mechanism which, except in very special cases, is non–rational. The process through which expectations are formed systematically differs from the process through which the actual values are formed.

19

b)   Rational expectations (Lucas, 1972; Sargent, Wallace, 1973). In this case, it is assumed that agents can learn the process behind the changes in the relevant variables and formulate an unbiased estimator with the available information. This estimator becomes the basis for the formation of expectations, which may not systematically diverge from the actual process.

Rational expectations then implies that the expectations of agents can diverge from the actual process only in so far as it contains stochastic variations. Thus agents cannot be surprised by variations in the money stock and that all conscious economic policy is ineffective in the short run. With the introduction of rational expectations in the simple monetarist model, money becomes neutral even in the short run, and the line of division between short term disequilibrium situations and the long term steady state is eliminated. In this chapter we will concentrate on the case of adaptive expectations.

3.2.2   Friedman's theoretical model

Friedman's ambition was to construct a model that could explain 'a) the short run division of nominal income between prices and output, b) the short run adjustment of nominal income to a change in autonomous variables and c) the transition between this short run situation and a long run equilibrium described essentially by the quantity theory of money' (Friedman, 1970, p. 223). In a later paper Friedman (1971) develops his ideas regarding point (b) above and constructs a model for variations in the nominal income which implies cyclical variations in velocity.

From these papers, we get a monetarist model of inflation directed towards the short run effects of variations with an exogenous money supply. Friedman assumes that the division of the change in nominal income into price and output changes primarily depends on two factors: a) expectations about the price level and b) the level of current production relative to full employment output.

We can summarize the general Friedman model (see Frisch, 1977) with three equations for short term variations in inflation, growth rate of real income and velocity due to variations in money supply. We then get

$$\pi_t = \pi_t^* + \alpha(y_t - y_t^*) + \gamma[\text{Log}X_t - (\text{Log}X_t)^*] \qquad (3.2)$$

$$x_t = x_t^* + (1 - \alpha)(y_t - y_t^*)$$
$$- \gamma[\text{Log}X_t - (\text{Log}X_t)^*] \qquad (3.3)$$

$$y_t = y_t^* + \frac{1}{1 - \beta s}(m_t - y_t^*) \qquad (3.4)$$

where π is the rate of inflation, y the rate of growth in nominal incomes, X real income, X^* full employment real income, x the growth in real income, m the growth of money supply, β the adjustment coefficient of the expected nominal income, and s the relative change in velocity with regard to changes in the nominal interest rate. All expected values (denoted by *) are generated by

$$z_t^* = \beta z_{t-1} + (1 - \beta) z_{t-1}^* \qquad (3.5)$$

Friedman's model shows all the traits we have ascribed to the monetarist view of inflation:
1)   In the long run inflation is determined by the growth of the money stock per produced unit of output. This is due to the fact that velocity is assumed to be

constant or a stable function of the variables which are fairly stable in the long run. This requires, in turn, a stable money demand function.

2) From the short term aggregate supply function we have that divergences from the long term trend of real income (full employment growth) depend on differences between the expected and the actual rate of inflation (the acceleration theorem). When π^* adjusts to π, which is the result of endogenous expectations, we get $x_t = x_t^*$ (the transitority theorem). Finally, if we assume that all firms are in equilibrium (on their notional labour demand curves) we have that the real wage moves counter cyclically, that is to say, it increases in depressions and falls in booms.

3) The theorem of procyclical variations in velocity.

4) The long term neutrality of money and the NUR—hypothesis. In steady state we have that

$$x_t = x_t^* \qquad (3.6)$$

The growth of real income now becomes completely independent of m and depends only on real factors. Money is neutral and in the long run there is no link between inflation and the activity level.

The simple model of inflation which we present in the next section is primarily aimed at investigating the relationship between money supply per produced unit and inflation (point 1), that is, the behaviour of the velocity of money.

The versions of Friedman's model which we will consider in sections 3.3 and 3.4 are primarily meant to investigate the validity of the short term aspects of the monetarist approach (points 2 and 3) under different assumptions concerning the process of expectations formation. The NUR hypothesis is discussed in section 3.5.

3.3 A simple monetarist inflation model with exogenous money supply

3.3.1 *Model presentation*

We begin by presenting a simple empirical monetarist inflation model with exogenous money supply (cfr Fernandez, 1979). The main differences between this model and the Friedman model described above are the following: this model has no explicit mechanisms through which differences between the expected and the actual values of the independent variables affect the dependent variable and it does not differentiate between price and output effects of changes in the value of money (the independent variable is the growth rate in the volume of money per manufactured unit). The model can, however, give us some insights regarding the behaviour of velocity in the long and short runs.

We assume a money demand function which is given by

$$M^d = APXe^{-\gamma_0 r}. \qquad (3.7)$$

The money supply can be considered exogenously determined and is given by

$$M^s = \overline{M}. \qquad (3.8)$$

Equilibrium is assumed to be determined on the money market according to

$$M^s = M^d = M. \qquad (3.9)$$

21

By putting (3.9) in (3.7) we get

$$M = APXe^{-\gamma_0 r} \qquad (3.10)$$

which after logarithmic differentiation gives

$$\frac{d\log M}{dt} = \frac{d\log P}{dt} + \frac{d\log X}{dt} - \gamma_0 \frac{dr}{dt} \qquad (3.11)$$

Using previously introduced notation we may write this as

$$m_t = \pi_t + x_t - \gamma_0(1-L)r_t \qquad (3.12)$$

where L is a lag operator so that $L^n r_t = r_{t-n}$.

The nominal interest rate, r, is assumed to be a function of the real interest rate, ρ, which is assumed to be constant, and of the expected inflations rate, π_t^*. We then have

$$r_t = \rho + \pi_t^* \qquad (3.13)$$

Let us assume that the expected inflation rate is a function of past inflation rates according to

$$\pi_t^* = \gamma_1(L)\pi_t \qquad (3.14)$$

where the function $\gamma_1(L)$ expresses a lag structure.

If we insert (3.14) into (3.13) and assume ρ to be constant we get

$$m_t = \pi_t + x_t - \gamma_0(1-L)\gamma_1(L)\pi_t \qquad (3.15)$$

We denote

$$\gamma_2(L) = \gamma_0(1-L)\gamma_1(L) \qquad (3.16)$$

and insert it in (3.15). This gives us

$$m_t = \pi_t + x_t - \gamma_2(L)\pi_t \qquad (3.17)$$

Rearranging this we get

$$\pi_t = \frac{1}{1 - \gamma_2(L)}(m_t - x_t) \qquad (3.18)$$

In (3.18) we have an empirically testable model. The inflation rate here is a function of the growth rate of money supply per unit of output, and functions within a lag structure, i.e. inflation is determined by both current and earlier values of the money supply's growth rate per manufactured unit. The on average constant velocity

22

during the period studied implies in this model that the coefficients on the $(m-x)$ terms should sum to approximately one.

In this model, we can explicitly introduce changes in velocity. We can, for instance, introduce it as a trend change by letting coefficient A in (3.10) vary with time (multiply with e^{at}). We then get

$$m_t = a + \pi_t + x_t - \gamma_0 (1 - L)r_t \tag{3.19}$$

instead of (3.12). Equation (3.18) now becomes

$$\pi_t = b + \frac{1}{1 - \gamma_2(L)} (m_t - x_t) \tag{3.20}$$

where $b = - \dfrac{a}{1 - \gamma_2(L)}$.

One may interpret the constant b in (3.20) as the trend change in velocity during the surveyed period, if the change in velocity is uncorrelated with $(m-x)$.

We will use models (3.18) and (3.20) to test the relationship between money supply per total output and inflation thereby enabling us to examine the stability in the velocity of money in the long run as well as short run. In the model without a constant term, (3.18), the value of $1/(1-\gamma_2(L))$, that is the sum of parameters of the current and lagged $(m - x)$ variables, is a measure of variations in average velocity during the sample period. If $1/(1-\gamma_2(L))$ is equal to 1, it means that the velocity was on average kept constant during the period; if $1/(1-\gamma_2(L))$ is greater than 1, then the average velocity had increased during the period and the opposite being true for $1/(1-\gamma_2(L))$ less than 1. In model (3.20) the constant term b may be interpreted as the average growth rate of velocity during the period in question, where there is no correlation between between $(m - x)$ and the velocity.

3.3.2   Estimation of the model

In this section, we shall reformulate the previous models into concrete estimatable forms and account for the results of estimations on Uruguayan data for the period $1956 - 85$.

The formulation of concrete estimatable versions of models (3.18) and (3.20) depends on assumptions about the lag structure. Two major variants exist: a) One can assume a specific lag structure, for example a geometrically distributed lag structure, and use those techniques which exist to estimate them. b) One can choose an arbitrary number of lags and empirically investigate their significance.

We did estimate models with different forms of geometrically distributed lag structures (normal geometric lag and geometric lags with the top within certain time limits), but there was no case where we got better results than in the model with an empirically determined number of lagged $(m - x)$ variables. This made us decide to investigate the lag structure of the models empirically.

3.3.2.1   Estimations with annual data. We will here estimate stochastic versions of (3.18) and (3.20), namely

$$\pi_t = b_0 (m_t - x_t) + ... + b_n (m_{t-n} - x_{t-n}) + u_t \tag{3.21}$$

23

$$\pi_t = a + b_0 (m_t - x_t) + \ldots + b_n (m_{t-n} - x_{t-n}) + u_t' \qquad (3.22)$$

with annual data where the number of lagged $(m - x)$ variables varies from 0 to 4. Estimates are for the period $1956 - 85$ and for subperiods $1956 - 74$ and $1975 - 85$, which we have already characterized as periods of a closed and an open economy, respectively.

As our measure of inflation, we use the increase from December to December, in the consumer price index. For money growth per total output, we use the growth rate of M1, alternatively M2, minus the growth rate of GDP [1]. M1 is defined as cash with the public plus private deposits on current account. M2 is defined as cash with the public plus all deposits in commercial banks.

The different variants of the model seemed to be strongly significant [2] (see table 3.1). In practically all cases we got an F—value, which showed that the models were significant at the 5 per cent level [3], even if the F—value for models (3.22) was considerably lower in the period 1975—85.

The relationship between $(m-x)$ and inflation proved significant at the 5 per cent level only during the current year. This is true for practically all the estimated models. No lagged $(m - x)$ variable is significant at that level, and after two lags, the variable was in all cases totally insignificant.

Parameters for the $(m - x)$ variables are not significantly different from 1 at the 5 per cent level in any models for the period $1956 - 74$, but for the subperiods $1975 - 85$ they are. If we compare the results we obtained from version (3.21) as well as (3.22) of our model, we detect important differences between estimations for periods $1956 - 74$ and $1975 - 85$.

We get the following results for the period 1956—74:

a)   The intercept in model (3.22) is never significantly different from 0 at the 10 per cent level.

b)   The sum of the parameters for $(m - x)$ variables in model (3.21) is not influenced by the introduction of an intercept.

c)   The sum in (3.21) as well as (3.22) is insignificantly different from 1 at the 5 per cent level.

For the period $(1975 - 85)$ we have that:

a)   The intercept in model (3.22) is always positive and significantly different from 0 at the 10 per cent level.

b)   The sum of the parameters for $(m - x)$ variables in model (3.22) is significantly less than 1 at the 5 per cent level.

c)   In model (3.21) the sum is not significantly different from 1.

We found that in both models (3.21) and (3.22), and above all, during the current year, that the relationship between the volume of money per unit of output and inflation is significant, although less marked in the last sub—period.

The long term relationship between $(m - x)$ and π appears stable during the entire sample period, which implies that the velocity has been constant in the long run.

The short term relationship between $(m - x)$ and π is also stable during the first subperiod. No systematic short term disturbances in the relationship between the volume of money per manufactured unit and inflation is visible before 1975.

After the mid 1970's, we instead find that this relationship is disturbed by short term movements in the velocity. This is especially notable for M2 and implies a weakened relationship between $(m - x)$ and π in model (3.21).

As we shall see in the next section, this phenomenon goes hand in hand with changes in economic policy which took place in the mid 1970's implying a liberalization of capital and currency markets. The public could then vary the money supply via changes in the international reserves. With a system where the exchange rate is not automatically adjusted to short term variations in the inflation rate ('dirty float' or 'crawling peg') the public can change the reserves when their inflation expectations change. Under these circumstances inflation affects money supply and this becomes endogenously determined, at least in the short run.

Table 3.1
Simple model. Estimations with annual data

Period	Depend. var.	Constant	Independent variables $(m2_t-x_t)$	$(m2_{-1}-x_{-1})$	$(m2_{-2}-x_{-2})$	$(m2_{-3}-x_{-3})$	F	R^2	DW
1956-85	π_t		1.0277 (14.302)				204.552	0.8758	1.883
1959-85	π_t		1.0609 (6.220)	0.0901 (0.405)	0.2428 (-1.102)	0.1099 (0.602)	43.369	0.8829	1.771
1956-85	π_t	9.2876 (1.211)	0.8782 (6.159)				37.928	0.5753	1.896
1959-85	π_t	23.4534 (1.945)	0.8827 (4.763)	0.0262 (0.123)	-0.2915 (-1.390)	-0.0302 (-0.162)	7.621	0.5808	2.004
1956-74	π_t		1.2317 (13.046)				170.186	0.9044	2.442
1959-74	π_t		1.3705 (6.382)	0.1544 (0.635)	-0.4267 (-1.657)	0.0862 (0.367)	37.173	0.9253	2.530
1956-74	π_t	-0.9420 (-0.110)	1.2488 (6.827)				46.610	0.7327	2.460
1959-74	π_t	4.3058 (0.301)	1.3357 (5.309)	0.1362 (0.524)	-0.4404 (-1.620)	0.0609 (0.236)	8.421	0.7538	2.556
1975-85	π_t		0.8426 (10.221)				104.467	0.9126	1.885
1975-85	π_t		0.8047 (2.971)	-0.0252 (-0.057)	-0.1080 (-0.260)	0.1838 (0.675)	20.102	0.9199	2.153
1975-85	π_t	22.9125 (1.990)	0.5169 (2.889)				8.346	0.4812	2.158
1975-85*	π_t	56.7866 (7.938)	0.4635 (4.975)	-0.1330 (-0.986)	-0.1765 (-1.282)	-0.2214 (-2.124)	24.641	0.9610	

* Yule-Walker's estimator with $\rho = 2$.

Table 3.2
Simple model. Estimations with quarterly data

Period	Depend. var.	Const.	$(m2_t-x_t)$	$(m2_{-1}-x_{-1})$	$(m2_{-2}-x_{-2})$	$(m2_{-3}-x_{-3})$	$(m2_{-4}-x_{-4})$	$(m2_{-5}-x_{-5})$	$(m2_{-6}-x_{-6})$	$(m2_{-7}-x_{-7})$	F	R^2	DW
II/75-IV/85*	π_t		0.2305 (2.180)	0.1943 (1.980)	0.2356 (2.385)	0.2199 (1.884)				0.1357 (1.200)	41.872	0.8808	
II/76-IV/85*	π_t		0.2393 (2.347)	0.1975 (1.828)	0.3010 (2.801)	0.2034 (1.736)	-0.1459 (-1.256)	0.0391 (0.327)	-0.0708 (-0.595)		33.713	0.9284	
II/75-IV/85*	π_t	4.5670 (1.741)	0.1876 (1.605)	0.1142 (0.991)	0.1314 (1.135)	0.1074 (0.834)					2.483	0.3110	
II/76-IV/85	π_t	8.0447 (3.836)	0.2461 (2.258)	0.1344 (1.236)	0.2325 (2.114)	0.1424 (1.176)	-0.2209 (-1.796)	-0.0287 (-0.229)	-0.1711 (-1.381)	-0.0687 (-0.569)	3.040	0.4739	1.266
II/75-IV/82	π_t		0.1728 (1.348)	0.1548 (1.141)	0.2570 (1.917)	0.1885 (1.490)					40.312	0.8704	1.262
II/76-IV/82*	π_t		0.1849 (1.595)	0.1141 (1.003)	0.3308 (2.763)	0.1703 (1.396)	-0.1193 (-0.867)	0.0006 (0.005)	0.0116 (0.099)	0.1015 (0.823)	24.671	0.9463	
II/75-IV/82	π_t	2.1987 (0.969)	0.1330 (0.987)	0.1226 (0.876)	0.2200 (1.575)	0.1400 (1.027)					3.224	0.3593	1.323
II/76-IV/82*	π_t	6.4456 (1.437)	0.1418 (1.170)	0.0936 (0.845)	0.3285 (2.788)	0.1789 (1.470)	-0.1627 (-1.158)	-0.1052 (-0.752)	-0.1291 (-0.863)	-0.0127 (-0.088)	3.405	0.7237	
I/83-IV/85	π_t		0.3831 (1.687)	0.3043 (1.578)	0.1724 (0.864)	0.4304 (1.288)					26.679	0.9303	1.527
I/83-IV/85	π_t		0.1871 (0.512)	0.1891 (0.595)	-0.0952 (-0.298)	0.4111 (1.117)	-0.0464 (-0.126)	0.2179 (0.551)	0.2171 (0.520)	0.5797 (1.329)	12.112	0.9604	1.522
I/83-IV/85	π_t	7.9900 (1.768)	0.3322 (1.629)	0.1364 (0.696)	0.0407 (0.212)	-0.0017 (-0.004)					1.002	0.3641	2.007
I/83-IV/85	π_t	9.1526 (2.595)	0.0685 (0.287)	-0.0580 (-0.258)	-0.2968 (-1.355)	-0.0077 (-0.257)	-0.0257 (-0.109)	0.3236 (1.261)	0.2879 (1.070)	0.6341 (2.262)	1.952	0.8388	2.337

Table 3.2 (continued)

			$(m3_t-x_t)$	$(m3_{-1}-x_{-1})$	$(m3_{-2}-x_{-2})$	$(m3_{-3}-x_{-3})$	$(m3_{-4}-x_{-4})$	$(m3_{-5}-x_{-5})$	$(m3_{-6}-x_{-6})$	$(m3_{-7}-x_{-7})$			
II/75-IV/85*	π_t		0.1824 (3.254)	0.3186 (5.770)	0.1340 (2.419)	0.1314 (2.336)					61.874	0.9161	
II/76-IV/85*	π_t		0.2273 (3.498)	0.3771 (5.066)	0.1775 (2.699)	0.1360 (2.621)	0.0007 (0.014)	-0.0243 (-0.374)	-0.0876 (-1.178)	0.0062 (0.093)	49.296	0.9499	
II/75-IV/85*	π_t	-2.4395 (-0.679)	0.2175 (2.859)	0.3592 (4.395)	0.1744 (2.135)	0.1663 (2.175)					5.591	0.5041	
II/76-IV/85*	π_t	-3.1151 (-0.438)	0.2409 (3.312)	0.4018 (4.265)	0.2086 (2.134)	0.1742 (1.708)	0.0392 (0.381)	0.0067 (0.069)	-0.0643 (-0.693)	0.0193 (0.259)	4.996	0.6665	
II/75-IV/82*	π_t		0.2440 (2.370)	0.1922 (1.371)	0.0471 (0.330)	0.1757 (1.194)					30.601	0.8390	
II/76-IV/82*	π_t		0.2867 (4.324)	0.2151 (2.180)	0.1426 (1.297)	0.1929 (1.934)	0.2778 (2.896)	0.2032 (1.906)	-0.3627 (-3.384)	-0.2601 (-2.517)	53.288	0.9744	
II/75-IV/82	π_t	-6.7550 (-1.613)	0.2855 (2.348)	0.3131 (1.955)	0.1788 (1.098)	0.3407 (1.797)					4.194	0.4217	1.246
II/76-IV/82*	π_t	-7.2329 (-1.128)	0.3136 (3.695)	0.3144 (2.543)	0.2196 (1.717)	0.2473 (2.010)	0.3372 (2.603)	0.2449 (1.730)	-0.2963 (-2.065)	-0.1842 (-1.384)	6.338	0.8298	
I/83-IV/85	π_t		0.3190 (6.289)	0.3644 (9.992)	0.1844 (5.070)	0.1558 (4.102)					154.190	0.9872	2.451
I/83-IV/85	π_t		0.2954 (2.669)	0.3238 (5.062)	0.1318 (2.370)	0.1486 (3.379)	0.0094 (0.198)	-0.0052 (-0.069)	0.0410 (0.611)	0.0900 (1.435)	60.321	0.9918	2.370
I/83-IV/85	π_t	1.0355 (0.377)	0.2926 (3.313)	0.3477 (5.905)	0.1667 (2.751)	0.1413 (2.541)					8.823	0.8345	2.409
I/83-IV/85	π_t	2.8886 (0.329)	0.2785 (2.054)	0.2989 (2.847)	0.0981 (0.816)	0.1081 (0.811)	-0.0313 (-0.232)	-0.0356 (-0.283)	0.0176 (0.170)	0.0071 (0.948)	3.209	0.8954	2.458

* Yule–Walker's estimator with $\rho = 2$.

27

In order to study the short term relationship between the volume of money per unit of output and inflation after the beginning of 1975, we shall employ quarterly models in the next section.

3.3.2.2   *Estimations with quarterly data.* For the estimation of quarterly models, we use data which we seasonally adjust using moving averages. We estimate models (3.21) and (3.22) with three to seven lagged (m − x) variables.

Given that during the time after the mid 1970's, it became more and more common to use the dollar as a means of payment and store of value in Uruguay, we employ a third measure of money, namely M3. This is defined as M2 plus public borrowing of foreign exchange in commercial banks.

We carried out estimations for the entire period, I/1976 − IV/1985, and for two subperiods, i.e. 1/1976 − IV/1982 [4] and I/1983 − IV/1985. This periodization is motivated by changes in exchange rate policy which led to a change–over from the 'crawling peg' system to floating exchange rates in November 1982 [5].

Model (3.21) was significant in all cases and can explain a lot of the variation in the price level during all the periods. As a rule this is also true for (3.22), except in the second subperiod, where M1 and M2 models showed F–values which were not significant at the 5 per cent level. In general, M1 and M3 models had higher F– and R^2–values than M2 models.

As far as M1– and M2–models are concerned the estimations with quarterly data give us that as a rule [6]:

a)   The intercept in model (3.22) is positive and significant at a 10 per cent level.

b)   The sum of the parameters for (m − x) variables in model (3.22) are significantly different from 1 at a 5 per cent level.

c)   The sum is not significantly different from 1 at the same level in model (3.21).

This is precisely the same pattern we got in estimations with annual data for the same period and imply a stable long run velocity, while in the short run, it varied and was negatively correlated with money growth.

These conditions also exist in estimations for subperiod I/1976 − IV/1982, but only for M2 models. In period I/1983 − IV/1985 we get the pattern once more in both M1 and M2 models.

Estimations of M3 models give us a different picture. For all periods, we see that:

a)   The intercept is insignificant at the 5 per cent level in model (3.22).

b)   The parameter sum for (m − x) variables is in most cases not significantly different from 1 whether in (3.21) or (3.22) models.

This implies that the negative correlation of variations in the volume of money and velocity, which exists for M1 and M2 during the period after 1975, is not as marked as for M3 which shows a more stable short term relationship to inflation than the other money aggregates.

3.3.2.3   *An explanation to the short term relationship between the growth of the volume of money and velocity after 1975.* An explanation of the situation which existed after the mid 1970's concerning the relationship between variations in money growth   and velocity go hand in hand with the political economic measures which were taken at that time. As we have already seen, these implied a liberalization of the international capital movements and of all types of exchange transactions. These new circumstances, together with the imposition of an exchange regime which did not automatically allow the adjustment of the exchange rate to changes in the public's demand for nominal balances, led to a situation where the public was unable to influence the supply of money through changes in reserves, according to their expectations about inflation.

During the period 1975–78, when a 'managed float' existed in the exchange market, the authorities seem to have kept control over money supply in the long run. But after the central bank interfered in the exchange market to stabilize the short term variations in the exchange rate, money supply became endogenous in the short run.

Between 1979 – 82, the exchange rate policy changed to a 'crawling peg' system with a devaluation programme which was fixed and known in advance. Under such conditions, the authorities' control of the volume of money was limited, even in the long run.

That money supply became endogenous does not mean that the relationship between the volume of money and inflation becomes more unstable in the short run. In order for a situation like that we find in Uruguay after the mid 1970's with a marked anti–cyclical variation in velocity to arise one needs other factors, i.e.

a) that the change in reserves in the face of the authorities' changes in internal credit is strong enough to further counterbalance the latter's effects on money supply.

b) that the monetary authorities' changes of domestic credit, e.g. financing of the budget deficit in the Central Bank, and its effects on inflation expectations, also makes the public change the velocity of money.

c) that foreign exchange becomes a common means of payment and store of value in the economy and that the public also reacts to changed inflation expectations by moving the bank assets between local and foreign currency.

With conditions a and b or a and c fulfilled, we can get a negative relationship between the growth of the volume of money and velocity as the one we found after 1975.

During the period 1975 – 79, there existed nearly total freedom in the exchange transactions while the exchange rate policy was characterized, as already mentioned, by the 'crawling peg' system for commercial currency transactions and 'dirty float' for financial transactions. Under such conditions, we know that variations in the Central Bank's credit to the public sector have a significant effect on the inflation expectations of the public. These are increased when credit increases over the 'normal' rate and decrease in the opposite case. If the velocity varies in relation to inflation expectations, and thereby with the Central Bank's financing of the budget, we have a double effect of the increased credit to the public sector. On the one hand, the revised inflation prognoses of the public means that people change the reserves and on the other hand, that velocity changes.

If a reduction of reserves caused by an increase of the Central Bank's budget financing is greater than this, the money supply is reduced with the increase of internal credit and vice versa. If, at the same time, the velocity is positively correlated with variations in the Central Bank's credit to the public sector, we have a negative short run relationship between money growth and velocity. This results in a positive but less than proportional, or, even a negative relationship between inflation and the volume of money per unit of output. The case in Uruguay seems to be the former.

A similar result is obtained in a situation where foreign exchange is used as money. Then M3, which includes that foreign exchange loans, will vary less than the local money aggregates of M1 and M2. If M3 is the relevant money aggregate, the inflation rate is determined by it and we then get a situation where the growth rate in M3 does not show any systematic relationship to the velocity, while M1 and M2 are negatively correlated with it. Such a situation can, among other things, give rise to a negative relationship between M1 and M2 growth rates and inflation. This takes place if it is mainly by shifting deposits between local and foreign exchange that the agents react to changed inflation expectations and the bank systems reserves change less than domestic credit. If, instead, agents behaviour implies a significant change in the bank systems reserves so that they vary more than internal credit, we get a positive but less than proportional relationship between M1 or M2 growth rates and inflation. The last appears to be the case in Uruguay after the mid 1970's.

That this mechanism has been in function after the mid 1970's is indicated by the estimation results we accounted for above, where M3 shows a more stable short term relationship to inflation than the other money aggregates.

During 1979, there was a change over to totally fixed exchange rates. There was one market for all types of transactions, the exchange rate fixed by the authorities. Changes in the exchange rate would be periodical and were announced a year in advance, the devaluation rate was to be held below the inflation rate and to be reduced. Under such a regime, the mechanism which we described above should be weakened to the extent a pre–announced exchange rate would increase the confidence of the agents in the future value of the local currency. This actually seems to have been the case during the years 1979 − 80, but already in 1981, the situation had begun to change.

In addition to the increasing difficulties in the trade balance due to the high exchange rate and an approaching recession, there was growing suspicion of the officially fixed exchange rate. The same anti–cyclical movements in the circulation rate which we found after 1975, for M2, appear once more during 1981. Every increase of the Central Bank's credit to the public sector was met once again by greater decreases in the international reserves. These experienced, especially under 1982, an enormous decline.

In November 1982, when the situation was getting out of hand, there was a change over to floating exchange rates (clean float). However, the distrust of the Peso was so strong that the negative relationship between the budget deficit and the reserves continued, in spite of the new policy. The increase in the exchange rate did not stop right away the general demand for the dollar, as inflation expectations increased. The negative relationship between M1 and M2 growth rates and their velocity continued throughout the period 1983 − 85. During this period, we also find that the average velocity accelerates for M1 and, especially, for M2.

That the short term relationship between inflation and M1 is disturbed only after 1981 is entirely in line with the above argument. It is only after a critical situation like the one that existed at the beginning of the 1980's that the public change their most liquid assets, that is the cash in hand and the check accounts to foreign exchange.

3.3.2.4   *Some general conclusions.* Our analyses with both annual and quarterly data show that our simple model is useful in the explanation of inflationary phenomena during the survey period. This is true for both M1 and M2 models. As a rule, the models showed an F–value which was significant at the 5 per cent level.

The relationship between these variables seemed very significant during the current year, but weaker for earlier values of the rate of money growth. This situation is especially prominent in the period before 1975.

The results can, however, not be taken as a proof that inflation is caused by money growth. One must be cautious when interpreting correlation as a causal connection between these two variables. Especially concerning the period after the mid 1970's our observations in this chapter strengthen the theoretical presumption that money supply is, at least in the short run, endogenous during the period.

As mentioned, the model gives a significant explanation of the long term relationship between $(m − x)$ and π. This relationship seemed very stable in the long run during the survey period. The velocity for M1 and M2 does not seem to have had any systematic long term variations, either during the entire period 1956–85 or when analyzed by subperiods, except probably for the period after 1982, when an acceleration seems to have taken place.

The model also shows a good ability to describe the relationship between $(m − x)$ and π in the short term, even if this is less obvious after 1975, especially for M2. Considering this short term relationship, two different periods can be distinguished according to our results. Before 1975, it is the short term relationship between $(m − x)$ and π which is stable and no systematic relationship between the growth of money and the velocity exists, neither for M1 or M2.

After the beginning of 1975, however, there are clear signs of a negative relationship between the growth rate of these money aggregates and the velocity, which weakened the short term relationship between money growth per unit of output and inflation. This is especially so for M2 during the entire period after 1975 and for

30

M1 after the beginning of the 1980's.

As we saw above, these conditions went hand in hand with the economic and political changes which took place in the mid 1970's and in particular with the critical economic situation which existed at the beginning of the 1980's.

That one gets a more stable short term relationship between M3 and inflation than between M1 or M2 and inflation during 1975–85 implies that the money aggregate which includes borrowing in foreign exchange, provides a better definition of the volume of money during the period, at least for short term analysis.

3.4 An empirically testable version of Friedman's model

3.4.1 *Derivation of the model*

The purpose of this section is to derive a testable version of Friedman's inflation model (see section 3.2.2), which explicitly contains the most important theoretical features in the monetarist view of inflation. Such a model should allow us to test the distribution in the short run, of the effects of variations in the growth rate of the volume of money on inflation, output and velocity.

To derive a testable version of Friedman's model implies that one has to make some assumptions about the process of expectations formation. In this section we assume that expectations are adaptive in accordance with Friedman's original model.

To derive a testable, reduced form for inflation we start from the system:

$$\pi_t = \pi_t^* + \alpha(y_t - y_t^*) + \gamma[\text{LogX}_t - (\text{LogX}_t)^*] \tag{3.23}$$

$$y_t = y_t^* + \frac{1}{1 - \beta s}(m_t - y_t^*) \tag{3.24}$$

$$\pi_t^* = \beta\pi_{t-1} + (1-\beta)\pi_{t-1}^* \tag{3.25}$$

$$y_t^* = \beta y_{t-1} + (1-\beta)y_{t-1}^* \tag{3.26}$$

From the system (3.23–3.26) we can derive the reduced form

$$\pi_t = \delta_0 m_t - \delta_1 m_{t-1} + \delta_2 m_{t-2} - \delta_3 y_{t-1} + \delta_4 y_{t-2} + \delta_5[\text{LogX}_t - (\text{LogX}_t)^*]$$
$$- \delta_6[\text{LogX}_{t-1} - (\text{LogX}_{t-1})^*] + \pi_{t-1}. \tag{3.27}$$

In this equation the parameters are defined as follows:

$$\delta_0 = \frac{1}{1 - \beta s} \gtrless 0 \tag{3.28}$$

$$\delta_1 = \frac{\alpha(1-\beta)}{(1-\beta s)}(1 + \frac{1}{\beta s}) \gtrless 0 \tag{3.29}$$

$$\delta_2 = \frac{\alpha(1 - \beta)(1 - \beta)}{(1 - \beta s)\beta s} \gtrless 0 \tag{3.30}$$

Given that α and β are assumed to lie between 0 and 1, δ_0, δ_1 and δ_2 are positive if $0 < s < 1$. This is an assumption by Friedman (Friedman, 1971, p. 332) who makes it a condition for the dynamic stability of the system. Furthermore, $\delta_1 > \delta_2$ under that assumption. We see that δ_0 positively depends on α, β and s, while both δ_1 and δ_2 positively depend on α.

From (3.27) we also see that

$$\delta_3 = \frac{\alpha\beta}{1 - \beta s} - \frac{\alpha(1 - \beta)}{\beta s} \gtreqless 0 \qquad (3.31)$$

and

$$\delta_4 = [\frac{\alpha\beta}{1 - \beta s} - \frac{\alpha(1 - \beta)}{\beta s}](1-\beta) \gtreqless 0 \qquad (3.32)$$

With a sufficiently low value of s (near 0) δ_3 and δ_4 can be negative. We also have that $|\delta_3|>|\delta_4|$. Both δ_3 and δ_4 positively depend on α and are unspecified on β and s.

Lastly, we have in (3.27) that

$$\delta_5 = \alpha > 0 \qquad (3.33)$$

$$\delta_6 = \gamma(1-\beta) > 0. \qquad (3.34)$$

In order to find out about the short term effects of money growth on real income, we shall also derive a reduced form for real income growth rate from Friedman's model. We assume the system

$$x_t = x^* + (1 -\alpha)(y_t - y_t^*) - \alpha[LogX_t - (LogX_t)^*] \qquad (3.35)$$

$$y_t = y_t^* + \frac{1}{1 - \beta s} (m_t - y_t^*) \qquad (3.36)$$

$$x_t^* = \beta x_{t-1} + (1-\beta)x_{t-1}^* \qquad (3.37)$$

$$y_t^* = \beta y_{t-1} + (1-\beta)y_{t-1}^* \qquad (3.38)$$

From this system we derive the following reduced form for the growth rates of real income:

$$x_t = \xi_0 m_t - \xi_1 m_{t-1} + \xi_2 m_{t-2} - \xi_3 y_{t-1} + \xi_4 y_{t-2} \qquad (3.39)$$
$$+ \xi_5 [LogX_t - (LogX_t)^*] - \xi_6 [LogX_{t-1} - (LogX_{t-1})^*] + \pi_{t-1}.$$

where

$$\xi_0 = \frac{1 - \alpha}{1 - \beta s} \gtreqless 0 \qquad (3.40)$$

$$\xi_1 = \frac{(1-\alpha)(1-\beta)}{1 - \beta s} (1 - \frac{1}{\beta s}) \gtreqless 0 \qquad (3.41)$$

32

$$\xi_2 = \left(\frac{1 - \alpha}{1 - \beta s}\right) \frac{(1 - \beta)^2}{\beta s} \gtrless 0 \tag{3.42}$$

$$\xi_3 = \frac{(1 - \alpha)\beta}{1 - \beta s} - \frac{(1 -\alpha)(1 - \beta)}{\beta s} \gtrless 0 \tag{3.43}$$

$$\xi_4 = \frac{(1-\alpha)\beta}{1 - \beta s} - \frac{(1-\alpha)(1-\beta)}{\beta s}(1-\beta) \gtrless 0 \tag{3.44}$$

$$\xi_5 = \alpha > 0 \tag{3.45}$$

$$\xi_6 = \gamma(1-\beta) > 0. \tag{3.46}$$

Given that $0<\alpha<1$ and that $0<\beta<1$ ξ_0, ξ_1 and ξ_2 are greater than 0 if $0<\beta s<1$. With very low values of s ξ_3 and ξ_4 can be negative ($|\xi_3|>|\xi_4|$).

3.4.2   *Estimation of the model*

In this section we present results from estimations of reduced forms of Friedman's model, (3.27) and (3.39). The main purpose is to test short term aspects of the monetarist approach to inflation, that is:

1)   That it is the unpredictable portion of increases in the volume of money growth rate which has a positive but temporal effect on real income.

2)   That these unpredictable rises in the money growth rate also have a positive effect on the velocity, so that it moves pro cyclically.

In the Friedman model with adaptive expectations, all these short term effects depend on the value of parameters α, β and s. These effects are summarized by the value of parameter $\alpha/(1-\beta s)$ which gives an expression for the effects of the unpredictable portion of the volume of money growth on inflation. Under the present assumption about α and s, $\alpha/(1-\beta s)$ should be positive. If the indicated short term effects exist, $\alpha/(1-\beta s)$ should be different from 1. It should be less than 1 if the effect of real income is the strongest, and greater than 1 if it is the velocity effect which is the strongest instead. There are also possibilities that both effects compensate each other and that $\alpha(1-\beta s)$ is not significantly different from 1 in spite of the fact that both effects are important. Given that there are no theoretical reasons to assume such a situation, we say that in such a situation, both effects are unimportant.

In the real income equation (3.35), the short term effects of the parameter $(1-\alpha)/(1-\beta s)$ are given. Here, we see that a value on a parameter which is greater than 0 should imply that unpredicted variations in the volume of money have effects on real income.

3.4.2.1   *Estimations with annual data.* We estimate stochastic versions of models (3.27) and (3.39) as first difference equations, that is

$$\pi_t-\pi_{t-1} = a + \delta_0 m_t-\delta_1 m_{t-1}+\delta_2 m_{t-2}-\delta_3 y_{t-1}+\delta_4 y_{t-2}$$
$$+\delta_5[LogX_t-(LogX_t)^*]+\delta_6[LogX_{t-1}-(LogX_{t-1})^*]+u_t \tag{3.47}$$

$$x_t-x_{t-1}= b+\xi_0 m_t-\xi_1 m_{t-1}+\xi_2 m_{t-2}+\xi_3 y_{t-1}+\xi_4 y_{t-2}$$
$$+ \xi_5[LogX_t-(LogX_t)^*] - \xi_6[LogX_{t-1}-(LogX_{t-1})^*] +u_t'. \tag{3.48}$$

We estimate models (3.47) and (3.48) with annual data for the period 1958–85 [7] as well as for subperiods 1958–74 and 1975–85 (see table 3.3). We estimate both models for M1 and M2. In order to get the capacity variable $\text{LogX}-(\text{LogX})^*$, we need a measure of full employment real income, X^*. We get this by estimating the growth rate of real income between business cycle peaks, that is for the period 1958–75 and 1975–81. We used the historical growth rate between 1956–75 to get full employment real income during the years 1975–85.

Estimations of the inflation model (3.47), for the period 1957 – 85, give us signs of the parameters, as well as the relationship between them, which, with the exception of the capacity variables, correspond quite well with the theoretical model. To a lesser degree, this is also the case for subperiods 1958–74.

When it comes to m– and y–variables, we see that the sign and value relationship between the parameters are generally speaking in accordance with the predictions of theory except in cases where the t–values are very low. During the subperiod 1975–85, the signs and relationships between the m– and y–parameters are instead inconsistent with the theory.

In the case of the capacity variables, signs of the parameters and in most cases the relationships between these is the opposite of the theoretical model.[8] This may imply that there were no significant capacity restrictions during the period, which corresponds quite well with the fact that the economy was clearly below full employment during most of the sample period.

The inflation models were generally not significant at a 5 per cent level except for the M1– model during 1958–85 and the M2–model during 1975–85.[9] The models' R^2s are also relatively high for the period 1958–85 as well as for subperiod 1958–74.

As far as the significance of the variables [10] is concerned, it is only m which is significant at the 5 per cent level in some cases (M1– and M2–models during period 1958–85 and M2 models during the period 1958–74). Otherwise we find that in the subperiod 1975–85, y is also significant at that level in M2 models.

The theoretical model parameters, α, β and s are over–identified in our reduced form (3.47), where we have five parameters $(\delta_0 - \delta_4)$ to identify them. We tried to identify them on the basis of the volume of money variable parameters, δ_0, δ_1 and δ_2. Since most of the parameters in the reduced forms were insignificant, there were no usable results for the theoretical model parameters.

Regarding the real income model (3.48), the parameter signs are not consistent with the theoretical model. The F–value for the real income model is significant at the 5 per cent level in all periods except the last one, but the significance of the model in all cases mainly depends on the capacity variables. These variables, whichhave a sign opposite to the theoretical model, are the only ones that are significant at the 5 per cent level.

Attempts at the identification of parameters in the theoretical model gave arbitrary results in all the real income equations.

A summary of the results from the analysis of annual data: In brief, estimations with annual data of the Friedman inflation model with adaptive expectations did not give results that were better than the simpler model in the preceding section. Regarding the significance of the dependent variable as well as the explanatory power of the model, the results obtained were worse than in the previous model.[11]

When it came to the short term effects of unpredicted variations in the money supply, it was not possible to draw any conclusions.

In the estimations of the real income equations the impact of money growth on variations in the real income was insignificant in all cases.

There are significant differences between results from the period 1975–85 and those of the earlier period. In the reduced form of the inflation model, the signs of the parameters are not consistent with the theoretical model. Parameter δ_0 is much lower

Table 3.3
The Friedman model with adaptive expectations. Estimations with annual data

Period	Depend. var.	Const.	Independent variables $m2_t$	$m2_{t-1}$	$m2_{t-2}$	y_{t-1}	y_{t-2}	$LogX_t-(LogX_t)$	$LogX_{t-1}-(LogX_{t-1})$	F	R^2	DW
1958-85*	$\pi_t-\pi_{t-1}$	13.0903 (1.292)	0.7911 (3.654)	-0.6331 (-1.664)	0.0432 (0.122)	-0.2532 (-0.963)	-0.1408 (-0.573)	-143.2056 (-1.234)	211.1787 (1.314)	3.688	0.6720	
1958-85	x_t-x_{t-1}	-0.3769 (-0.230)	-0.0095 (-0.368)	0.0459 (1.380)	0.0040 (0.111)	-0.0259 (-0.807)	-0.0340 (-1.246)	60.4929 (3.915)	-95.9973 (-4.816)	6.077	0.6802	1.748
1958-74	$\pi_t-\pi_{t-1}$	10.5465 (0.260)	1.0416 (1.353)	-0.7618 (-0.910)	-0.2320 (-0.218)	-0.1371 (-0.226)	0.2925 (0.488)	-197.0132 (-0.280)	505.9231 (1.017)	1.318	0.5062	2.737
1958-74	x_t-x_{t-1}	-3.7241 (-1.551)	-0.0502 (-1.104)	0.0950 (1.919)	0.0219 (0.348)	-0.0222 (-0.618)	-0.0645 (-1.824)	18.0466 (0.435)	-107.8458 (-3.669)	5.988	0.8232	1.421
1975-85	$\pi_t-\pi_{t-1}$	35.3450 (0.677)	0.2825 (0.704)	0.6911 (1.818)	-0.5498 (-1.147)	-1.4671 (-2.955)	0.2935 (0.823)	-77.8416 (-0.314)	69.4625 (0.266)	3.520	0.8914	2.744
1975-85*	x_t-x_{t-1}	19.0377 (2.643)	-0.0480 (-0.989)	-0.0423 (-0.849)	-0.0418 (-0.863)	-0.0842 (-1.364)	-0.0652 (-1.449)	129.7935 (3.083)	-137.9870 (-3.143)	15.287	0.9935	

* Yule-Walker's estimator with $\rho = 2$.

35

than 1 whereas in the M2 model, the parameter δ_3 is now significant, with a negative value. These results imply that the short term relationship between inflation and the volume of money changed after the mid 1970's. In order to analyze this further we also estimate (3.47) and (3.48) with quarterly data for the period after the beginning of 1975.

3.4.2.2   *Estimations with quarterly data.* We carried out estimations of models (3.47) and (3.48) with quarterly data for the period IV/1975–IV/1985, using the method of the moving average. We got the nominal income growth rate by calculating the growth rate of the production index times the consumer price index. Full employment real income was obtained using the already described method of increasing GDP growth in the base period with its historical growth rate between business cycle peaks. We carried out estimations for the money aggregates M1, M2 and M3 as defined in the previous section.

The results of estimations for the period IV/75–IV/85 shall be analyzed here, as well as for subperiods IV/75–IV/82 and I/83–IV/85. We also estimate the model for the period III/81–IV/85 which includes the depression years, i.e. after the unsuccessful stabilization attempt towards the end of the 1970's.

Estimation of the inflation model gave us for all periods, and money aggregates, signs of the parameters which did not conform with the theoretical model (see table 3.4).[12] Apart from the capacity variables, which had the wrong signs in the annual estimations, we also got signs on m– and y–variables which did not agree with the theoretical assumptions of the model. Identification of parameters from the theoretical model proved difficult and the results were unrealistic.

For periods IV/75–IV/85 and IV/75–IV/82, the F–value of the inflation models was significant at the 5 per cent level. R^2 was around 0.50 for all money aggregates during these periods. For the subperiod I/83–IV/85, the models were not significant at the 5 per cent level, while R^2 was around 0.80.

The money variable showed parameters which were positive and, in most cases significant at the 5 per cent level, except in the last subperiod. Of the other explanatory variables it was only Y_{t-1} which appeared significant at this level (except one for M1– and M3–models in the last subperiod). The parameters for Y_{t-1} were negative.

In the model of real income, we see that in all cases, very high F– and R^2–values are obtained, but that these mainly depend on the capacity variables which are highly significant. The volume of money and nominal income variables are in all cases more significant than in the annual model. This is the case for periods IV/75–IV/85 and IV/75–IV/82, where M_t and Y_{t-1} are in most cases significant at the 5 per cent level. The money and nominal income variables have in all cases a negative effect on the growth of real income.

A summary of the results from the analysis with quarterly data: From our estimations with quarterly data, we got inflation models which were significant and had high R^2s except for the last subperiod. In subperiod 1/1983 – IV/1985, the model was not significant at the 5 per cent level but showed a higher R^2. If we compare these results with those of models in the former section [13], we find that as a rule, Friedman's model shows better results in the last subperiod.

As with the annual model for the same period 1975–85, the signs of the parameters in quarterly inflation models is inconsistent with the theory behind the model. The theoretical parameters of the model cannot be solved, thus it is impossible to draw clear conclusions concerning the short term effects of unpredicted money growth.

The real income models are very significant and have very high R^2 values.

Table 3.4
The Friedman model with adaptive expectations. Estimations with quarterly data

Period	Dependent variables	Constant	Independent variables $m2_t$	$m2_{t-1}$	$m2_{t-2}$	y_{t-1}	y_{t-2}	$LogX_t-(LogX_t)$	$LogX_{t-1}-(LogX_{t-1})$	F	R^2	DW
IV/75-IV/85	$\pi_t-\pi_{t-1}$	-0.9429 (-0.388)	0.3019 (2.166)	0.2957 (2.046)	0.3351 (2.072)	-0.7495 (-4.365)	-0.3743 (-2.174)	-98.3221 (-2.939)	86.5032 (2.643)	3.677	0.4382	2.336
IV/75-IV/85	x_t-x_{t-1}	5.0252 (5.312)	-0.0084 (-1.629)	-0.0392 (-1.655)	-0.1273 (-2.021)	-0.1641 (-2.454)	0.1329 (2.137)	156.1414 (11.989)	-159.3703 (-12.508)	30.803	0.8673	2.008
IV/75-IV/82	$\pi_t-\pi_{t-1}$	0.1449 (0.030)	0.2835 (1.532)	0.1722 (0.828)	0.4084 (1.829)	-0.8035 (-3.840)	-0.2788 (-1.346)	-63.1559 (-1.558)	67.4939 (1.570)	2.557	0.4601	2.139
IV/75-IV/82	x_t-x_{t-1}	2.8209 (1.754)	-0.1479 (-2.419)	-0.0357 (-0.520)	-0.0663 (-0.900)	-0.1587 (-2.296)	0.2059 (3.009)	146.0305 (10.903)	-170.9455 (-12.039)	32.606	0.9157	2.010
I/83-IV/85	$\pi_t-\pi_{t-1}$	6.0141 (0.381)	0.5259 (1.256)	0.3936 (1.270)	0.4606 (1.205)	-1.3542 (-2.096)	-0.5134 (-1.390)	-215.3198 (-2.084)	213.7295 (1.825)	2.474	0.8124	2.643
I/83-IV/85	x_t-x_{t-1}	-1.7018 (-0.297)	-0.2520 (-1.653)	-0.1388 (-1.231)	-0.3906 (-2.808)	0.5725 (2.434)	-0.0791 (-0.589)	236.1910 (6.281)	-257.3719 (-6.036)	11.091	0.9510	2.789
			Independent variables $m3_t$	$m3_{t-1}$	$m3_{t-2}$	y_{t-1}	y_{t-2}	$LogX_t-(LogX_t)$	$LogX_{t-1}-(LogX_{t-1})$			
IV/75-IV/85	$\pi_t-\pi_{t-1}$	-4.7599 (-1.452)	0.2564 (2.811)	0.3220 (3.319)	-0.0233 (-0.236)	-0.4589 (-2.999)	0.0611 (0.428)	-48.4039 (-1.677)	41.3197 (1.416)	3.999	0.4589	2.386
IV/75-IV/85	x_t-x_{t-1}	4.4455 (3.520)	-0.0876 (-2.494)	-0.0179 (-0.479)	0.0954 (2.507)	-0.3481 (-5.906)	0.0036 (0.066)	136.9086 (12.314)	-143.6600 (-12.780)	32.955	0.8749	1.666
IV/75-IV/82	$\pi_t-\pi_{t-1}$	2.2830 (0.474)	0.4188 (3.231)	0.1790 (0.843)	-0.1641 (-0.720)	-0.7252 (-3.612)	0.0028 (0.014)	-33.6338 (-1.032)	101.7938 (2.344)	3.168	0.5136	1.709
IV/75-IV/82	x_t-x_{t-1}	1.3574 (0.815)	-0.1381 (-3.082)	0.0186 (0.253)	0.1175 (1.492)	-0.2210 (-3.184)	0.0760 (1.119)	135.9476 (12.072)	-178.2556 (-11.875)	33.101	0.9169	1.147
I/83-IV/85	$\pi_t-\pi_{t-1}$	3.4923 (0.328)	0.3357 (1.485)	0.2144 (1.000)	-0.2239 (-1.013)	0.7193 (0.787)	-0.2041 (-0.320)	-3.8767 (-0.037)	49.5841 (0.556)	3.895	0.8721	2.426
I/83-IV/85	x_t-x_{t-1}	-2.0236 (-0.367)	-0.1925 (-1.643)	-0.0198 (-0.178)	0.1626 (1.421)	-0.7128 (-1.505)	0.0649 (0.196)	79.3604 (1.458)	-118.7757 (-2.571)	7.877	0.9324	2.263

However, they also have signs which are inconsistent with the theoretical model. Even though the m— and y—variables are now more significant than in the annual model, the high F— value of the model is mainly the result of the capacity variables. The volume of money and nominal income variables have negative effects on variations in the real income, which is against the basic theory.

3.4.2.3   *Some general conclusions.* We can draw some general conclusions from the former analysis of Friedman's model with adaptive expectations.

Almost invariably, the inflation models gave quite bad results. A look at the F— and R^2—values show that Friedman's model with adaptive expectations gives worse results than the simpler model we used in section 3.3. This model gives better results only for certain periods and money aggregates.

No significant results about the short term effects of unpredicted money growth could be obtained.

For the period after the beginning of 1975, we see that the estimation results differ from those for the earlier period and, to a lesser extent, from estimations for the whole period. In both the annual and quarterly models, we saw that a) the sign differs totally from those in the theoretical model, b) parameter $\delta_o = \alpha(1-\beta s)$ is less than 1 even in the annual models, and c) that parameter δ_4 becomes negative and significant.

These changes in δ_0 and δ_3 after 1975 are not consistent with the existence of the effects of unpredicted growth of money supply on real income or velocity as alleged by the monetarists. A positive effect of unpredicted money supply growth after 1975 should imply a decrease in δ_0, which we actually got, but also a decrease in the absolute value of δ_3, through either a decrease in α and/or in βs. A positive effect on velocity should imply, through an increase in s, both an increased δ_0 and a decreased δ_3.

However, changes in the inflation model's parameters after 1975 can be related to changes in the economic policy of those years. Uruguay liberalized the economy, especially the financial transactions. In an economy with free capital and exchange rate markets and fixed exchange rates, the public may change the volume of money supply which eventually becomes endogenous. An increase in the inflation rate can then, in a given period, cause the public to reduce international reserves and thereby the growth rate in money supply in the following period. In this way, the inflation rate in the period can also be brought down. If we assume that y is a good 'proxy' for π_{t-1}, we can have an explanation for the negative relationship between $(\pi_t - \pi_{t-1})$ and y_{t-1} which we get in our model after 1975.

It was also this type of mechanism that we found in the preceding chapter to lay behind the short term anti—cyclical movements in velocity for M1 and M2. For such a pattern to arise, it is also necessary that the velocity accelerates with increased inflation in the preceding period. This is because the public, faced with increased inflation expectations, directly increase the velocity of money or move part of their bank assets to deposits in foreign exchange. These conditions would be reflected in our inflation model with M1 and M2 when the parameter becomes considerably less than 1, which was actually the case during the period after 1975.

This type of mechanism, with the ability to explain changes in the parameters during the period after 1975, is precisely the same as that used in the preceding chapter to explain changes in the relationship between inflation and (m—x). As already mentioned, this implies an anti—cyclical movement in velocity which reduces the effect of variations in M1 and M2 on the inflation rate.

Regarding estimations of the real income model, we find that the results are inconsistent with the theoretical model and that the money variables have no

38

significant effect on real income or, as is the case after 1975, have a negative effect on it.

In brief, we see that the monetarist model with exogenous money supply implies that the impact that unpredicted money supply has on real income and velocity and which disrupt the relationship between inflation and the volume of money growth did not exist during the sample period. Evidence shows that short term variations in velocity after 1975, were negatively correlated with the variations in the volume of money. Thus they show a pattern which is the opposite of the one shown by the Friedman model.

3.5 The neutrality of money and the natural rate of unemployment hypothesis

In this chapter, we shall apply two models which are especially aimed at studying the neutrality of money assumption in a situation of equilibrium [14]. The point of departure is that in equilibrium, i.e. when the expectations are correct, there is no 'trade off' between inflation and the real output level. In monetarist theory this is related to the hypothesis of a natural rate of unemployment (NUR—hypothesis) which is totally dependent on real factors that act on the supply side of the economy.

The two models to be studied in this chapter are: a) the expectations augmented Phillips curve and b) Lucas' model (Lucas, 1973) for a 'trade off' between inflation and real income under the assumption of rational expectations.

3.5.1 *The expectations augmented Phillips curve*

The NUR hypothesis implies that in equilibrium conditions the activity level in the economy is totally independent of monetary factors, and therefore totally independent of inflation, that is, money is neutral.

According to monetarists, equilibrium in an economy, that is when actual and expected quantities are equal, is compatible with any anticipated inflation rate. The inflation rate depends on the money growth rate. In such a state, the activity level in the economy is dependent on real factors only and unemployment is equal to NUR (Friedman, 1968; Laidler, 1975; Phelps, 1979). The 'trade off' between inflation and unemployment is for monetarists a temporary phenomenon which depends on the economy's disequilibrium, that is, by how much the anticipated inflation rate differs from the actual. This is primarily due to the unexpected changes in the growth rate of money supply (Friedman, 1971). Such divergences must be temporary with an endogenous process of expectations generation. If the expectations are rationally generated, divergences, with regard to the systematic variations in the money supply, are non—existent (Lucas, 1972; Sargent, Wallace, 1976).

The relationship between inflation, the activity level, and expectations is normally presented with the use of an expectations augmented Phillips curve

$$\pi_t = f(U_t) + a\pi_t^* \qquad (3.49)$$

where U is some measure for unemployment and where the parameter a is equal to one.

When equilibrium prevails we have $\pi_t = \pi_t^*$ and $\pi_t = \dfrac{f(U_t)}{(1-a)}$. This function, which gives all combinations of π and U that are consistent with a fully anticipated inflation rate, has no solution at a=1. Thus π is no longer a function of U and the long term Phillips curve is a vertical line which crosses the U—axis at a point which is totally independent of the monetary side of the economy. This point indicates the natural unemployment level for a certain combination of real factors.

This condition has usually been used to test the NUR hypothesis through testing

39

the value of the a parameter in (3.49). It is assumed that the expected rate of inflation π_t^* is a function of π's previous history according to;

$$\pi_t^* = \sum_{i=1}^{n} v_i\, \pi_{t-i}. \tag{3.50}$$

By inserting (3.50) into (3.49) we get

$$\pi_t = f(U_t) + a(v_1\pi_{t-1} + ... + v_n\pi_{t-n}) \tag{3.51}$$

where the a parameter can be estimated when a further assumptions is made, that is, that

$\sum_{i=1}^{n} v_i = 1$. If on estimating

$$\pi_t = f(U_t) + av_1\pi_{t-1} + .. + av_n\pi_{t-n} \tag{3.52}$$

we get that $\sum_{i=1}^{n}$ (av) is not significantly different from 1, it is assumed that a is not different from 1. This procedure has obvious limitations and has been strongly criticized (Santomero & Seater, 1978), as we shall see in the next section.

An expectations augmented Phillips curve from Friedman's inflation model can be written as

$$\pi_t = \pi_t^* + b(y_t - y_t^*) + b[LogX_t - (LogX_t)^*]. \tag{3.53}$$

We assume adaptive expectations for π and y, i.e. that

$$\pi_t^* = \beta\pi_{t-1} + (1-\beta)\pi_{t-1}^* \tag{3.54}$$

$$y_t = \beta y_{t-1} + (1-\beta)y_{t-1}^* \tag{3.55}$$

By developing these so that

$$\pi_t^* = \beta\pi_{t-1} + (1-\beta)\pi\beta_{t-2} + (1-\beta)^2 \beta\pi_{t-3} + ... \tag{3.54'}$$

and

$$y_t = \beta y_{t-1} + (1-\beta)\beta y_{t-2} + (1-\beta)^2\beta y_{t-3} + ... \tag{3.55'}$$

and putting them into (3.54) and using a Koyck transformation we get

$$\pi_t - (1-\beta)\pi_{t-1} = \beta\pi_{t-1} + by_t - b\beta y_{t-1} + \tag{3.56}$$
$$b[LogX_t - (LogX_t)^*] - b(1-\beta)[LogX_{t-1} - (LogX_{t-1})^*]$$

or

$$\pi_t = \gamma_1\, \pi_{t-1} + \gamma_2 y_t + \gamma_3 y_{t-1} + \tag{3.57}$$

$$\gamma_4[\text{LogX}_t - (\text{LogX}_t)^*] + \gamma_5[\text{LogX}_{t-1} - (\text{LogX}_{t-1})^*]$$

where $\gamma_1 = 1$ and $\gamma_2 = \gamma_4$.

Equation (3.57) is an empirically testable augmented Phillips curve. π_{t-1} is included in the equation as a 'proxy' for π_t^* and the test of the NUR hypothesis implies testing whether γ_1 is significantly different from 1 or not.

3.5.1.1   *Estimation of the model.* We estimate the model (3.57) using more realistic forms, that is

$$\pi_t = b + c_1 y_t + c_2 y_{t-1} + d_1 [\text{LogX}_t - (\text{LogX}_t)^*] + \qquad (3.58)$$
$$d_2[\text{LogX}_{t-1} - (\text{LogX}_{t-1})^*] + e_1\pi_{t-1} + e_2\pi_{t-2} + e_3\pi_{t-3} + u_t$$

where the public's inflation estimator is given by $\sum\limits_{i=1}^{3} v_i \pi_{t-i}$ instead of π_{t-1}.

We undertook estimations of (3.58) with annual data for the period 1956–85, and for subperiods 1956–67 and 1968–85. The criteria for periodization was that while during 1957–67 inflation was rising, the period 1968–85 shows variations in inflation without any clear trend.

Estimation of (3.58) gave us results which were not compatible with the theoretical structure of the model. The sign of the parameters was wrong almost all the time. The sum of the e's was also negative and significantly different from 0.

The last mentioned result can depend on the fact that π_t and π_{t-1} are highly correlated with y_t and y_{t-1}, which had positive, significant parameters in the estimations.

We therefore excluded the y variables and estimated the simpler models.

$$\pi_t = b + c\,[\text{LogX}_t - (\text{LogX}_t)^*] + d_1\,\pi_{t-1} + d_2\,\pi_{t-2}$$
$$+ d_3\pi_{t-3} + d_4\,\pi_{t-4} + d_5\pi_{t-5}\,u_t \qquad (3.59)$$

and

$$\pi_t = b + c(\frac{1}{U_t}) + d_1\,\pi_{t-1} + d_2\,\pi_{t-2} + d_3\pi_{t-3}$$
$$+ d_4\,\pi_{t-4} + d_5\pi_{t-5} + u_t \qquad (3.60)$$

where U is unemployment as a percentage of the work force. Equation (3.60) was estimated only for period 1965–85 [15].

In all cases, the F–values showed that the models were not significant at the 5 per cent level. We also found that all activity variables $(\text{LogX}_t - (\text{LogX})^*)$ as well as $(1/U_t))$ were not significant at the 5 per cent level. At the same time, the sum of the e–parameters was in most cases significantly different from 1 at the 5 per cent level and was at times negative.

We estimated equivalent models with quarterly data, that is;

$$\pi_t = b + \sum_{i=0}^{3} c_i [\mathrm{Log}X_{t-i} - (\mathrm{Log}X_{t-i})^*] + \sum_{i=1}^{8} e_i \pi_{t-i} + u_t \qquad (3.61)$$

$$\pi_t = b + \sum_{i=0}^{3} c_i \left(\frac{1}{U_{t-1}} \right) + \sum_{i=1}^{8} e_i \pi_{t-i} + u_t \qquad (3.62)$$

for the period III/75–IV/85 and III/77–IV/85 [16].

Model (3.62) was significant at the 5 per cent level but not (3.61). In both cases, the activity variables were not significant or had the wrong sign. The sum of e–parameters was always significantly different from 1 at the 5 per cent level.

In brief, it can be said that all estimated models were scarcely significant and gave results which were contradictory. On the one hand, this indicates that there was no positive relationship between inflation and the activity level. On the other hand, we found that as a rule, the sum of π_{t-i} parameters in the annual as well as quarterly analysis was significantly less than 1. As already mentioned, this would imply that parameter a in (3.49) is lower than 1 and that even in the long run, there is a relationship between inflation and the activity level.

Against the former conclusion one can, however, argue (see Santomero & Seater, p. 528) that the procedure used to estimate parameter a implies that in $\pi_i^* = \sum_{i=1}^{n} v_i \pi_{t-i}$ it

is assumed that $\sum_{i=1}^{n} v_i = 1$, which is not theoretically justified. The actual inflation

process does not have to have such strong auto–correlation so that $\sum_{i=1}^{n} v_i = 1$. Should

this be the case, then use of the assumption that $\sum_{i=1}^{n} v_i = 1$ in the public's inflation

estimator is the same as assuming an adaptive schedule for the expectations of the public, when the actual sequence is not adaptive, is an ad hoc procedure.

3.5.1.2   *Estimation of the model without the assumption* $\sum_{i=1}^{n} v_i = 1$. We tried

another method to estimate a. We assumed, in line with the theory of rational expectations, that the public generates a real value estimator of π_t. We estimated

this in two variants, that is, $\hat{\pi}_t = \sum_{i=1}^{n} v_i \pi_{t-i}$ and $\tilde{\pi}_t = \sum_{i=1}^{n} v_i ml_{t-i}$, which replaced

$\pi_t^* = \sum_{i=1}^{n} v_i \pi_{t-i}$ in (3.50). The estimated value of inflation $\hat{\pi}_t$ or $\tilde{\pi}_t$ was later included

in (3.49) instead of π_t^*. Lastly, we estimated (3.49) with $\hat{\pi}_t$ or $\tilde{\pi}_t$ as independent variables.

The estimators used by the public to make their prognoses about inflation imply, as seen in the former section, that the public is aware of the structure of the inflation process and can build an estimator with more information than that in the available observations.

Testing parameter a in the model

$$\pi_t = f(U_t) + a\hat{\pi}_t \qquad (3.63)$$

using an OLS estimator of π as an explanation variable to estimate a model whose independent variable is π implies a very doubtful procedure. This method ought to give us information concerning the value of parameter a. On the one hand, it allows us to differentiate parameter a from $\sum_{i=1}^{n} v_i$. On the other hand, the divergence in model (3.63) of the a:s from 1 depends on how strong the correlation of other explanatory variables with π is.

In a model with two variables, we have that

$$\hat{\beta}_2 = \frac{m_{y2}m_{33} - m_{y3}m_{23}}{m_{22}m_{33} - m_{23}^2}$$

where $m_{jk} = \sum_{i=1}^{n} (X_{ji} - \overline{X}_j)(X_{ki} - \overline{X}_k)$, X_2 and X_3 are explanatory variables and Y is the dependent variable. If X_2 is an OLS estimator of Y, we have that $m_{y2}/m_{22}=1$ [17] and $\hat{\beta}_2$'s divergence from 1 depends on the difference between m_{y3} and m_{23}. The greater the absolute difference between m_{y3} and m_{23} is, that is the difference between X's correlation with Y and its correlation with the other independent variable X, the more $\hat{\beta}_2$ differs from 1.

From the former argument, we have that in model (3.63), the value of parameter a gives us a measure of how strong the relationship between inflation and the activity level is when expectations about inflation are included as explanatory variables in the model. That is, parameter a in model (3.49) becomes less than 1 if U is negatively correlated with current inflation and at the same time weakly correlated with the expected inflation and vice versa. This is consistent with the logic of the model.

With the described method, we estimated annual and quarterly models of the expectations augmented Phillips curve.

$$\pi_t = b + c[LogX_t - (LogX_t)^*] + a\pi_t^* + u_t \text{ and} \qquad (3.64)$$

$$\pi_t = b + c(-\frac{1}{U_t}) + a\pi_t^* + u_t \qquad (3.65)$$

and with quarterly data

$$\pi_t = b + \sum_{i=0}^{3} c_i[LogX_{t-i} - (LogX_{t-i})^*] + a\pi_t^* + u_t \qquad (3.66)$$

and

$$\pi_t = b + \sum_{i=0}^{3} c_i \frac{1}{U_{t-1}} + a\pi_t^* + u_t \qquad (3.67)$$

We used two variants as estimators for inflation, namely

$$\pi^*_t = \hat{\pi}_t = c + \sum_{i=1}^{5} v_i \, \pi_{t-i} + v_t \qquad (3.68)$$

and

$$\pi^*_t = \tilde{\pi}_t = c + \sum_{i=1}^{5} v_i \, ml_{t-i} + u_t \qquad (3.69)$$

for annual analysis and

$$\pi^*_t = \hat{\pi}_t = c + \sum_{i=1}^{8} v_i \, \pi_{t-i} + u_t \qquad (3.70)$$

$$\pi^*_t = \tilde{\pi}_t = c + \sum_{i=1}^{8} v_i \, ml_{t-i} + u_t \qquad (3.71)$$

for quarterly analysis. The results for the given period are shown in tables 3.5 and 3.6.

In all cases, we got models which were significant at the 5 per cent level. Both the F–value and R^2 were in most cases much higher in models with $\tilde{\pi}_t$, which proved a better estimator for inflation than $\hat{\pi}_t$ Regarding the activity level variables, LogX–(LogX)* was never significant at the 5 per cent level and often had a negative sign. In most cases, U had the right sign, but was, with the exception of $(1/U_{t-3})$ in the quarterly model with $\hat{\pi}$, not significant.

In all cases, it was clear that parameter a was not significantly different from 1 at the 5 per cent level. The results we got mean that when we estimated the models and $\sum_{i=1}^{n} v_i$ differed from 1, the estimations we got for a did not significantly differ from 1.

Table 3.5
An expectations augmented Phillips curve (estimations with annual data)

Period 1955–85

$$\pi_t = -1.9041 \; -0.8028 \; (\mathrm{LogX}_t - (\mathrm{LogX}_t)^*) + 0.9347 \; \hat{\pi}_t$$
$$ (-0.141) \;\; (-1.434) (3.746)$$
$$F=8.674 \quad R^2 = 0.3912 \quad DW=1.983$$

$$\pi_t = -4.6470 \; -1.0495 \; [\mathrm{LogX}_t - (\mathrm{LogX}_t)^*] + 0.9650 \; \tilde{\pi}_t$$
$$ (-0.279) \;\; (-1.781) (3.111)$$
$$F=6.320 \quad R^2 = 0.3189 \quad DW=1.926$$

Period 1955–67

$$\pi_t = -9.8643 \; -3.1497 \; [\mathrm{LogX}_t - (\mathrm{LogX}_t)^*] + 0.8206 \; \hat{\pi}_t$$
$$ (-0.752) \;\; (-1.375) (3.177)$$
$$F=11.457 \quad R^2 = 0.7180 \quad DW=1.605$$

$$\pi_t = -5.0218 \; -1.9011 \; [\mathrm{LogX}_t - (\mathrm{LogX}_t)^*] + 0.883 \; \tilde{\pi}_t$$
$$ (-0.572) \;\; (-1.160) (5.516)$$

Period 1968–85

$$\pi_t = -0.0862 \; + 0.0479 \; [\mathrm{LogX}_t - (\mathrm{LogX}_t)^*] + 1.0083 \; \hat{\pi}_t$$
$$ (-0.006) \;\; (0.102) (3.877)$$
$$F=8.199 \quad R^2 = 0.5223 \quad DW=1.795$$

$$\pi_t = -3.5085 \; + 0.6622 \; [\mathrm{LogX}_t - (\mathrm{LogX}_t)^*] + 1.1558 \; \tilde{\pi}_t$$
$$ (-0.366) \;\; (1.761) (6.420)$$
$$F=21.890 \quad R^2 = 0.7448 \quad DW=1.621$$

Period 1965–85

$$\pi_t = -9.3331 \; + 0.9151 \; (1/u_t) + 0.9870 \; \hat{\pi}_t$$
$$ (-0.307) \;\; (0.405) (3.014)$$
$$F=4.841 \quad R^2 = 0.3629 \quad DW=1.908$$

$$\pi_t = -24.8163 \; +1.9137 \; (1/u_t) + 1.0688 \; \tilde{\pi}_t$$
$$ (-0.748) \;\; (0.856) (3.051)$$
$$F=4.958 \quad R^2 = 0.3684 \quad DW=2.019$$

Table 3.6
An expectation augmented Phillips curve (estimations with quarterly data)

Period 1/1975–IV/1985

$$\pi_t = -0.9638 -10.3333 \ [LogX_t-(LogX_t)^*] +66.6085 \ [LogX_{-1}-(LogX_{-1})^*]$$
$$\quad (-0.297) \quad (0.378) \qquad\qquad\qquad\qquad (1.937)$$
$$-51.8857 \ [LogX_{-2} -(LogX)_{-2}^*] \ -13.8876 \ [LogX_{-3} -(LogX)_{-3}^*] + 1.0557 \ \hat{\pi}_t$$
$$\quad (-1.652) \qquad\qquad\qquad\qquad (-0.497) \qquad\qquad\qquad\qquad (3.665)$$

$$F=5.093 \quad R^2=0.4212 \quad DW=1.881$$

$$\pi_t = -0.7631 + 10.0463 \ [LogX_t - (LogX_t)^*] \ -15.1125 \ [LogX_{-1} -(LogX)_{-1}^*]$$
$$\quad (-0.404) \quad (0.494) \qquad\qquad\qquad\qquad (-0.567)$$

$$-25.9340 \ [(LogX_{-2} -(LogX)_{-2}^*]+33.9006 \ [(LogX_{-3} - (LogX _{-3})^*]+1.0731 \ \tilde{\pi}_t$$
$$\quad (-1.025) \qquad\qquad\qquad\qquad (1.407) \qquad\qquad\qquad\qquad (6.387)$$

$$F=11.923 \quad R^2=0.6301 \quad DW=2.208$$

Period IV/1976–IV/1985

$$\pi_t = 8.9619 + 0.1945 \ (1/U_t) - 0.1831 \ (1/U_{-1})+ \ 0.6671 \ (1/U_{-2})$$
$$\quad (1.795) \quad (0.357) \qquad (-0.239) \qquad\quad (-0.863)$$

$$-1.1796 \ (1/U_{-3}) + 0.6390 \ \hat{\pi}_t$$
$$\quad (-2.085) \qquad\quad (2.181)$$

$$F=4.973 \quad R^2=0.4704 \quad DW=1.803$$

$$\pi_t = 3.4626 + 0.1848 \ (1/U_t) \ -0.1447 \ (1/U_{-1}) + 0.1611 \ (1/U_{-2})$$
$$\quad (1.103) \quad (0.467) \qquad (-0.259) \qquad\quad (0.284)$$

$$-0.4284 \ (1/U_{-3}) + 0.8784 \ \tilde{\pi}_t$$
$$\quad (-0.975) \qquad\quad (5.788)$$

$$F=14.253 \quad R^2=0.7179 \quad DW=2.220$$

3.5.1.3   *Conclusions.* The previous analysis with the expectations augmented Phillips curve offered some implications of the impact of inflation on the activity level.

There is no possibility of a permanent 'trade off' between the activity level and inflation and when the expectations conform with actual inflation, the latter becomes totally independent of the activity level in the real sector.

In view of results for the real variables, which become non significant and/or had the wrong sign, the 'trade off' between the activity level and inflation may not be so obvious, not even in the short run. This result is consistent with estimations in the previous section which showed that the growth of money, within the course of one year, was completely carried over to inflation.

The above results support the NUR hypothesis, since this implies that the activity

46

level of the real sector becomes totally independent of monetary policy when the expectations of agents are realized independently of monetary policy measures. However, we will discuss this result further below.

3.5.2 *Lucas' model for 'trade off' between inflation and the activity level*

A different method to test the hypothesis that in equilibrium the activity level is independent of variations in the inflation rate has been developed by Lucas (1973). His theory 'will not place testable restrictions on the coefficients of estimated Phillips curves or other single equation expressions of the trade–off. They will not, for example, imply that money changes are linked to price level changes with a unit coefficient, or that "long run" (in the usual distributed lag sense) Phillips curves must be vertical. They will (as we shall see below) link supply parameters to parameters governing the stochastic nature of demand shifts' (Lucas, 1973, p. 326).

In Lucas' model, the supply of commodities in market z is given by

$$y_{t(z)} = y_{nt} + y_{ct(z)} \tag{3.72}$$

where y is the logarithm of a trend component in supply

$$y_{nt} = \alpha + \beta t \tag{3.73}$$

common for all markets and $y_{ct(z)}$ is the logarithm of a cyclical component in market z.

We also have that

$$y_{ct(z)} = \alpha[P_{t(z)} - E(p_t/I_{t(z)})] + \lambda y_{ct-1(z)} \tag{3.74}$$

where $|\lambda| < 1$, i.e. that $y_{ct(z)}$ is a function of divergences between the actual commodity price in market z, $P_{t(z)}$, and the general anticipated price level   given information, also in market z, $E(P_t|I_{t(z)})$, and a lagged component. The expectations of the agents are rationally generated and $E(P_t|I_{t(z)})$ is a real value estimator of P_t. This is equal to the current average price level, given $I_{t(z)}$, the information available in market z and t. Agents do not know the general price level, P_t, for certain, but are assumed to know its distribution which is $N(P_t,\sigma^2)$.

The price in market z can be expressed as

$$P_{t(z)} = P_t + z \tag{3.75}$$

where z is the divergence from the average price in market z and has a distribution characterized as $z \sim N(o,\sigma_z^2)$.

We also have that

$$E(P_t|I_{t(z)}) = E(P_t|I_{t(z)},\overline{P}_t) = (1-\theta)P_{t(z)} + \theta\overline{P}_t \tag{3.76}$$

where $\theta = \tau^2/(\sigma^2 + \tau^2)$; i.e. the anticipated general price level in market z is the measured mean value of the commodity price in market z and the average general price level with the weights dependent on the variance of the general price level and z price.

Inserting (3.74) and (3.76) into (3.72) and rearranging gives

47

$$y_{t(z)} = y_{nt} + \theta\gamma[P_{t(z)} - \overline{P}_t] + \lambda y_{ct-1(z)} \tag{3.77}$$

and the average for all markets becomes

$$y_t = y_{nt} + \theta\gamma[P_t - \overline{P} + \lambda[y_{t-1} - y_{nt-1}]. \tag{3.78}$$

Furthermore, Lucas assumes a nominal demand function for commodities given below in logarithmic form

$$x_t = y_t + P_t. \tag{3.79}$$

Changes in the aggregate demand, Δx_t, are assumed to have a distribution characterized by $x \sim N(\delta, \sigma_x^2)$.

The general price level, P_t, is assumed to be a function of x' and y:s history and that of y_{nt} according to

$$P_t = \pi_0 + \pi_1 x_t + \pi_2 x_{t-1} + \pi_3 x_{t-2} + \dots + \eta_1 y_{t-1} \tag{3.80}$$
$$+ \eta\, y_{t-2} + \dots + \xi_\delta y_{nt}.$$

The P_t, which is anticipated on the basis of available information in period t, is

$$\overline{P}_t = \overline{P}_0 + \pi_1(x_{t-1} + \delta) + \pi_2 x_{t-1} + \dots$$
$$+ \eta_1 y_{t-1} + \dots + \xi_0 y_{nt} \tag{3.81}$$

Our assumption of equilibrium in the commodity market allows us to eliminate y from (3.78) and (3.79) and by substituting P_t and $\overline{P}_t$ with (3.80) and (3.81) we get an identity in x, y and y_{nt} which can be used to get the value of the parameters. The solutions for P_t and y become

$$P_t = \frac{\theta\,\gamma\,\delta}{1 + \theta\gamma} - \lambda\beta + \frac{1}{1 + \theta\gamma} + \frac{\theta\gamma}{1 + \theta\gamma} x_{t-1}$$
$$- \lambda y_{t-1}(1-\lambda)y_{nt} \tag{3.82}$$

and

$$y_t = \frac{\theta\,\gamma\,\delta}{1 + \theta\gamma} + \lambda\beta + \frac{\theta\gamma}{1 + \theta\gamma} \Delta x_t - \lambda y_{t-1}$$
$$- (1-\lambda)y_{nt} \tag{3.83}$$

respectively.

In terms of y_{ct} and ΔP_t and given that $\pi = \theta\gamma/(1 + \theta\gamma)$ we get from (3.82–3.83) that

$$y_{ct} = -\pi\delta + \pi\Delta x_t + \lambda y_{ct-1} \qquad (3.84)$$

and

$$P_t = -\beta + (1 - \pi)\Delta x_t + \pi\Delta x_{t-1} - \lambda\Delta y_{ct-1} \qquad (3.85)$$

Model 3.84–85 implies that: a) variations in commodity demand have an immediate effect on real income and a lagged effect which decreases geometrically, b)price effects in the first period are equal to one minus the real effect and c) the rest of the price effect comes in the next period.

Lucas' model incorporates 'rational expectations', where the distribution of demand shock effects between real and nominal demand depends on the relative variability of aggregate demand and that of relative prices and through their effects on the rational estimations of the agents. The greater the tendency to regard variations in market prices as outcomes of variations in the general price level, the less are the effects on production and vice versa. However, without introducing an ad–hoc term (3.77), that is $y_{ct-1(z)}$, (see Gordon, 1981), this model could not generate a cyclical pattern in production.

The model can be used to test neutrality of money and the NUR hypotheses. Defining π in terms of θ and γ and θ in terms of σ^2 and τ^2 we have that

$$\pi = \frac{\tau^2\gamma}{\sigma^2 + \tau^2(1 + \gamma)} \qquad (3.86)$$

and that $\sigma^2 = 1/(1+\theta\gamma)^2 \, \sigma_x^2$ we have that

$$\pi = \frac{\tau^2\gamma}{(1 - \pi)^2\sigma_x^2 + \tau^2(1 + \gamma)} \qquad (3.87)$$

If τ^2 and γ are constants, we have that $\pi \to \dfrac{\gamma}{1 + \gamma}$ when $\sigma_x^2 \to 0$ and $\pi \to 0$ when $\sigma_x^2 \to \infty$. The test then composes an examination of the correlation between π's size and the variance of aggregate demand, σ_x^2, for different countries and for different periods in one country.

3.5.2.1   *Estimation of the model* [18]. Lucas uses the model (3.84–85) to examine the relationship between the variance of commodity demand, σ_y^2, and the distribution between the real and nominal effects of variations in demand, which are given by the size of the the the π parameter, in different countries. We shall use the model to analyze the inflation process in Uruguay during different time periods.

The periods chosen are characterized by different sizes in variance, σ_y^2, of the nominal demand growth rate. The latter is used instead of the variance in demand because in a land with high inflation, this tends to be greater in later periods, irrespective of the variability in demand.

We also used the model to estimate the relative distribution of variations in nominal demand between price and output effects. We therefore estimate the model also for the whole period.

For a measure of nominal demand, we used nominal GDP. The cyclical components of nominal demand and the real product were taken as divergences from logarithmic growth curves for these variables.

Estimations with annual data: We estimated with annual data the following models

$$LogX_{ct} = a + by_t + cLogX_{ct-1} + u_t \qquad (3.88)$$

$$\pi_t = d + (1-b)y_t + by_{t-1} - cx_{ct-1} + u'_t \qquad (3.89)$$

for the period 1957–85 [19] and for subperiods 1957–69 and 1970–85. Periods that showed the largest differences in the variance in the growth rate of the nominal product were chosen. These were 0.102 for 1957–69 and 0.069 for 1978–85 [20].

Lucas asserts that his test 'involves two steps. First, within each country (11) and (12) [3.88–89 in our case] should perform reasonably well. In particular, under the presumption that demand fluctuations are the major source of variation in $\Delta P_t(\pi_t)$ and y_{ct} $(LogX_{ct})$ the fits should be "good". The estimated values of π (b) and λ (c) should be between zero and one. Finally, since (11) and (12) involve five slope parameters but only two theoretical ones, the estimated π (b) and λ (c) values obtained from (11) should work reasonably well in explaining variations in p.' (Lucas, 1973, p 330). We shall analyze these relationships in our estimations and the results are presented in table 3.7.

For all subperiods, we got values of b which were between 0 and 1, while for c, we got values which were either less than 0 or greater than 1. The first was the case for the inflation equations for the periods 1957–85 and 1957–69. The second being the case for the real income equation in the period 1970–85 and for the inflation equation for the same period, even if divergence from 1 in the last case was negligible. However, it should be noted that in none of these cases was c significantly different from 1 at the 5 per cent level.

With the exception of the real output equation in the period 1957–69, the fit of the model is fairly good (R^2 lies between 0.45 and 0.80).

Lastly, when we use b and c estimations from the real output equations in the inflation equations, we still get quite an acceptable fit (R^2 between 0.40 and 0.60).

The F–values for both equations are high for 1957–85 and for the subperiod 1970–85. On the other hand, it is not significant at the 5 per cent level for the equations of the period 1957–85. The F–values are especially low for the real income equations, which indicates that variations in the nominal product had no impact on output during the period.

Regarding Lucas' test for the relationship between σ_y^2 and b, we find that in period 1957–69 (when σ_y^2 is greatest), b in the real income equation, is much lower than in the period 1970–85 (when σ_y^2 is least). The inverted relationship is true for (1–b) in the inflation equation. These results support the hypothesis that it is only unexpected variations in nominal demand which influence the agents' production decisions and that there is no 'trade–off' between the 'expected' inflation and the activity level, this being true even in the short run.

50

Table 3.7
Lucas' model for the 'trade off' between inflation and real product (estimations with annual data)

Period 1957 – 85.

$$\text{LogX}_{ct} = -0.0323 + 0.648y_t + 0.8934 \text{ LogX}_{ct-1}$$
$$(-1.777) \quad (1.566) \quad (6.468)$$
$$F = 22.678 \quad R^2 = 0.6447$$

$$\pi_t = 0.1084 + 1.2221y_t - 0.1851y_{t-1} + 0.2795x_{ct-1}$$
$$(0.963) \quad (4.090) \quad (-0.581) \quad (0.200)$$
$$F = 8.426 \quad R^2 = 0.5130 \quad DW = 2.830$$

Period 1959–69.

$$\text{LogX}_{ct} = -0.0133 + 0.0214y_t + 0.0172 \text{ LogX}_{ct-1}$$
$$(-0.880) \quad (0.579) \quad (0.048)$$
$$F = 0.175 \quad R^2 = 0.0374 \quad DW = 1.613$$

$$\pi_t = 0.1350 + 1.4130y_t - 0.4816y_{t-1} + 4.8841X_{ct-1}$$
$$(0.659) \quad (2.307) \quad (-0.769) \quad (1.129)$$
$$F = 2.173 \quad R^2 = 0.4490 \quad DW = 2.877$$

Period 1970–85.

$$\text{LogX}_{ct} = -0.1396 + 0.2777y_t + 1.3343 \text{ LogX}_{ct-1}$$
$$(-3.267) \quad (3.215) \quad (6.713)$$
$$F = 24.991 \quad R^2 = 0.8196 \quad DW = 1.542$$

$$\pi_t = 0.0631 + 1.2267y_t - 0.0621y_{t-1} - 1.0664X_{ct-1}$$
$$(0.384) \quad (3.770) \quad (-0.167) \quad (-0.825)$$
$$F = 6.893 \quad R^2 = 0.6740 \quad DW = 2.834$$

Looking at the distribution of nominal demand shocks between output and inflation, we find that in all periods, parameter (1–b) in the inflation equation is not significantly different from 1. Parameter b in the real production equation is always near 0. This implies that most of the nominal demand variations influence inflation already during the first year. This fits very well with Lucas' view of an economy with high inflation, where the agents have learnt to identify variations in prices in their own markets with those in the general price level.

Estimations with quarterly data: We estimated (3.88–89) with seasonally adjusted quarterly data (see table 3.8) for period III/1975–IV/1978 and subperiods III/1976–II/1980 and III/1980–IV/1985. The last two periods showed the largest differences in the growth rate of demand variance, 18.215 and 38.649 respectively.

In relation to the annual models, we also find here that the value of b always is between 0 and 1 and this was also the case with c values in the real product equations. In the inflation equations, c was instead always less than 0, even though never significantly different from 0 at the 5 per cent level. The fit of the models is good in all cases with R^2 which varies between 0.60 and 0.85.

Lastly, we see that the fit of the inflation equations with b and c parameter

Table 3.8
Lucas' model for the 'trade off' between inflation and real product (estimations with quarterly data)

Period III/1975 − IV/1985.

$$\text{LogX}_{ct} = -0.0318 + 0.3099y_t + 0.9991 \ \text{LogX}_{ct-1}$$
$$(-3.629) \quad (4.204) \quad (18.375)$$

$$F=174.431 \ R^2=0.9018 \ DW=2.633$$

$$\pi_t = 0.0294 + 0.7607y_t + 0.0020y_{t-1} + 0.3244x_{ct-1}$$
$$(2.419) \quad (8.739) \quad (0.018) \quad (1.664)$$

$$F=32.771 \ R^2=0.7266 \ DW=1.905$$

Period III/1976−II/1980

$$\text{Logx}_{ct} = -0.0562 + 0.4072y_t + 0.465 \ \text{LogX}_{ct-1}$$
$$(-4.837) \quad (4.606) \quad (0.292)$$

$$F=10.754 \ R^2=0.6419 \ DW=1.393$$

$$\pi_t = -0.0058 + 0.6583y_t + 0.3639y_{t-1} + 0.1939X_{ct-1}$$
$$(-0.185) \quad (3.555) \quad (1.641) \quad (0.591)$$

$$F=7.281 \ R^2=0.6651 \ DW=1.761$$

Period III/1980−IV/1985

$$\text{LogX}_{ct} = -0.0221 + 0.2535y_t + 0.8325 \ \text{LogX}_{ct-1}$$
$$(-2.195) \quad (2.697) \quad (4.622)$$

$$F=12.129 \ R^2=0.6062 \ DW=2.609$$

$$\pi_t = 0.0353 + 0.6294y_t + 0.1608y_{t-1} + 0.4472X_{ct-1}$$
$$(3.077) \quad (5.448) \quad (1.109) \quad (1.890)$$

$$F=27.110 \ R^2=0.8443 \ DW=1.849$$

estimations from the real output equations is also relatively good, with R^2 which lies between 0.40 and 0.60.

The relationship between σ_y^2 and the b parameter is once again negative in the real income equations and the parameter is much larger in the period, III/1976−II/1980, where σ_y^2 is lower. This supports the hypothesis of no 'trade off' between the activity level and inflation above that which is caused by unexpected variations in nominal demand. In the inflation equations, we found no relationship between (1−b) parameter and σ_y^2.

Regarding the distribution of nominal demand growth into price and real output effects, we find that in all periods, inflation seems to absorb the greater part of nominal demand growth already during the first quarter. Parameter (1–b) in the inflation equations shows a value that lies between 0.60 and 0.75 and is always significant at the 5 per cent level. The effect on real output during the first quarter is also significant in all periods with a value on parameter b which lies between 0.25 and 0.40. In all cases, the sum of b and (1–b) was near 1.

We shall summarize below the main conclusions from the analysis with Lucas' model:

a)   In both the annual and quarterly models, we found a negative correlation between σ_y^2 and parameter b in the real output equation. This result supports Lucas' hypothesis that the more variable is nominal demand, the less is its impact on the agents' production decision. This is because agents generate expectations in a rational way and learn to distinguish between variations in the general price level and variations in the relative prices. The results indicate that money is neutral, even in the short run, and affects production only when changes in it are unexpected.

b)   Variations in the growth of demand during the first year and especially during the first quarter are mostly due to inflation. However, the effects on real output within the first year are significant (except in period 1959–1968). These effects are especially large and are very significant in the first quarter.

Lastly, we should point out that equation (3.87) above implies that the effects of variations in nominal demand on real output are assumed to be geometrically decreasing after period t, which, as we shall see later, need not be the case in Uruguay, especially with regard to quarterly models. The fact that the effects on real output do not weaken after period t could be the cause of instability in parameter c in our estimations in this section.

3.5.3   *Some general conclusions*

The study of the augmented Phillips curve and Lucas' model, which we used to test the neutrality of money seem to point in the same direction, that inflation and the activity level are not only independent in the long run, but their relationship is weak in the short run too. In this direction point the insignificant coefficients for the real variables in the Phillips curve and the relationship between output variations and 'unidentified' demand variations in Lucas' test.

This result supports the NUR hypothesis in that it implies a very weak relationship between inflation and the output level, even in the short run. However, to the extent that all effects of demand variations on the real product would also be weak and temporary, the result does not have to support the NUR hypothesis .

These two implications of the NUR hypothesis – lack of a connection between inflation and the activity level and the inability of nominal demand variations to influence real output – are placed equally within the monetarist world. This is due to the fact that monetarists argue that all variations in income depend on real or imagined changes in relative prices. In other theoretical contexts, these aspects do not have to be interconnected.

As we shall see in the coming section, the fact that the activity level is independent of inflation also in the short run, does not mean that it is independent of the level of aggregate demand in a disequilibrium model.

3.6   Inflation, output variations and the real wage. A tentative explanation of the patterns 1955–85

3.6.1   *The volume of money growth, inflation and output variations*

The earlier sections offered some results which uphold the monetarist view of the effects of money growth on the price and output levels. We saw that:
1) The 'trade off' between inflation and the activity level was weak and very temporary so that variations in the volume of money in the first quarter went into inflation. Practically all the analysed models confirmed this.
2) In section 3.5, no results indicated any special relationship between output and unexpected money growth, but this could be, among other things, because our money supply functions do not successfully differentiate between expected and unexpected growth of money supply.

In simpler terms, the impression we got is that in the short run, agents ascribe all the variations in prices to variations in the general price level. Real effects of monetary policy seem weak and short lived, a consequence of the quick adjustment of expectations to the inflation rate.

It is unclear, however, to what extent these results are due to the characteristics of the models. The monetarist model assumes that the real effects of variations in nominal demand can only take place while price expectations are adjusted. This is the case, for example, in Lucas' model, which assumes that real effects diminish geometrically after period t. The series of events behind such models are as follows: An increase in money growth accelerates inflation. This creates a gap between expected and the actual inflation and causes the real wage to decrease. When employees modify their expectations, the nominal and the real wages increase once again. Production declines and the price level increases further. Variations in the real output must, on the whole, take place before the expectations and inflation have adjusted completely to the new equilibrium situation.

If we take into consideration the fact that short term variations in output could depend on factors other than temporary differences between actual and expected variations in the price level, and also extend our analysis in time, we could get results which do not fit well in the framework of the monetarist model.

If we were to compare, on a yearly basis, the relationship between money growth on one hand and that between money growth and real income growth on the other, we would find (see table 3.9) that most of the real effects of money growth occur after the impact on the price level has been fully realized. This implies that the real effects of money growth could depend on factors other than false expectations about the rate of inflation.

For the whole period 1956–85, the impact on inflation appears to be fully effected during the first year, while output effects are positive and significant only during the second year. During 1956–74, the growth of the volume of money growth seems to have real negative effects during the first year and positive ones during the following year.

The special pattern we got for the period 1956–74 can be explained in a number of ways. A possible explanation is that the inflation, which accelerates due to increases in money growth, has a negative effect on consumption because the consumers cannot differentiate between the general and relative price increases (Deaton, 1977) [21]. Another possible explanation is that under fixed exchange rates, inflation has a negative effect on exports which is later stimulated through devaluation.

Finally, this pattern indicates that on the one hand, the real effects caused by variations in nominal demand are not of a temporary nature as suggested by some of the previous models. On the other hand, it is clear that these effects can be independent of expectations and dependent on variations in effective demand, which is incompatible with the monetarist approach.

54

Table 3.9
The relationship between real income and the growth of the volume of money (estimations with annual data)

Period 1956–85

$$\S \quad x_t = -1.1389 \;\; -0.0535T \;\; -0.0245ml_t \;\; +0.0797ml_{-1} \;\; +0.0425ml_{-2}$$
$$(-0.758) \;\; (-0.662) \;\; (-1.214) \;\; (3.664) \;\; (2.102)$$

$$-0.0279ml_{-3}$$
$$(-1.246)$$

$$F=5.089 \quad R^2=0.6182$$

$$x_t = -1.3433 \;\; -0.1579T \;\; +0.0209m2_t \;\; +0.0846m2_{-1} \;\; +0.0237m2_{-2}$$
$$(-1.069) \;\; (-1.685) \;\; (0.781) \;\; (2.922) \;\; (0.819)$$

$$-0.0272m2_{-3}$$
$$(-0.938)$$

$$F=4.947 \quad R^2=0.5076 \quad DW=1.600$$

Period 1956–74

$$x_t = 0.2668 \;\; +0.1302T \;\; -0.0625ml_t \;\; +0.0496ml_{-1} \;\; +0.0292ml_{-2}$$
$$(0.204) \;\; (0.689) \;\; (-2.138) \;\; (1.927) \;\; (1.127)$$

$$-0.0303ml_{-3}$$
$$(-1.029)$$

$$F=1.679 \quad R^2=0.3924 \quad DW=1.674$$

$$x_t = 0.1741 \;\; +0.0730T \;\; -0.0776m2_t \;\; +0.0700m2_{-1} \;\; +0.0495m2_{-2}$$
$$(0.143) \;\; (0.289) \;\; (-2.072) \;\; (2.099) \;\; (1.1437)$$

$$-0.0369m2_{-3}$$
$$(-0.953)$$

$$F=1.836 \quad R^2=0.4588 \quad DW=1.864$$

Period 1975–85

$$x_t = 10.7070 \;\; -0.5973T \;\; +0.0604ml_t \;\; +0.0672ml_{-1} \;\; +0.0787ml_{-2}$$
$$(0.940) \;\; (-1.812) \;\; (1.905) \;\; (1.654) \;\; (1.747)$$

$$-0.0870ml_{-3}$$
$$(-2.034)$$

$$F=11.261 \quad R^2=0.9184 \quad DW=2.520$$

$$\S \;\; x_t = 6.6485 \;\; +0.4887T \;\; +0.0862m2_t \;\; +0.0358m2_{-1} \;\; +0.0410m2_{-2}$$
$$(0.673) \;\; (-1.749) \;\; (2.252) \;\; (0.809) \;\; (0.897)$$

$$-0.0464ml_{-3}$$
$$(-1.347)$$

$$F=4.445 \quad R^2=0.9222$$

§ Yule–Walker estimators with $\rho = 2$.

Table 3.10

The relationship between inflation and the growth of the volume of money (estimations with annual data)

Period 1956–85

$$\pi_t = \underset{(7.437)}{0.9523ml_t} \underset{(0.548)}{+0.0908ml_{t-1}} \underset{(-0.855)}{-0.1370ml_{t-2}} \underset{(1.080)}{+0.1582ml_{t-3}}$$

$$F=56.799 \quad R^2=0.9081 \quad DW=2.028$$

$$\pi_t = \underset{(5.706)}{1.0390m2_t} \underset{(0.021)}{+0.0051m2_{t-1}} \underset{(-1.099)}{-0.2714m2_{t-2}} \underset{(1.089)}{+0.2146m2_{t-3}}$$

$$F=36.393 \quad R^2=0.8636 \quad DW=1.703$$

Period 1956–74

$$\pi_t = \underset{(6.582)}{1.1775ml_t} \underset{(0.279)}{+0.0554ml_{t-1}} \underset{(-1.447)}{-0.2934ml_{t-2}} \underset{(0.901)}{+0.1689ml_{t-3}}$$

$$F=37.739 \quad R^2=0.9264 \quad DW=2.024$$

$$\pi_t = \underset{(5.927)}{1.4419m2_t} \underset{(0.3\ 9)}{+0.0216m2_{t-1}} \underset{(-1.793)}{-0.5317m2_{t-2}} \underset{(0.536)}{+0.1440m2_{t-3}}$$

$$F=33.071 \quad R^2=0.9168 \quad DW=2.568$$

Period 1974–85

$$\pi_t = \underset{(2.333)}{0.6066ml_t} \underset{(1.103)}{+0.4602ml_{t-1}} \underset{(-0.697)}{-0.3078ml_{t-2}} \underset{(0.940)}{+0.3119ml_{t-3}}$$

$$F=19.925 \quad R^2=0.9088 \quad DW=1.507$$

$$\pi_t = \underset{(1.816)}{0.5774m2_t} \underset{(0.854)}{+0.4281m2_{t-1}} \underset{(-1.071)}{-0.5401m2_{t-2}} \underset{(1.276)}{+0.4228m2_{t-3}}$$

$$F=14.442 \quad R^2=0.8784 \quad DW=1.163$$

3.6.2   *The growth of real wages over the business cycle in the period 1955–85. A possible disequilibrium explanation*

A crucial issue with regard to the cause of short term variations in the real product, divergences between the expected and the actual variations in the price level or variations in effective demand, is the relationship between those variations and the real wage, i.e. the behaviour of the real wage during an economic boom.

As we saw in section 3.3, a direct consequence of the monetarist analysis of the business cycle is that the real wage must move anti–cyclically. From the monetarist point of view, the business cycle itself depends on misconceptions among the workers concerning the real wage level, which in turn depends on faulty expectations about inflation. If a decrease in nominal wages is taken to be a decline in real wage by the employees, it will bring about a recession and a reduction in the supply of labour. If, on the other hand, the labour demand curve has a negative slope, the real wage must then go up. The opposite result can be found during an economic boom when an increase in nominal wage is taken for an increase in the real wage. Consequently, movements in the real wage are not cyclical.

We shall now analyse the relationship between the cyclical variations in real output and the real wage in Uruguay during 1955–85.

Estimation with annual data (table 3.11) shows a negative relationship between real output and the real wage for the whole period 1955–85, which is primarily due to a long term diminishing real wage. An analysis of shorter periods shows that the negative relationship existed mainly after 1972 while for the period 1955–71, the relationship was positive.

Table 3.11

The relationship between real income and real wage (annual data)

Period 1955–85

$$X_t = 39143.70 - 140.13 \left(\tfrac{W}{P}\right)_t$$
$$\quad (18.982) \quad (-6.391) \qquad F=61.588 \quad R^2=0.8725$$

Period 1955–71

$$X_t = 15957.04 + 68.92 \left(\tfrac{W}{P}\right)_t$$
$$\quad (5.093) \qquad (2.396) \qquad F=13.760 \quad R^2=0.7605$$

Period 1972–85

$$X_t = 39329.63 - 127.00 \left(\tfrac{W}{P}\right)_t$$
$$\quad (12.583) \quad (-2.994) \qquad F=24.987 \quad R^2=0.8823$$

Note: Yule–Walker estimators.

In a quarterly analysis (table 3.12) for the period after the mid 1970's, we see that during I/1975 – IV/1985, a period consisting of a complete business cycle, with a peak during the second quarter of 1981, the relationship between the real product and the real wage is not significant. This is due to the fact that during the increasing activity phase of the business cycle, I/1975 – IV/1979, the relationship is negative, while it is positive during the decline.

We have a distinctive pattern for real wage development in connection with short term variations in the real product, which does not correspond to the monetarist assumptions for the existence of an business cycles since the real wage does not move cyclically. Even if, in the long run, the real wage shows a negative relationship with real output, it is primarily due to a long term trend. On top of the business cycle, on the other hand, the real wage shows no negative relationship to the activity level.

A possible explanation for the relationship between the real wage and the business cycle in Uruguay during the last thirty years, is based on the existence of a permanent disequilibrium situation of excess supply. Although it is consistent with the course of events during the period in question, this obviously needs a broader analysis. [22]

Given disequilibrium in the economy, not in the monetarist sense but in the sense that the agents find themselves off their notional supply and/or demand curves (Barro, Grossman, 1976), the real product is then no longer determined by the level of real wages or the marginal product of labour, but by demand. The level of real output consequently becomes independent of the price level even in the short run, but is sensitive to changes in the effective demand. [23]

This situation exists when the level of real output is sensitive to variations in the effective aggregate demand. The level of the real wage can be independent of and even positively related (which is the most plausible) to the real product during the

Table 3.12
The relationship between real income and real wages (quarterly data)

Period 1/1975–IV/1985

$$x_t = 96.0277 + 0.2137(\tfrac{W}{P})_t - 0.1891(\tfrac{W}{P})_{t-1}$$
$$(8.823) \quad (1.387) \quad (-1.240) \qquad F=67.988 \quad R^2=0.8774$$

Period 1/1975–IV/1979

$$x_t = 140.2792 - 0.2594(\tfrac{W}{P})_t - 0.3267(\tfrac{W}{P})_{t-1}$$
$$(12.180)(-1.327) \quad (-1.575) \qquad F=20.374 \quad R^2=0.8534$$

Period 1/1980–IV/1985

$$x_t = 70.7467 + 0.6113 \, (\tfrac{W}{P})_t - 0.0598(\tfrac{W}{P})_{t-1}$$
$$(5.519) \quad (2.426) \quad (-0.237) \qquad F=77.494 \quad R^2=0.8635$$

Note: Yule–Walker estimators.

business cycle.

Uruguay's economy possibly entered a disequilibrium situation, characterized by insufficient demand in the mid 1950's, owing to, among other things, the tremendous decline in export income, which took place at that time. This had a negative effect on several components of aggregate demand. This indicates that the real wage level during 1955–71 is positively correlated with variations in the real product. This implies that it was determined by demand factors. For such a disequilibrium situation to exist, the price level should be inflexible downwards, which is a possible assumption for Uruguay at that time. [24]

Furthermore, in a situation where the income effect is stronger than the substitution effect, which is the case of Uruguay's economy, we have a labour supply curve which turns downwards at a sufficiently low w/p.

In figures 3.1 and 3.2, we represent the goods and labour markets in a disequilibrium situation of excess supply. X^d and $X^{d'}$, are, respectively, the notional and the effective commodity demand, N^d and $N^{d'}$, the notional and effective labour demand and X^s and N^s are the supply of goods and labour. This is characterized by the features indicated above. Lastly, we have that N is employment and X, produced output. In equation form, we have that

$$X^d = X^d \left(\tfrac{W}{P}, E\right) \qquad (3.90)$$

$$X^{d'} = X^{d'}\left(\tfrac{W}{P}, E, N\right) \qquad (3.91)$$

$$N^d = N^d\left(\tfrac{W}{P}\right) \qquad (3.92)$$

$$N^{d'} = N^{d'}(X) \qquad (3.93)$$

$$X^s = X^s \left(\tfrac{W}{P}\right) \qquad (3.94)$$

$$N^S = N^S \left(\frac{W}{P}\right) \qquad (3.95)$$

where E is export revenue and $E_0 > E_1$.

At point A, where the notional demand and supply curves intersect, there is equilibrium in the goods and labour markets. A decline in export from E_0 to E_1 causes a cumulative process where both the goods and the labour markets are out of equilibrium, with effective demand curves instead of notional ones. The economy is brought to point A' which is a quasi equilibrium point with excess supply on both the goods and the labour markets.

Under these circumstances, a decline in real wage implies no increase in production but rather an increase in unemployment (for example from A'–A to B'–B in figure 3.2) due to the increased labour supply which follows a decline in real wage.

If we introduce one more element into the picture, that is, that the decline in W/P could increase the demand for the foreign commodity, we find that reductions in W/P reduce demand restrictions on the goods and the labour market and increase production. Under these circumstances, there can be a negative relationship between the real wage and production.

Given the above assumptions, we can now define the relationship between production and real wage in Uruguay during 1955–85. It is represented in figure 3.3, which shows the labour market in a disequilibrium with excess supply.

In the period 1955–71 there were temporary variations in the effective aggregate demand. These, which could be assumed to have been mainly due to variations in international demand, caused changes in employment and the real wage. In terms of figure 3.3, the situation could be described as temporary variations in effective demand around line N^d, and of the real wage between $(W/P)^*$ and $(W/P)'$. Every increase in demand implies a decrease in unemployment and (W/P) then tends to increase and vice versa. Thus the real wage moves pro–cyclically.

That equilibrium was not regained through fiscal policy measures may be due to the fact that decline in export income also created restrictions on the supply side. This was obviously the case for large parts of the industrial sector, which used imported capital and raw materials. Under these circumstances, disequilibrium could not be eliminated by expansion of domestic demand.

The period 1972–81 was characterized by export–led growth. The basis for this was a declining real wage brought about by government wage controls and the forbidding of union activities. The fall in the real wage reduced the demand restrictions by increasing exports and caused production and employment to increase along line A'–D' in the figure. During the first part of the process (distance A'–B') both employment and unemployment may increase, owing to the increased labour supply, which was a consequence of the decline in real wage. This was actually the case during 1972–77, when a drastic decline in real wage, increased both unemployment and total employment. After a certain point, the increase in employment was greater than increase in labour supply and unemployment began to decrease (Line B'–D'). This finally led to, in 1980–81, a small increase in the real wage (Line C'– D'). In 1981 when the foreign demand began to fall due to internal and external reasons, employment and production fell back and (W/P) began to fall again in line with rising unemployment (Line D'–E').

The pattern described above for real output and real wage corresponds well with that which we determined empirically for the period 1955–85 and especially for the period I/1975–IV/1985, where real wage moved anti–cyclically in the increasing activity period of the cycle and pro–cyclically during the peak and decline.

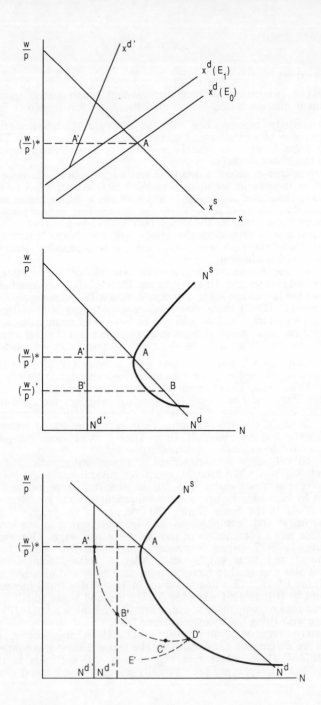

Figures 3.1, 3.2 and 3.3

3.7 Conclusions

We shall now draw some general conclusions from our analysis of Uruguay's inflationary process based on monetarist inflation models, which have exogenous money supply.

We found that the relationship between money growth and inflation was significant during the period of study and that the variable explains much of the variations in the price level, even if, especially after the mid 1970's, when the economy was opened, a lot is left unexplained by our models.

The relationship between the growth of the volume of money per produced unit and inflation appeared stable in the long run, which implies that during the sample period, there were no permanent changes in velocity.

The velocity does not either show any systematic variations in the short run until the mid 1970s. After 1975, however, short term variations in velocity for monetary aggregates M1 and M2 began to take place. These variations did not affect the relationship between inflation and the monetary aggregate with deposits in foreign exchange, that is M3, to the same extent.

These short term variations in velocity, which disturb the relationship between inflation and M1 and M2, were a result of the liberalization of capital movements which, when exchange rates are not completely flexible ('managed float'), implies the endogenisation of money supply, at least in the short run. This occurs when the public response to variations in the expected inflation rate affect international reserves.

Even if such a situation does not in itself imply that the relationship between inflation and the growth of money supply per produced unit is disturbed, it provides a condition for such a situation to exist. In our case, other conditions were that to every abnormally large change in Central Bank credit to the public sector, there was a reaction from the public bringing changes 1) in other reserves (then the volume of money changes in the opposite direction to the central bank's credit) and 2) in the velocity of money or 3) by moving part of bank deposits between domestic and foreign exchange (the latter also used as money).

Such a relationship is partly connected to doubts about the future value of the domestic currency. These circumstances manifested themselves in the economic situation which existed at the beginning of the 1980's and which was such that even given flexible exchange rates, after November 1982, the pattern with short term variations in velocity persisted.

The growth of the volume of money seems to be carried over to inflation in a relatively short time (within the course of the year). Its effects on output are relatively weak and short lived. There is thus no permanent 'trade off' between output and inflation.

The weak relationship between inflation and the activity level does, however, not imply that variations in aggregate demand have no effect on the real income level. This should be the case within the framework of the monetarist theory, where demand variations can only influence output through their unpredictability. However, this was not the case in Uruguay. There were significant variations in real income after the adjustment in price expectations could be considered to have been completed. This implies that variations in output could depend on variations in the effective aggregate demand and that the situation must be analysed within the framework of a disequilibrium model.

A disequilibrium condition implies that the short term connection between inflation and output through W/P disappears, because output no longer depends on the latter. But output is still dependent on the effective demand level, so that it becomes sensitive to variations in aggregate demand. Under these circumstances, we find that 1) the relationship between inflation and the activity level ends without the relationship between the activity level and demand variations being eliminated and 2) that the relationship between the real wage level and the real output level is not of necessity negative as postulated by the monetarist view, but that it probably is

61

positive.

There are signs that the latter situation characterized Uruguay's economy during the period of study.

Notes

1. In table 3.2, results for M2 are shown. Results for M1 are shown in the appendix to section V in Giorgi (1987). We shall generally present the results for M2 and M3 using quarterly analysis for the period after 1975. Even though, in many cases, M1 results are statistically better than M2's, we assume that M2 is, according to the monetarist view, a more suitable definition of the volume of money.

2. When we used the model with lagged independent variables, we lost a corresponding number of observations at the beginning of the survey period.

3. This is true for all models except M1 with intercept and four lags in the period 1975 − 85.

4. Wen we estimated the model with seven lagged independent variables, we lost four more observations in the beginning of the survey period. It then begins I/1977.

5. The results for M2 are shown in the appendix to section V in Giorgi (1987).

6. The pattern of (3.21) is not valid for M1 in the period I/76 − IV/82. For M2 in the period 1/83 − IV/85 we also find that the sum of the parameters of the (m − x) variables is not different from 1. This, however, mostly depends on the fact that M2's average velocity is accelerating during the period. We also found that the sum of these parameter is considerably greater than 1 in model (3.22).

7. In the annual as well as quarterly models, observations at the beginning of the survey period are missing due to the lagged independent variables of the model.

8. When we lag the capacity variables for one period, we get, in most cases, the right sign and value relationship. However, this is not consistent with the logic of the model, since it is not possible that capacity restrictions have an effect on inflation after one year.

9. The results of estimations with M2 are shown in the table and those with M1 in appendix VI in Giorgi (1987).

10. When the signs disagree with the theoretical model the significance level is estimated by a two–sided test. In other cases, we use a one–sided test.

11. There was, however, an improvement in both F− and R^2−values during the last subperiod where the relationship between money and inflation is most unstable. This is contrary to the results from the simpler model in the preceding chapter, which imply a greater flexibility of the Friedman model to arrest temporary disturbances in the relationship between money and the price level.

12. We estimated the model with the lagged capacity variables for one period. We then got the right sign of the capacity variables, even if value relationship between these variables continued to conflict with the theoretical model in some cases. However, the changes in the model indicate no significant changes in the results of the model.

13. We got a better F− and R^2−values in the Friedman model with M2 for the whole period and with M1 and M2 for the last subperiod. This was true for both variants of the last subperiod, that is, III/81 and I/83–IV/85.

14. We say that money is neutral when there is equilibrium instead of saying that it is neutral in the long run. This formulation is more acceptable since, as we have seen, equilibrium exists in the short run too, according to the

theory of rational expectations.

15. We have no information on annual unemployment before 1965.

16. We have no information on quarterly unemployment before III/1977.

17. Given that $x_2 = \hat{y}$ (OLS–estimator of y) we have that $m_{y2} = \Sigma(y_i - \bar{y})\,(\hat{y}_i - \bar{y})^2 = \Sigma(\hat{y}_i - \bar{y})^2 + \Sigma e_i(\hat{y} - \bar{y}) = m_{22} + \Sigma e_i(\hat{y}_i - \bar{y})$. Given that $\Sigma e_i(\hat{y} - \bar{y}) = 0$, we then have that $m_{y2} = m_{22}$.

18. In this section, we return to the notation used previously: X = real product, x = the growth rate in real product, y = growth rate in nominal product or demand, π = the inflation rate and a c subscript signifies divergences from the trend for the variable in question.

19. We miss one observation when estimating the model.

20. We estimated (3.88–89) using the annual growth rate in the volume of money as the explanatory variable instead of the growth rate in nominal demand. We estimated models for both M1 and M2 and for the periods 1957–85, 1957–74 and 1975–85. In all cases, we got smaller b parameters in the real income equations than when we used variations in nominal demand, which implies that there are other reasons for the variations of the nominal demand equations than mere variations in the volume of money, and that these affect output.
For the period 1957–74, we found that parameter b in the real income equation was insignificant at the 5 per cent level in both M1 and M2 models. For period 1975–85, we found that M2 had a very positive effect on output.

21. That consumers do not differentiate between the general and relative price variations does not mean that agents on the labour market behave in a similar manner. In both cases, it has to do with agents who have different levels of organization and information possibilities.

22. There are, of course, also other possible interpretations of this relationship between real wage and output. There are some studies of disequilibrium econometrics for Uruguay (Rama, 1986; Licandro, 1987; Castel and Forteza, 1990). They identify three different macroeconomic regimes, in the fix–price theory sense, since 1975. They were classical unemployment 1975–78, repressed inflation 1979–81, and Keynesian unemployment 1982–87. During the first period there was thus according to this view a negative relationship between W/P and Y, while there was a positive relationship in the two latter periods. The view of events given in these studies is different than the one presented in this section.

23. In such a situation, variations in the volume of money growth would influence output not through variations in the real wage but through the real balance effect. But if expectations in the price level adjust quickly, this effect becomes temporary and thereby money policy becomes less effective. Such a situation can be characterized by the fact that the real output level is slightly sensitive to variations in the growth of the volume of money in the short run and totally independent in the long run. The delayed relationship between output and money in Uruguay can be explained by other means, for example, through the relationship between inflation and devaluation which existed during the period when the delayed effects of the growth of the volume of money on output was most obvious, that is before the mid 1970's.

24. Martin Rama disagrees with the interpretation of the the events given in this paragraph. He argues that lower export incomes may represent excess supply in the cattle raising sector, but not necessarily in the rest of the economy. Instead, lower export incomes led to a higher exchange rate. By that time, the only imports allowed in Uruguay were fuel and other inputs for the manufacturing sector. Therefore, higher import prices reduced the supply of goods.

4 Inflation and the balance of payments in a monetarist model for a small open economy: the case of Uruguay 1956–85

4.1 Introduction

In chapter 3, we applied variations of the standard monetary model of inflation for a closed economy. We now extend our analysis by applying the monetary model for an open economy i.e. a model with endogenous money supply, to analyze inflation and the balance of payments for the same period. The model is based on the monetary approach to the balance of payments (Johnson, 1972; Frenkel and Johnson, 1976).

The analysis will, in the main, be based on a model developed by Blejer and Leiderman (Blejer, 1977; Blejer and Leiderman, 1981) which differentiates between 'traded' and 'non–traded' goods. The introduction of 'non–tradables' into the model implies that variations in the domestic credit component of the monetary base can cause short run differences between domestic and international rates of inflation.

We shall also apply a modified version of this model which takes account of the imbalances in the real sector and their impact on inflation and the balance of payments. This we do by introducing into the model an augmented Phillips curve along the lines developed by Bruno (Bruno, 1977, 1979; Bruno and Sussman, 1979).

Like in the previous chapter, we investigate how well these models explain the inflationary process in Uruguay, given shifts in economic and political regimes. Particular note will be taken of the changes in trade and foreign exchange restrictions during the course of the sample period. Use of an open economy model allows us to focus on issues that were not taken up in chapter 3: the relative impact on inflation of domestic and external factors, the effect of changes in the exchange rate etc.

The chapter proceeds as follows: In section 2 we present the models used in the empirical applications, i.e. models incorporating non–tradables in their simpler and extended versions.

In section 3, we discuss the problems related to the derivation of reduced form estimation equations from the models presented in section 2, along with other econometric difficulties. We look at the formation of expectations, in particular the case of rational expectations, discussing different ways of modeling them empirically. We consider the problem of lagged variables in the models and methods to control and overcome the autocorrelation in the residuals.

Also this part gives an account of the periodization of the empirical analysis, with respect to the outline of the economic policy. It ends with a presentation of the data used in the estimations.

In sections 4 to 6, we present the results of our estimations and compare them with those from other studies in Uruguay as well as other countries. In section 7, we finally draw the most important conclusions from our findings.

4.2   The monetarist theory of inflation for an open economy

4.2.1   *The standard theory of inflation and the balance of payments*

The monetarist theory of inflation for an open economy is composed of two elements, namely global monetarism and the monetary approach to the balance of payments (Whitman, 1975).

According to the global view, international inflation depends on the excess of the growth rate in the international supply of money over that of international real production (Johnson, 1972; Branson, 1975; Dornbusch, 1980). In the long run, this determines every country's rate of inflation.

The main assumption for this is that the world economy is largely integrated, via fixed exchange rates between countries and the free flow of goods and capital across borders. Moreover, prices and interest rates tend to equalize across countries, consistent with the law of one price.

Under these circumstances, the global monetarist model of inflation is nothing more than the standard model for a closed economy (Friedman, 1968, 1970, 1971) applied at the international level. Like in the former, the global model implies that prices are flexible, money is neutral in the long run and output is given by the natural rate of employment.

The monetary approach to balance of payments explains a mechanism through which, in the long run, price levels are equalized across countries in spite of the fact that the products produced neither are perfect substitutes nor all traded internationally. Equalization of the national price levels takes place as the quantity of money, irrespective of origins, is divided among countries via their balance of payments. Thus money markets are cleared in each country via adjustment of supply to demand. Through this mechanism, the rates of inflation in the different countries converge to the international rate of inflation (Dornbusch, 1973, 1980; Johnson, 1972; Frenkel and Johnson, 1976; Frenkel and Mussa, 1985).

According to the monetary approach, the balance of payments is a monetary phenomenon. Thus equilibrium in the balance of payments is seen as equality between stocks, while flows — deficit or surplus — are temporary adjustments to reach equilibrium (Johnson, 1972; Frenkel and Johnson; 1976, Dornbusch, 1980).

In an open economy, the monetary base has two components, namely domestic credit and international reserves. The volume of money increases or decreases with variations in either one of these two components. In an open economy with fixed exchange rates, the desired stock of money balances can be reached via the inflow or outflow of international money (international reserves), in other words through the balance of payments. Thus it is the relationship between the actual and desired stock of balances which determines the balance of payments equilibrium, while a deficit and surplus in the balance of payments are nothing more than self–adjusting mechanisms which guarantee stock equilibrium in the long run.

As already noted, the discrepancies between the desired and the actual stock of real balances in an open economy could be eliminated in two ways; via variations in domestic credit or variations in international reserves. Given fixed exchange rates, this implies that the volume of money is kept outside the control of the monetary authorities. Monetary policy cannot, at least in the long run, affect the price level, but is on the other hand the main equilibrating factor of the balance of payments

65

(Dornbusch, 1980; Frenkel and Mussa, 1985; Marston, 1985). For example, if the growth of domestic credit exceeds the rate of international inflation plus the rate of growth in real output, the actual stock of real balances will be greater than the desired. The surplus will, as a result, move abroad in the form of a balance of payments deficit.

Accordingly, a devaluation would only have passing effects on the balance of payments. These effects, which do not depend on variations in the current account but on those in the demand for real balances, are self–adjusting and therefore temporary (Dornbusch, 1973, 1980).

How long the effects of a devaluation, or the variations between the domestic and international inflation caused by the domestic monetary policies, last would depend on such factors as the share of non–tradables in the economy and the types of adjustment mechanisms at work to realize stock equilibrium on the money market. Adjustment of the supply and demand for real balances can take place in different ways depending on the country's trade regime. It could be via the current or capital account, in the latter if free capital movements are allowed, or via a combination of the two. Free capital movements do, of course, imply that the adjustment process is smoother and quicker (Frenkel, 1976; Swoboda, 1976).

4.2.2   *A short run model with non–tradables*

In the long run equilibrium the adjustment process has been completed and the actual inflation is equal to the expected rate of inflation and the actual stock of money to the desired stock of real balances. Here we will analyse the effects on inflation and balance of payments of the different economic policies in a short run perspective, given a set of regimes describing the country's relationship to the world economy. We, therefore, need a model which takes into consideration the factors which influence and delay the process of adjustment towards equilibrium. We assume a short run perspective so that the instantaneous equilibrium (when expectations have been realized), within the scope of the model, is not the same as the long run one (when adjustment of actual to desired stocks has taken place) (Blejer, 1977; Blejer and Leiderman, 1981; Frenkel and Mussa, 1985).

We distinguish between tradables and non–tradables (Blejer, 1977; Blejer and Leiderman, 1981; Dornbusch, 1980). This implies that domestic monetary policy (i.e. variations in domestic credit) has, in the short run, not only effects on the balance of payments but also on inflation, and that the level of domestic inflation could deviate from the world level. This is because the price for non–tradables, and thereby the relative price between tradables and non–tradables, is affected by the disequilibrium in the money market caused by variations in domestic credit. The size and persistence of these price effects depend on the share of non–tradables in the economy and on the elasticity of the relative price with respect to the disequilibria on the money market i.e. on how the adjustment mechanism between desired and actual stocks of money operates. This is something that is related to the country's external trade regimes, i.e. trade policy, constraints on capital movements, exchange rate policy etc.

In the long run, according to the monetary approach to the balance of payments, adjustment is achieved by the whole effect of domestic monetary policy bearing on the balance of payments, while domestic inflation converges to the world level. Frenkel and Mussa observe that 'the major innovations resulting from the introduction of non–traded goods are that we allow for variations in the relative price of non–tradable goods and in the general domestic price level along the path of convergence to long run equilibrium' (Frenkel and Mussa, 1985, p. 703).

We introduce, finally, the concept of alternative cost for holding money in the money demand function, in other words we incorporate agents' expectations on inflation as an argument in this function.

The model is put together along the lines of Blejer and Leiderman (Blejer, 1977; Blejer and Leiderman, 1981) and we get the following money market equations:

$$M_s = a(R+D) \qquad (4.1)$$

M_s is the nominal supply of money, R is domestic credit, D the level of international reserves and a the multiplier of the monetary base. In the following equation

$$M_d = Pm_d \qquad (4.2)$$

we give the expression for the nominal demand for money, M_d, with P as the price level and m_d, the real demand for money. Next we have the real demand for money

$$m_d = f(y,P_e^*) \qquad (4.3)$$

where y is real income and P_e^* is the expected rate of inflation. We assume that the money market clears in each period, and this requires us to have a flow equilibrium

$$M_s^* = M_d^* \qquad (4.4)$$

where *, in this chapter, indicates rate of growth. By logarithmic differentiation we get

$$a^* + (1-\gamma)R^* + \gamma D^* = P^* + m_d^* \qquad (4.5)$$

where $\gamma = D/(R+D)$ and P^* is the domestic rate of inflation.
In (4.5) we have not assumed that the adjustment to the long term equilibrium has been completed within a single period, since P^* on the right hand side need not equal the international level of inflation (or international inflation plus the change in the exchange rate). Accordingly we have the following expression for domestic inflation

$$P^* = \lambda P_T^* + (1-\lambda)P_{NT}^* \qquad (4.6)$$

where P_T^* is the rate of growth of the traded goods price index, P_{NT}^* the rate of growth of the non–tradables price index and λ is the share of traded goods in the economy.
We also have that

$$P_T^* = P_w^* + \epsilon^* \qquad (4.7)$$

and

$$P_{NT}^* = P_T^* + \theta\Omega \qquad (4.8)$$

where P_w^* is the rate of world inflation, ϵ^* the variation in the exchange rate, Ω is a measure of ex ante monetary imbalance and θ is the elasticity of the relative non–tradables price with regard to the ex ante monetary imbalance. θ is always positive. We thus see that the change of prices for non–traded goods depends on the change of prices for traded goods and the ex ante imbalance on the money market. By inserting and simplifying we get

$$P^* = \xi(P_w^* + \epsilon^*) + (1-\xi)(\gamma D^* + a^* - m_d^*) \qquad (4.9)$$

which is the reduced form for inflation, expressed as a function of international inflation, variations in the exchange rate and imbalances in the money market. The relative weight of the first two factors versus the third, depends on the parameter $\xi = [1+(1-\lambda)\theta]^{-1}$, whose size itself depends on $(1-\lambda)$, the share of non–tradables in the economy, and θ, the elasticity of the relative price with respect to the ex ante imbalance on the money market (Blejer, 1977; Blejer and Leiderman, 1981). When we finally insert (4.9) into (4.5) and solve for $(1-\gamma)R^*$ we get

$$(1-\gamma)R^* = \xi(P_w^* + \epsilon^* + m_d^* - \gamma D^* - a^*) \qquad (4.10)$$

which is the reduced form for the balance of payments, which is dependent on the foreign inflation, the change in the exchange rate, and the imbalances on the money market. The speed of adjustment depends, on the other hand, on the parameter that we analyzed above.

Equation (4.9) shows that for the level of domestic inflation, given a fixed exchange rate ($\epsilon^* = 0$), to equal the international level, even in the short run, demands that $(\gamma D^* + a^* - m_d^*) = P_w^*$ or, assuming a constant multiplier for the monetary base, $(\gamma D^* - m_d^*) = P_w^*$. Assuming constant international inflation and that $m_d^* = y^*$, we see that growth in the domestic credit component of the monetary base should be equal to $(P_w^* + y^*)$ for the economy to remain in equilibrium with the same level of inflation as the world. As shown by equation (4.10), this is also the condition for the balance of payments to remain in equilibrium. Each deviation from the condition $\gamma D^* = P_w^* + y^*$ results in differences between domestic and international levels of inflation and deficit or surplus in the balance of payments (Blejer, 1977).

4.2.3   *A model with non–tradables and disequilibrium in the real sector*

In the previous model, it was assumed that all short run effects resulting from ex ante imbalances in the money markets affect the price level and that there is no effect on the activity level. The model thus assumes full employment, all the time, or, equivalently, that agents have perfect foresight with regard to changes in the price level.

Let us now relax the latter assumption, and allow for the fact that unexpected variations in the price level could cause variations in the activity level. We modify the previous model in this direction by adding the growth rate of nominal wages , w^*, as an argument in the non–tradables price equation and by incorporating an augmented Phillips curve to determine w^* (Bruno, 1978; Bruno and Sussman, 1979). We replace (4.8) with

$$P_{NT}^* = a_1 w^* + a_2 P_T^* + \theta\Omega \qquad (4.11)$$

and define

$$w^* = bP_e^* + \phi(\ell) \tag{4.12}$$

where P_e^* is the expected rate of inflation and ℓ is the excess demand in the labour market.

We also define

$$P_e^* = (1-\lambda)P_{NTe}^* + \lambda P_T^* \tag{4.13}$$

where P_{NTe}^* is the rate of expected inflation for non–tradables and where perfect foresight, regarding international prices, has been assumed (Bruno, 1979; Dornbusch, 1980).

On inserting (4.13) into (4.12) we get

$$w^* = b(1-\lambda)P_{NTe}^* + b\lambda P_T^* + \phi(\ell) \tag{4.14}$$

We now specify the real money demand function in (4.3) as

$$m_d = ye^{\delta P_e^*}, \qquad \delta \! < \! 0 \tag{4.3'}$$

which after logarithmic differentiation, yields

$$m_d^* = y^* + \delta(P_e^* - P_{e_{-1}}^*) \tag{4.3''}$$

By inserting (4.14) into (4.3'') and using $\Omega = \gamma D^* + a^* - P^* - y^*$ we get

$$\Omega = \gamma D^* + a^* - P^* - y^* - \delta[(1-\lambda)P_{NTe}^* + \lambda P_T^* - (1-\lambda)P_{NTe_{-1}}^* - \lambda P_{T_{-1}}^*] \tag{4.15}$$

which, together with (4.14), is inserted in (4.11) to get

$$P_{NT}^* = a_1[(1-\lambda)P_{NTe}^* + b\lambda P_T^* + \phi(\ell)] + a_2 P_T^* + \theta\{\gamma D^* + a^* - P^* - y^* - \delta[(1-\lambda)P_{NTe}^* + \lambda P_T^* - (1-\lambda)P_{NTe_{-1}}^* - \lambda P_{T_{-1}}^*]\} \tag{4.16}$$

Inserting (4.7) into (4.16) and rearranging we get

$$P_{NT}^* = [a_1 b(1-\lambda) + \theta\delta(1-\lambda) - \delta(1-\lambda)]P_{NTe}^* + \delta(1-\lambda)P_{NTe_{-1}}^* +$$
$$(a_1 b\lambda + a_2 - \theta\delta\lambda - \delta\lambda)(P_w^* + \epsilon^*) + \delta\lambda(P_w^* + \epsilon^*)_{-1}$$
$$+ a_1\phi(\ell) + \theta(\gamma D^* + a^* - P^* - y^*) \tag{4.17}$$

which when inserted in (4.6) yields

69

$$P^* = \lambda(P_w^* + \epsilon^*) + (1-\lambda)\{[a_1 b(1-\lambda) + \theta\delta(1-\lambda) - \delta(1-\lambda)]P_{NTe}^* +$$

$$\delta(1-\lambda)P_{NTe_{-1}}^* + (a_1 b\lambda + a_2 - \theta\delta\lambda - \delta\lambda)(P_w^* + \epsilon^*)$$

$$+ \delta\lambda(P_w^* + \epsilon^*)_{-1} + a_1\phi(\ell) + \theta(\gamma D^* + a^* - P^* - y^*)\} \qquad (4.18)$$

Rearrangement gives

$$P^* = \frac{[\lambda + (1-\lambda)(a_1 b\lambda + a_2 - \theta\delta\lambda)]}{1 + (1-\lambda)\theta}(P_w^* + \epsilon^*) \qquad (4.19)$$

$$+ \frac{(1-\lambda)\theta\delta\lambda}{1+(1-\lambda)\theta}(P_w^* + \epsilon^*)_{-1} + \frac{(1-\lambda)[(a_1 b(1-\lambda) - \theta\delta(1-\lambda)]}{1 + (1-\lambda)\theta}(P_{NTe}^*) +$$

$$\frac{(1-\lambda)^2\delta\theta}{1+(1-\lambda)\theta}(P_{NTe_{-1}}^*) + \frac{(1-\lambda)a_1}{1+(1-\lambda)\theta}\phi(\ell) + \frac{(1-\lambda)\theta}{1+(1-\lambda)\theta}(\gamma D^* + a^* - y^*)$$

Equation (4.19) is a reduced form for inflation, given as a function of international inflation plus variations in the exchange rate, the expected inflation for non–tradables, the activity level and variations in the domestic–credit component of the monetary base in excess of the growth of real output.

Inserting (4.6) in (4.3''), and the result together with (4.19) into (4.15) and rearranging gives us

$$(1-\gamma)R^* = \frac{[\lambda + (1-\lambda)(a_1 b\lambda + a_2 - \theta\delta\lambda) + \delta\lambda]}{1 + (1-\lambda)\theta}(P_w^* + \epsilon^*) -$$

$$\frac{\delta\lambda}{1+(1-\lambda)\theta}(P_w^* + \epsilon^*)_{-1} + \frac{\{(1-\lambda)[(a_1 b(1-\lambda) - \theta\delta(1-\lambda) + \delta(1-\lambda)]\}}{1 + (1-\lambda)\theta}$$

$$P_{NTe}^* - \frac{(1-\lambda)\delta}{1+(1-\lambda)\theta}P_{NTe_{-1}} + \frac{(1-\lambda)a_1}{1+(1-\lambda)\theta}\phi(\ell) +$$

$$\frac{1}{1+(1-\lambda)\theta}(\gamma D^* + a^* - y^*) \qquad (4.20)$$

which is the reduced form for the balance of payments, where the latter is a function of the same variables as inflation in equation (4.19).

Analysis of the inflation equation, (4.19), shows that it includes two different kinds of arguments, on the one hand $(P_w^* + \epsilon^*)$ and P_{NTe}^*, which represent the factors which determine inflation under long term equilibrium conditions, while $\phi(\ell)$ and $(\gamma D^* + a^* - y^*)$ represent the impact of short run disequilibrium factors.

To analyze the equation further, we need to make a clear distinction between the two different equilibrium situations to which we referred above with respect to the money market: the short run flow equilibrium, which implies that agents' price expectations coincide with actual inflation, and the long run stock equilibrium, which implies that the process of adjustment, via the balance of payments, is complete.

When we are in flow equilibrium, all monetary imbalances are predictable and their effects are wholly on the level of inflation. These effects are given by the coefficients of the P_{NTe}^* variables. Under these circumstances, variations in the domestic component part of money supply have no real effects and ϕ as well as θ are equal to 0.

If we further assume that $a_1+a_2=1$, and that also $b=1$, which is wholly in line with the monetarist approach, the sum of coefficients for the $(P_w^*+\epsilon^*)$ and P_{NTe}^* variables are equal to 1.[1] This implies that we are in flow equilibrium.

For also stock equilibrium to obtain, we must have $(P_w^*+\epsilon^*)=P_{NTe}^*$. This implies that domestic inflation (given fixed exchange rates) is equal to international inflation and that the rate of growth of the domestic–credit component of money supply is equal to the growth rate of real income plus international inflation. Thus $(\gamma D^*+a^*-y^*)=(P_w^*+\epsilon^*)$ is a direct consequence of $P_{NTe}^*=(P_w^*+\epsilon^*)$

When not in stock equilibrium, θ and ϕ both differ from 0 and the sum of the coefficients of $(P_w^*+\epsilon^*)$ and P_{NTe}^* is less than 1. This last result could, however, also depend on another factor, namely that $b<1$. Both $\theta>0$ and $b<1$ depend on the fact that expectations are not adjusted frictionlessly or that there exist rigidities in prices which means that the expectations of agents' are not fully reflected in their behaviour. This results in real imbalances, of a relatively long duration, so that ϕ also exceeds 0.

With regard to the balance of payments equation, (4.20), the coefficients for P_{NTe}^* and $(P_w^*+\epsilon^*)$ sum, under flow equilibrium conditions, to 1. The stock equilibrium condition is that $(P_w^*+\epsilon^*)=P_{NTe}^*=(y^*-\gamma D^*-a^*)$. This implies that like in the previous model, the condition for equilibrium in the balance of payments (under fixed exchange rates) is that the rate of growth of domestic credit is equal to international inflation plus the growth in the real product.

4.3   Empirical models for inflation and the balance of payments

4.3.1   *Econometric specification of the models*

In this section, we provide the specifications necessary to make the reduced forms for inflation and the balance of payments in our models in sections 4.2.2 and 4.2.3 empirically testable. In this respect, we shall mainly take into consideration four aspects: a) specification of expectations; b) specification of a testable version of the real demand for money function; c) specification of lag structure; d) the problem of autocorrelation.

a) Specification of expectations.   In both the inflation and balance of payments equations in the two models, there are variables which are based on expected values. In the first model, the expected rate of inflation is included in the determination of the demand for money and is part of the money market imbalance which is given by the term $(\gamma D^*+a^*-m_d^*)$. In the second model, the expected rate of inflation of 'non–tradables' is a direct argument in our reduced forms.

The first question concerns the approach to be used regarding the generation of agents' expectations. We use OLS estimates for the expected values. To derive the former, we assumed that agents base their estimators on a number of variables, correlated to the target variables, which they know in advance (Barro, 1977, 1978).

We formulate the public's estimator for the rate of inflation as a function of lagged values of the following variables: the rate of international and domestic inflation, rate of change of the exchange rate, rate of growth of real production, and rate of growth of domestic credit and bank advances. In choosing independent variables for this estimator, we follow Blejer's and Leiderman's work (1981).

With regard to the public's estimator of the rate of inflation for 'non–tradables', we used the same function as in the previous case, with the exception that the aggregate rate of inflation is replaced with the growth rate of the price level for 'non–traded goods'.

For the model in section (4.2.3), the one with imbalances in the real sector, we also use a different formulation to introduce expected 'non–tradables' inflation. The reason, as we shall clarify later on, is that both variants of our inflation model can be used to undertake a special test of the validity of the monetarist assertion that predicted and unpredicted rates of growth of the volume of money have different effects on the price level and production.

The alternative we use is as follows: starting from equations (4.11), (4.12), and (4.7), the growth rate of the price level for 'non–tradables' can be expressed as a function of the rate of growth of the international price level and the exchange rate plus the imbalance on the money market, i.e.

$$P^*_{NT} = f\{(\gamma D^* + a^* - y^*), (P^*_w + \epsilon^*)\} \tag{4.21}$$

If P^*_{NTe} is an unbiased estimator of P^*_{NT}, it follows that

$$P^*_{NTe_t} = \beta_0 (\sum_0^\infty w^i L^i (\gamma D^* + a^* - y^*)_t)$$

$$+ \beta_1 (\sum_0^\infty v^i L^i (P^*_w + \epsilon^*)_t) + u_t \tag{4.22}$$

where $\beta_0 + \beta_1$ can be assumed to sum to 1. In (4.22), as in all the following functions,

$$L^i(x_t) = x_{t-i} \text{ and } \sum_0^\infty x^i = 1.$$

b) Specification of the real demand for money function. We specify the real demand for money as a linear function of current and lagged values of the real output and the expected rate of inflation plus lagged values of the real demand for money itself. We then get

$$m^*_d = \alpha_0 (\sum_0^\infty w^i L^i (y^*_t)) + \alpha_1 (\sum_0^\infty z^i L^i (Pe_t))$$

$$+ \alpha_2 (\sum_0^\infty \eta^i L^{i+1} (m^*_{d_t})) + u_t \tag{4.23}$$

c) Specification of the lag structure. We choose to determine the lag structure of our inflation and balance of payments models empirically. This is done by estimating models with different numbers of lags and examining their performance, in general, and the significance of the variables in particular. In the model using yearly data, we use up to four lags, and in the quarterly variant, up to seven lags.

Using the solutions to the problems of empirical specification that we outlined above, we were finally able to derive the following estimating models for inflation and balance of payments.

Our reduced forms (4.9) and (4.10) in section 4.2.2 becomes

$$P_t^* = \mu(\overset{\infty}{\underset{0}{\Sigma}}b^i L^i (P_w^* + \epsilon^*)_t)$$

$$+ (1-\mu)(\overset{\infty}{\underset{0}{\Sigma}}c^i L^i (\gamma D^* + a^* - m_d^*)_t) + u_t \qquad (4.24)$$

and
$$(1-\gamma)R_t^* = \mu(\overset{\infty}{\underset{0}{\Sigma}}d^i L^i (P_w^* + \epsilon^* + m_d^* - \gamma D^* - a^*)_t) + u_t \qquad (4.25)$$

where m_d^* was generated using the predicted values from the estimation of (4.23).

Our reduced forms (4.19) and (4.20) in section 4.2.3 become, using the first specification variant for expectations,

$$P_t^* = \Psi_0((\overset{\infty}{\underset{0}{\Sigma}}e^i L^i + \overset{\infty}{\underset{0}{\Sigma}}e^i \frac{(1-\lambda)\theta}{1+(1-\lambda)\theta} \frac{\delta \lambda}{} L^{i+1})(P_w^* + \epsilon)_t)$$

$$+ \Psi_1((\overset{\infty}{\underset{0}{\Sigma}}f^i L^i + \overset{\infty}{\underset{0}{\Sigma}}f^i \frac{(1-\lambda)^2}{1+(1-\lambda)\theta} \frac{\delta \theta}{} L^{i+1})(P_{NTe_t}^*)) \qquad (4.26)$$

$$+ \Psi_2(\overset{\infty}{\underset{0}{\Sigma}}\xi^i L^i (\ell_t)) + \Psi_3(\overset{\infty}{\underset{0}{\Sigma}}h^i L^i (\gamma D^* + a^* - y^*)_t) + u_t$$

$\Psi_0 = [\lambda + (1-\lambda)(a_1 b\lambda + a_2 - \theta\delta\lambda)]/(1+(1-\lambda)\theta)$
$\Psi_1 = \{(1-\lambda)[a_1(1-\lambda) - \theta\delta(1-\lambda)]\}/(1+(1-\lambda)\theta)$
$\Psi_2 = [(1-\lambda)a_1 \phi]/(1+(1-\lambda)\theta)$
$\Psi_3 = [(1-\lambda)\theta]/(1+(1-\lambda)\theta)$

and

$$(1-\gamma)R^* = \Pi_0((\overset{\infty}{\underset{0}{\Sigma}}m^i L^i - \overset{\infty}{\underset{0}{\Sigma}}m^i \frac{\delta\lambda}{1+(1-\lambda)\theta} L^{i+1})(P_w^* + \epsilon^*)_t)$$

$$+ \Pi_1((\overset{\infty}{\underset{0}{\Sigma}}n^i L^i - \overset{\infty}{\underset{0}{\Sigma}}n^i \frac{(1-\lambda)\delta}{1+(1-\lambda)\theta} L^{i+1})(P_{NTe_t}^*) + \Pi_2((\overset{\infty}{\underset{0}{\Sigma}}o^i L^i (\ell_t))$$

$$- \Pi_3((\overset{\infty}{\underset{0}{\Sigma}}\varphi^i L^i (\gamma D^* + a^* - y^*)_t) + u_t' \qquad (4.27)$$

where

$\Pi_0 = [\lambda + (1-\lambda)(a_1 b\lambda + a_2 + \theta\delta\lambda) + \delta\lambda]/(1+(1-\lambda)\theta)$
$\Pi_1 = \{(1-\lambda)[a_1 b(1-\lambda) - \theta\delta(1-\lambda)] + \delta(1-\lambda)\}/(1+(1-\lambda)\theta)$
$\Pi_2 = [(1-\lambda)a_1 \phi]/(1+(1-\lambda)\theta)$
$\Pi_3 = 1/(1+(1-\lambda)\theta)$

Using the other variant for the specification of expectations, which is derived by inserting (4.22) into (4.26) and (4.27) and rearranging we get

$$P^*_t = (\Psi_0 + \exists_1 \Psi_1)((\Sigma q^i L^i + \Sigma q^i \frac{(1-\lambda)\ \theta\ \delta\ \lambda}{1+(1-\lambda)\theta}\ L^{i+1})(P^*_w + \epsilon^*)_t)$$

$$+((\exists_0 \Psi_1)(\Sigma s^i(1 + \frac{(1-\lambda)^2}{1+(1-\lambda)}\frac{\delta}{\theta}\frac{\theta}{\theta}\ L^{i+1}) +$$

$$\Psi_3(\Sigma h^i L^i)(\gamma D^* + a^* - y^*)_t + \Psi_2(\overset{\infty}{\underset{0}{\Sigma}} \xi^i L^i(\ell_t)) + u_t \qquad (4.28)$$

and

$$(1-\gamma)R^*_t = (\Pi_0 + \exists_1 \Pi_1)((\Sigma \zeta^i L^i + \Sigma \zeta^i \frac{\delta\lambda}{1+(1-\lambda)\theta}\ L^{i+1})(P^*_w + \epsilon^*)_t)$$

$$+((\exists_0 \Pi_1)(\Sigma \beta^i(1 - \frac{(1-\lambda)\delta}{1+(1-\lambda)\theta}\ L^{i+1}) - \Pi_3(\Sigma \varphi^i L^i))(\gamma D^* + a^* - y^*)_t)$$

$$+\Pi_2(\Sigma o^i L^i(\ell_t)) + u_t \qquad (4.29)$$

where if $\exists_0 + \exists_1 = 1$, we have, when b=1 and $\theta = 0$, that the sum of the parameters for the variables $(P^*_w + \epsilon^*)$ and $(\gamma D^* + a^* - y^*)$ are equal to 1 in equation (4.28) and to zero in equation (4.29). This would imply that our theoretical conclusions in section 2.3 are valid.

As we have said before it is possible by using both variants of the inflation model (4.26) and (4.28), to test the validity of the assumption of 'rational' expectations. If the expected part of the imbalance in the monetary market has an effect on inflation which is clearly separate from the unexpected, then the variable P_{NTe} shall have a separate effect on P^* irrespective of whether $(\gamma D + a^* - y^*)$ is included in the model or not. By using the models (4.26) and (4.28) we can perform an F–test of the significance of current and lagged values of P and thereby test the theory that predicted and unpredicted changes in money supply have different effects (Barro, 1977, 1978).

d) The problem of autocorrelation. Taking into consideration the type of data we use and the type of tests we apply in the empirical section of the study, we need to control for the occurrence of autocorrelation in the residuals. This can be carried out through a variety of methods.

In all cases, we undertake the DW–test for the first order autocorrelation. We also examine autocorrelation of higher order by estimating the autocorrelation coefficients using the Yule–Walker method. We carry out a second order analysis for the annual model and a fourth order analysis for the quarterly model. When we get coefficients which are significant at the 5 per level or in some cases find that there are marked differences in t–values between the OLS and YW estimations of the models' parameters, we use the latter ones, instead of the former.

4.3.2 *Periodization and data specification*

As mentioned earlier, we carried out our analysis for the period 1956–85, but this was divided into different subperiods, taking account of the changes in the country's external regime.

There were three important aspects that we, in this respect, paid particular attention to: variations in foreign capital and trade transaction, together with changes in the exchange rate regime.

The most important subdivision of our study period was the one motivated by liberalization measures in September 1974. Before this, capital transactions were strictly controlled and some quantitative restrictions for foreign trade were also applied. This meant that the country could, for all practical purposes, be considered a closed economy. The adjustment mechanism for the money market, through international reserves, was slow and the authorities could thus keep the volume of money in control over a long period. After September 1974, the adjustment mechanisms became smoother and faster, mainly via the liberalization of the international capital flows.

We also periodized the analysis, taking into consideration changes in the exchange rate policy. Between 1975–85, when the economy could be said to have been open, we identify three subperiods. Estimations are carried out for a) the period 1975–78, where one had a dual–exchange rate regime with a floating financial rate and a 'crawling peg' for commercial transactions; b) the period 1979–82, when a single rate based on a 'crawling peg' announced in advance, was in operation; c) the period 1983–85, when a unique floating exchange rate based on a reasonably 'clean float' was used.

Our analysis is carried out using both annual and quarterly data. Taking into consideration the number of observations, analysis based on annual data is carried out for only the subperiods 1956–74 and 1975–85. Quarterly data are utilized only after III/67, but with this limitation, we carry out quarterly analysis for all subperiods.

The data we used were mostly from Uruguay's Central Bank and Uruguay's Central Statistical Office. From these sources we found the data to construct the following series.

The rate of inflation is defined as CPI's growth rate.

The rate of inflation of non–tradables is defined as the growth rate of the index for housing costs and the costs of other services, each weighted by its own weight in the CPI.

The growth rate of the exchange rate is defined as the growth rate of the commercial dollar rate.

The growth rate of real production is defined as the growth rate of GNP.

The growth rate of the Central Bank's international reserves and domestic credit, as well as the entire banking system's domestic credit, were taken directly from the Central Bank's series.

The growth rate of the volume of money refers to M2 defined as notes and coins outside the bank system plus check credits or interest bearing deposits in the bank system in domestic currency.

The rate of unemployment is defined as the number of unemployed divided by the entire manpower. This variable is used in a standardized form as $\text{Log}(U/1-U)$ where U is the rate of unemployment

The activity level, which is a variable used as an alternative to the the the rate of unemployment, and which is defined as $(\log Y - \log \hat{Y})$, where Y is the real product and $\hat{Y}$ is the full employment real product. The latter is derived by taking an exponential growth path through the business cycle peaks.

For the the growth rate of international inflation, we used the rate of inflation in the developed countries. The source of this information was the IMF–series.

4.4   Results of the analysis of the model with non–traded goods

In this section we shall report the most important results from the estimates of the model with non–tradable goods. The model is estimated annual and quarterly data for the periods, 1956 – 85 and III/67 – IV/85.

The division of the period of investigation was done as suggested in the previous section and we shall, above all concentrate on the comparison of results from estimates of these different subperiods. [2]

In the text and tables below, we use the following name for variables:

$$TTPRIS = P^*_t$$

$$TTRESERV = (1-\gamma)R^*_t$$

$$PRISINT = (P^*_w + \epsilon^*)_t, \ PRISINTL1 = (P^*_w + \epsilon^*)_{t-1} \ etc$$

$$CREDINT = (\gamma D^* + a^* - m^*_d)_t, \ CREDINTL1 = (\gamma D^* + a^* - m^*_d)_{t-1} \ etc$$

$$PMOBALS = (P^*_w + \epsilon^* + m^*_d - \gamma D^* - a^*)_t$$

$$PMOBALSL1 = (P^*_w + \epsilon^* + m^*_d - \gamma D^* - a^*)_{t-1} \ etc.$$

4.4.1 *The analysis of the results for periods with different external regimes*

4.4.1.1 *Estimates with annual data.* Estimates of (4.9–10) for the entire period 1956–85 (see table 4.1) give us a picture of an economy, where imbalances in the domestic monetary market are quickly corrected and have small effects on the inflation, but strong effects on the balance of payments. The imported inflation $(P^*_w + \epsilon^*)$ is transmitted fairly slowly by only a third during the first year.

Otherwise, the inflation equation is not markedly significant. The F–value is not significant at a 5 per cent level and PRISINT is the only variable which is significant at this level. The balance of payments equation, though, shows a better fit with high R^2 and F–values and implies that the adjustment mechanism would eliminate the money imbalance within the course of two years. The sum of coefficients for PMOBALS and PMOBALS1, which are highly significant, sum up to approx. 1.

Table 4.1
Results of estimations with annual data

Method: OLS   OLS
Period: 1956–85   1956–85
Dependent variable: TTPRIS   TTRESERV

Indep.var.	Coeff.	t–value	Indep.var.	Coeff.	t–value
CONSTANT	8.7478	0.5570	CONSTANT	−15.3882	− 1.6648
PRISINT	0.3557	3.2873	PMOBALS	0.4914	4.6837
PRISINTL1	0.1616	1.5178	PMOBALSL1	0.5178	4.9547
PRISINTL2	0.1712	1.7181	PMOBALSL2	0.1217	1.3408
PRISINTL3	0.1028	0.9980	PMOBALSL3	0.2311	2.6090
CREDINT	0.0849	0.5679			
CREDINTL1	− 0.0440	− 0.3001			
CREDINTL2	− 0.0937	− 0.6604			
CREDINTL3	− 0.0417	− 0.2705			

R^2=0.5286   F=2.2429 (0.0805) R^2=0.7176   F=12.0690 (0.000)
DW=1.427   DW=1.524

Method: OLS   YW
Period: 1956–74   1956–74

Dependent variable: TTPRIS   TTRESERV

Indep.var.	Coeff.	t–value	Indep.var.	Coeff.	t–value
CONSTANT	− 9.0760	− 0.6978	CONSTANT −	3.9293	− 0.445
PRISINT	0.2075	2.5443	PMOBALS	0.1387	1.859
PRISINTL1	0.0918	1.0238	PMOBALSL1	0.1409	1.453
PRISINTL2	0.0382	0.4359	PMOBALSL2−	0.0501	− 0.537
CREDINT	0.4758	2.8952	PMOBALSL3	0.1260	1.889
CREDINTL1	0.2176	1.2909			
CREDINTL2	0.1160	0.6876			

R^2=0.8295   F=6.4863 (0.0095) R^2=0.7302   F=3.1575
DW=2.004   NLAG=2

Method: OLS   OLS
Period: 1975–85   1975–85

Dependent variable: TTPRIS   TTPRIS

Indep.var.	Coeff.	t–value		Coeff.	t–value
CONSTANT	30.0522		1.3444	—	
PRISINT	− 0.2580	− 1.0436		− 0.1042	− 0.4412
PRISINTL1	0.2951	1.3339		0.4381	2.0964
PRISINTL2	0.4142	1.5095		0.5989	2.3394
CREDINT	0.2579	1.1889		0.2467	1.0559
CREDINTL1	− 0.0249	− 0.1477		− 0.0188	− 0.1040
CREDINTL2	− 0.1614	− 1.0111		− 0.2530	− 1.6265

R^2=0.5745   F=0.9001 (0.5684)   F=10.7367 (0.0099)
DW=1.905   DW=1.715

Method: OLS
Period: 1975–85

Dependent variable: TTRESERV

Indep.var.	Coeff.	t–value
CONSTANT	−18.3370	− 0.6794
PMOBALS	0.6533	2.1933
PMOBALSL1	0.3791	1.4060
PMOBALSL2	0.3090	1.1686

R^2=0.6016   F=3.5277 (0.0771)   DW=2.036

When we divide the data into the periods before and after 1974, we get a result which makes it possible for us to draw further conclusions concerning the relationship between the country's regime for foreign transactions and inflation and the factors determining the balance of payments.

For the period 1956–74, we get an inflation equation which has a high explanatory power and which is highly significant. The analysis of the particular variables show that it is those factors which affect balance in the domestic money market which also strongly influence inflation. International inflation and exchange rate changes now have less effect. Even if we get, for both the internal and external factors, significant coefficients at a 5 per cent level during the first year, only the coefficient on CREDINT is now near 0.50 while that for imported inflation (PRISINT) is about 0.20. The sum of the parameters for all the variables is insignificantly different from 1 at the 5 per cent level, which conforms with theory. The sum of the parameters on the PRISINT–variables implies that the μ–parameter lies between $0.20 - 0.30$.

The estimates from the equation of the balance of payments confirm this. This also implies that ϵ lies around 0.30 after four years. Moreover, there are no parameters in the equation which are significant at the 5 per cent level. This also means that the imbalances on the money market do not have any major effect on the balance of payments. However, the F–test gives significant results at the 5 per cent level, which may indicate multicollinearity between the variables.

For the period 1975–85, when the economy could be taken to have been open, the results of the inflation model are clearly worse. The F–test indicates that the model fits poorly and none of the variables shows t–values which are significant at the 5 per cent level. The sum of the parameters indicate that μ and $(1 - \mu)$ is clearly below 1 and $(1 - \mu)$ lies around 0.

If we, instead, estimate the model without an intercept, we get a picture which agrees better with the theory. The model now has a reasonable degree of explanation power. We also see that the sum of μ and $(1 - \mu)$ is again insignificantly different from 1 at the 5 per cent level, which is in agreement with theory. Now, however, the relative weight of both variables is changed. It is now the sums of the coefficients on the PRISINT variables (i.e. μ) which are insignificantly different from 1, while the sum of the coefficients of the CREDINT – variables is insignificantly different from 0. It is now international inflation, in particular, plus changes in the exchange market which affect inflation, while imbalances on the money market adjust quickly through the balance of payments. This is also confirmed by the estimates of the balance of payments equation, where the coefficient in the first period lies around 0.65. We get low F– and t–values for this model, probably because the number of observations is quite low.

We can draw some conclusions from these results. First of all, it has been seen that openness in the economy, as far as the international freedom of movement for both goods and capital is concerned has, as expected, a marked effect on the money market's adjustment mechanism through the balance of payments. Thereby, the authorities's ability to control the amount of money, and consequently, the importance of imbalances in the money market for inflation are reduced. In terms of our model, the opening up of the economy implies increases in $(1-\lambda)$ as well as θ, which would lead to an increase in μ, which is wholly in accordance with theory.

Even if we, during the period $1975 - 85$, did not have an immediate adjustment of the amount of money through the balance of payments, it is much faster than in the preceding period. From the theoretical point of view, a greater flexibility in the exchange market should be able to stop the effects of a great openness. Our estimates do not show this.

We shall take a closer look at this in the coming section by estimating the model with quarterly data and by refining the period division.

4.4.1.2   *Estimates with quarterly data.*   Our results from estimates with quarterly data generally confirm the conclusions we drew from the annual analysis. Estimates for the entire period $III/67 - IV/85$ (see table 4.2) with a number of lags which cover two years, give a value of μ which lies around 0.40 and a value of $(1-\mu)$ which is not significantly different from 0. On the other hand, it was only some of the lagged PRISINT–variables which were significant. Also, the inflation model has a low R^2–value and an insignificant F–value.

Table 4.2
Results of estimations with quarterly data

Method: OLS
Period: II/67–IV/85

OLS
II/67–IV/85

Dependent variable: TTPRIS

TTRESERV

Indep.var.	Coeff.	t–value	Indep.var.	Coeff.	t–value
CONSTANT	6.8130	3.5488	CONSTANT	2.3807	1.3044
PRISINT	0.0516	1.2456	PMOBALS	0.5303	8.8743
PRISINTL1	0.0759	1.7621	PMOBALSL1	0.0301	0.5072
PRISINTL2	0.0202	0.4552	PMOBALSL2	0.1084	1.8337
PRISINTL3	0.1111	2.4807	PMOBALSL3	0.1050	1.7698
PRISINTL4	0.0740	1.6358	PMOBALSL4	0.0512	0.8545
PRISINTL5	0.0084	0.1875	PMOBALSL5	0.1004	1.6216
PRISINTL6	0.0960	2.0942			
PRISINTL7	− 0.0074	− 0.1653			
CREDINT	0.0926	1.8736			
CREDINTL1	0.0463	0.8560			
CREDINTL2	− 0.0339	− 0.6302			
CREDINTL3	− 0.0205	− 0.4013			
CREDINTL4	0.0388	0.7724			
CREDINTL5	− 0.0617	− 1.1782			
CREDINTL6	− 0.0619	− 1.1725			
CREDINTL7	− 0.0010	− 0.0218			

R^2=0.3670   F=1.5221 (0.1372) R^2=0.6523   F=16.8885 (0.000)
DW=1.673   DW=1.708

Method: OLS
Period: II/67–III/74

OLS
II/67–III/74

Dependent variable: TTPRIS

TTRESERV

Indep.var.	Coeff.	t–value	Indep.var.	Coeff.	t–value
CONSTANT	0.5362	0.2163	CONSTANT	2.5253	1.1388
PRISINT	0.0868	1.4423	PMOBALS	0.2206	2.3503
PRISINTL1	0.0102	0.2215	PMOBALSL1	0.0623	0.6521
PRISINTL2	0.0570	0.8582	PMOBALSL2	0.0385	0.4018
PRISINTL3	− 0.0039	− 0.0778	PMOBALSL3	0.2109	2.1883
PRISINTL4	0.1835	2.7414	PMOBALSL4	0.1814	1.8615
PRISINTL5	− 0.0493	− 0.9533	PMOBALSL5	0.1150	1.1792
CREDINT	0.3405	2.5307			
CREDINTL1	− 0.2653	− 2.0934			

CREDINTL2	0.2741	2.3325
CREDINTL3	− 0.0055	− 0.0401
CREDINTL4	0.2129	1.7432
CREDINTL5	0.1751	1.1085

R^2=0.9282   F=6.4639 (0.0158) R^2=0.4998   F=1.9987 (0.1447)
DW=1.917   DW=2.059

Table 4.3
Results of estimations with quarterly data

Method: YW   YW
Period: IV/74–IV/85   IV/74–IV/85

Dependent variable: TTPRIS   TTPRIS

Indep.var.	Coeff.	t–value	Coeff.	t–value
CONSTANT	4.4758	1.527	——	——
PRISINT	0.0442	0.999	0.0710	1.745
PRISINTL1	0.1042	2.248	0.1293	2.971
PRISINTL2	0.0235	0.491	0.0523	1.190
PRISINTL3	0.1358	2.510	0.1710	3.522
PRISINTL4	0.0688	1.243	0.1047	2.102
PRISINTL5	0.0106	0.196	0.0374	0.743
PRISINTL6	0.0698	1.298	0.0981	1.976
PRISINTL7	0.1386	2.679	0.1619	3.347
CREDINT	0.0998	2.253	0.1093	2.507
CREDINTL1	0.0357	0.727	0.0360	0.744
CREDINTL2	− 0.0793	− 1.552	− 0.0838	− 1.669
CREDINTL3	− 0.0134	− 0.266	− 0.0163	− 0.328
CREDINTL4	0.1139	2.240	0.1139	2.256
CREDINTL5	− 0.1022	− 2.238	− 0.1179	− 2.675
CREDINTL6	− 0.1209	− 2.651	− 0.1270	− 2.859
CREDINTL7	0.0246	0.615	0.0250	0.623

R^2=0.6406   F=2.1389   F=18.1776
NLAG = 4   NLAG = 4

Method: YW   YW
Period: IV/74–IV/85   IV/74–IV/85

Dependent variable: TTPRIS   TTPRIS

Indep.var.	Coeff.	t–value	Coeff.	t–value
CONSTANT	8.6699	3.815	——	——
PRISINT	0.0550	1.182	0.1258	2.669
PRISINTL1	0.0809	1.646	0.1313	2.506
PRISINTL2	0.0070	0.139	0.0826	1.570
PRISINTL3	0.0876	1.519	0.1749	3.025

CREDINT	0.0845	1.757		0.1159	2.158
CREDINTL1	0.0124	0.279		− 0.0272	− 0.553
CREDINTL2	− 0.0300	− 0.653		− 0.0556	− 1.107
CREDINTL3	− 0.0247	− 0.621		− 0.0158	− 0.350

R^2=0.3893   F=1.6999   F=17.3804

NLAG = 4   NLAG = 4

Method: OLS
Period: IV/74–IV/85

Dependent variable: TTRESERV

Indep.var.	Coeff.	t–value
CONSTANT	1.4856	0.6095
PMOBALS	0.6399	9.1419
PMOBALSL1	0.0302	0.4291
PMOBALSL2	0.1414	2.0305
PMOBALSL3	0.0505	0.7319
PMOBALSL4	0.0268	0.3865
PMOBALSL5	0.0790	1.1060

R^2=0.7213   F=16.3910 (0.0000)

DW=1.507

The balance of payments equation strengthens the impression of a quick adjustment by showing a strongly significant coefficient on PMOBALS during the first quarter, with a value greater than 0.50. Besides, the balance of payments equation is highly significant and shows a moderately high R^2 (0.65).

In the subperiods (see tables 4.2 and 4.3), the relative influence of both PRISINT and CREDINT shows the same pattern as in the annual analysis. We find in the period III/67 − IV/74, that the sum of all coefficients (in an estimation with five lags) is not significantly different from 1, but that the greatest weight lies on CREDINT variables coefficients $(1-\mu)$ approximately 0.75, while μ lies around 0.25 − 0.30.

Between 1975–85 (see table 4.3) the opposite situation is predominant. When we estimate the inflation model without a constant term, we find that, in a seven lags model, μ is not significantly different from 1 and $(1-\mu)$ from 0 at the 5 per cent level. For the two subperiods, we get models which showed significant F–values.

These results are confirmed by the estimations of the balance of payments equations. We then get, for the period III/67 − IV/85 a model for the balance of payments which is not significant and shows a low R^2. All PMOBALS variables show low t–value (insignificant at a 5 per cent level). Even if their coefficients sum up to 1 in a five lags model, the adjustment is obviously slower with low coefficients in the first quarters.

In the second subperiod, the balance of payments model becomes highly significant and with a higher R^2. In a five lags model, the coefficients once again sum up to 1. Now, however, the greatest part of the adjustment is already accomplished during the first quarter. The PMOBALS coefficient lies around 0.65 for the first quarter and is highly significant.

These results obviously confirm our earlier impression that the balance of payments adjustment mechanism and the endogeneity of money supply are strengthened by the liberalization of foreign transactions and that its effects are not eliminated by the high flexibility in the foreign exchange market. In order to look at these conditions in detail, we exposed our models to finer period division which took into consideration variations in the exchange rate regime.

4.4.2   *Results of estimates for periods with different exchange rate regimes*

To examine the influence of different exchange rate regimes on the determinants of inflation, we divide the period 1975–85 into three different subperiods, which were characterized by different regimes. The period classification is as follows: 1) The period IV/74 – IV/78 was characterized by dual exchange rates. The commercial rate, a 'crawling peg', was adjusted according to the difference between the domestic and the foreign inflation. The rate for financial transactions was floating, but there was considerable central bank intervention in the market [3]. 2) The period 1/79–IV/82 was characterized by a unique exchange rate, the 'crawling peg', with exchange rate variations announced a year in advance. 3) During the period I/83–IV/85, there was a floating exchange rate regime.

In the first and third periods, the exchange rate may be considered to have been floating, since the financial rate was determined by the market during both periods. In the second period, there was instead a regime which with regard to monetary policy, is similar to that of a fixed exchange rate. Here, the exchange rate variations were fixed in advance and generally known, which meant that they were regarded as exogenous factors. Under such circumstances, the imbalances on the money market were corrected by the variations in the reserves.

According to our monetarist model, we would expect a lower μ in the first and third periods. However, we could not empirically find such results (see tables 4.4, 4.5 and 4.6).

Table 4.4
Results of estimations with quarterly data

Method: YW   YW
Period: IV/74–IV/78   IV/74–IV/78

Dependent variable: TTPRIS   TTPRIS

Indep.var.	Coeff.	t–value	Coeff.	t–value
CONSTANT	12.9862	2.281	—	—
PRISINT	0.4414	2.825	0.6707	5.709
PRISINTL1	− 0.9403	− 5.844	− 0.7057	− 5.533
PRISINTL2	0.3513	2.140	0.5840	4.605
PRISINTL3	0.0866	0.559	0.3672	3.139
CREDINT	0.2151	5.892	0.2067	5.207
CREDINTL1	− 0.0179	− 0.325	− 0.1085	− 2.567
CREDINTL2	0.0241	0.480	− 0.0537	− 1.288
CREDINTL3	− 0.0487	− 1.326	− 0.0507	− 1.221

R^2=0.9235   F=7.2431   F=35.8645
NLAG = 2   NLAG = 2

Method: OLS
Period: IV/74–IV/78

Dependent variable: TTRESERV

Indep.var.	Coeff.	t–value
CONSTANT	4.5021	1.5718
PMOBALS	0.9406	8.3262
PMOBALSL1	− 0.1068	− 0.8712
PMOBALSL2	0.1431	1.2123
PMOBALSL3	− 0.0573	− 0.4540

R^2=0.8761   F=21.2046 (0.0000)   DW=2.146

Table 4.5
Results of estimations with quarterly data

Method: OLS   YW
Period: I/79–IV/82   I/79–IV/82

Dependent variable: TTPRIS   TTPRIS

Indep.var.	Coeff.	t–value	Coeff.	t–value
CONSTANT	−17.2503	− 2.5444	——	——
PRISINT	− 0.0197	− 0.3538	0.0209	0.392
PRISINTL1	1.8348	1.3441	0.6643	0.472
PRISINTL2	0.7696	0.6642	0.3657	0.325
PRISINTL3	1.1691	1.5757	0.4571	0.629
CREDINT	0.0211	0.2298	− 0.0689	− 0.674
CREDINTL1	− 0.0514	− 0.5184	− 0.1385	− 1.243
CREDINTL2	0.0176	0.1822	− 0.0001	− 0.001
CREDINTL3	0.2249	2.0945	0.0751	0.824

R^2=0.7779   F=3.0647 (0.0789)   F=12.5871
DW=1.383   NLAG = 2

Method: OLS
Period: I/79–IV/82

Dependent variable: TTRESERV

Indep.var.	Coeff.	t–value
CONSTANT	− 2.0518	− 0.5505
PMOBALS	0.4784	3.7112
PMOBALSL1	0.1931	0.6720
PMOBALSL2	0.4112	1.4702
PMOBALSL3	0.1716	0.6966

R^2=0.6664   F=5.4939 (0.0111)   DW=1.615

Table 4.6
Results of estimations with quarterly data

Method: OLS
Period: I/83–IV/85

OLS
I/83–IV/85

Dependent variable: TTPRIS

TTPRIS

Indep.var.	Coeff.	t–value	Coeff.	t–value
CONSTANT	9.7807	2.2652	——	——
PRISINT	0.0991	0.6597	0.3871	3.3962
PRISINTL1	0.0441	1.1329	0.0873	1.8045
PRISINTL2	− 0.0213	− 0.4104	0.0638	1.2500
PRISINTL3	0.0976	1.7351	0.2034	4.5380
CREDINT	0.1751	2.4234	0.2565	2.8680
CREDINTL1	0.0207	0.2930	− 0.0250	− 0.2583
CREDINTL2	− 0.1075	− 1.6524	− 0.2002	− 2.7784
CREDINTL3	− 0.0457	− 1.0373	− 0.0541	− 0.8646

R^2=0.9237   F=4.5419 (0.1203)
DW=1.361

F=31.6219 (0.0023)
DW=2.609

Method: OLS
Period: I/83–IV/85

Dependent variable: TTRESERV

Indep.var.	Coeff.	t–value
CONSTANT	2.8607	0.3444
PMOBALS	0.7678	7.2198
PMOBALSL1	− 0.0269	− 0.2368
PMOBALSL2	0.0769	0.7303
PMOBALSL3	0.0193	0.2153

R^2=0.9150   F=18.8434 (0.0008)   DW=2.390

For the inflation model, we get, for both the first and third periods, a result very similar to that for the entire period IV/74–IV/85. When estimated with the restriction that the constant should be equal to 0 the models become highly significant. The sum of PRISINT variables coefficients is also (in the three lags models) not significantly different from 1 at the 5 per cent level, while the sum of CREDINT variables coefficients was not significantly different from 0. This implies that $\mu = 1$ and the effect of imbalances on the money market on inflation was of little importance.

The balance of payments model show in both these periods, that $\mu = 1$ and that the greatest part of the imbalance on the money market was already corrected during the first quarter, through variations in the reserves.

For the other period, 1/79 − IV/82, we see that the sum of the coefficients of the PRISINT variables was considerably greater than 1, though none of the coefficients is significant at the 5 per cent level. The sum of the parameters of the CREDINT

84

variable is as in the other periods, not significantly different from 0. However, the results from the inflation model for this period are probably greatly influenced by very strong devaluation expectations, which prevailed after 1980 and we cannot, in comparison to results from other periods, come to any clearcut conclusions.

In the balance of payments estimates, however, we got a result which clearly differed from the ones expected. In this period, with the exchange rate considerably more stable than in others, we found that the balance of payments model showed an adjustment process which was considerably slower than in the other periods. This was so, in spite of the strong devaluation expectations which prevailed during the period.

To sum up, we can say that the investigation does not give support to one of the fundamental monetarist ideas, namely that a more flexible exchange rate implies a smaller adjustment of the imbalances in the money market, through the balance of payments and a larger effect on the inflation rate.

4.4.3 Some conclusions from the assessment of the model with non–traded goods

We shall here try to summarize the major results from the preceding analysis based on our version of the Blejer and Leiderman model with non–tradables.

Except for the estimations for the entire 1956 – 85 period, which include different economic policy regimes, the inflation models are generally significant with a relatively high explanatory power. For the period after 1974 this holds only for the models which were estimated with the restriction that the constant was 0.

The balance of payments model shows, both with annual and quarterly data, moderately high R^2s (between 0.60 – 0.75), with F–values which are significant at the 5 per cent level. The exceptions are periods 1975–85, in the analysis with annual data, and III/67 – III/74 in the quarterly analysis.

The relative importance of the different variables of inflation (PRISINT which reflects imported inflation through variations in world inflation and in the exchange rate, and CREDINT which reflects imbalances in the money market caused by the domestic monetary policy) is very sensitive to the degree of economic openness. In a relatively closed economy, it is the domestic determinants which are most important, while the role of external inflation and fluctuations in the exchange rate increase in a relatively open economy. In terms of Blejer's and Leiderman's model, μ increases a great deal when the economy is opened. This is consistent with the logic of the model, since a freer regime for foreign transactions implies an increase in λ, which is the share of tradables in the economy and a reduction in θ, the price elasticity of the relative price with regard to the imbalances on the money market. The latter depends on the sluggishness in the adjustment of the volume of money through the balance of payments. Both changes point to an increase in μ when the economy is opened.

The former argument is confirmed by the estimation of the balance of payments model. This model turns out to be more significant in the period after 1974, i.e. for the period with an open economy, than for the preceding one. The parameter μ is now also near 1, which is in accordance with the results of estimations of the inflation model.

However, the former argument is only true when the exchange rate regime is not changed. A flexible exchange rate regime would, according to the logic of the model, imply a cut–off from the world market as far as the functioning of the money market is concerned, which in turn would eliminate the effects of a more open regime for capital and goods transactions. However, we got no evidence in our investigation to support the fact that a greater flexibility in the exchange rate regime would imply a greater role for domestic monetary policy in the inflation process, through its isolation of the local money market from foreign markets by variations in the exchange rate. This is rather strong evidence against the monetarist model for inflation and the monetary theory of the balance of payments. [4]

The evidence for a strongly negative relationship between imbalances on the local money market and variations in the reserves on one side and for a non–significant relationship between inflation and variations in domestic credit (which is two sides of the same coin) during a period with great flexibility on the exchange market comes from estimates of both the balance of payments and the inflation model.

Exchange rates which are floating or react in other ways to imbalances in the money market should, according to our model, neutralize adjustments in the volume of money through the reserves and imply a large θ and a low μ. This is not the case in our empirical investigation. For the two periods which had flexibility in the exchange markets (1974 − 78 and, less so, 1983 − 85) we get a high value for E in both equations.

There may be explanations for this indicating that the logic of the models does not agree with reality. We shall take up two such possibilities.

The first is an econometric explanation and is valid only for the inflation model. If, according to the logic of the model, every imbalance on the money market is counterbalanced by a change in the exchange rate, it would be natural that both explanatory variables PRISINT and CREDINT are highly correlated with one another. The insignificance of the CREDINT variables in the inflation model, could then be due to multicollinearity.

We have looked at this possibility but have not found a high level of multicollinearity between the two variables. We have regressed PRISINT against CREDINT variables and not obtained an especially high R^2. We also estimated the inflation model without PRISINT variables but did not obtain significant changes in the size or significance of the parameters of the CREDINT variables.

The other explanation is economic in nature. If the adjustment of the exchange rate to the imbalances in the money market is not instantaneous, and is only valid on average during a relatively long period, one finds that a crawling peg regime, or a dirty float, coupled with equilibrating intervention from the Central Bank cannot eliminate short term deficits and surpluses in the balance of payments. This holds true even if, in the long run, a balance of payments equilibrium prevails and the authorities once again can control money supply. This is the point that Blejer and Leiderman make on the consequences of using a crawling peg and could have been the case in Uruguay, during the period in question. However, our investigation does not seem to support this view.

This is because some facts emanating from the period do not agree with the fundamental logic in Blejer and Leiderman's model and the monetary approach to the balance of payments. The flexibility in the exchange rate does not seem to prevent the negative relationship between domestic credit and foreign reserves and thus variations in domestic credit are not significant factors in the explanation of the determinants of the inflation rate, not even in the short run.

The reason behind this may be that the basic assumptions in the model do not agree with the facts. One of these assumptions is that prices, as well as real interest rate, are equalized internationally. Nevertheless, this is not the case in Uruguay in the period after 1975. The era was characterized by large capital movements, set off by interest rate differences, and which led to a dramatic increase in reserves during the period 1975 − 81 (Astori, 1981, 1982; Macadar, 1982; Notaro, 1984). The rigidity in interest rate misalignment, which lay behind the influx of short term capital, was also one of the foremost reasons for the deep recession seen during the years 1982 − 84 (Astori, 1982; Notaro, 1984). This may have been due to a rigidity, but it could alternatively have been due to a gap between expected and actual devaluation rates once the stabilization policy became unsustainable.

4.5   Results from analyses of the model with real imbalances

In what follows we shall analyze results of the estimations of the model that we described in section 4.2.3.

The concept of flow disequilibrium in this model refers to a situation where there are differences between the expected and the real growth rates of the prices for non–tradables. This is because not all changes in domestic credit are wholly predicted by the agents. This being the case, the changes can have short term effects on real output, according to the monetarist theory (Friedman 1968, 1970, 1971; Lucas, 1972, 1973; Barro, 1977, 1978).

If we, wholly in line with the monetarist approach, assume that $b = 1$ and $a_1 + a_2 = 1$, the flow equilibrium will depend on parameter θ. This parameter now acquires a meaning different from that in the model from the former section. Here, parameter θ is instead a measure of the deviation between the expected and the actual development of the prices for non–traded goods.

From the analysis of model (4.19), we see that when $\theta > 0$ the sum of the parameters of $(P_w^* + \epsilon^*)$ and P_{NTe}^* is less than 1, while at the same time the parameter of $(\gamma D^* + a^* - y^*)$ is greater than 0. Following the logic of the model, the parameters of ϕ must also be greater than 0.

In model (4.20), we have that when $\theta > 0$ the sum of the parameters of $(P_w^* + \epsilon^*)$ and P_{NTe}^* is less than 1 and that the parameter of $(\gamma D^* + a^* - y^*)$ is greater than -1. According to the logic of the model, parameter ϕ should be greater than 0 here too.

When there is flow equilibrium and $\theta = 0$, the sum of the parameters of $(P_w^* + \epsilon^*)$ and P in (4.19) should instead be equal to 1, while those of parameters $(\gamma D^* + a^* - y^*)$ and ϕ should be equal to 0. In (4.20) the sum of parameters $(P_w^* + \epsilon^*)$ and p_{NTe}^* should be equal to 1, while that of parameter $(\gamma D^* + a^* - y^*)$ should be equal to -1. In the latter case, the sum of all these parameters under the flow equilibrium conditions is equal to 0. Parameter ϕ must also be equal to 0.

In models (4.19) and (4.20) we used two alternative variables to measure the level of activity. We used a capacity variable (CAPACID) which is defined as [(LogY–LogȲ)x100] where Y is real output and Ȳ is the full employment real output. We also used an unemployment variable (UNEMPLO) which was defined as [Log(U/(1–U)x100], where U is the level of unemployment as a percentage of the work force. Variable P_{NTe}^* (i.e. expected changes in non–traded goods prices) is called PEXNONT. Variable $(\gamma D^* + a^* - y^*)$ is called CRINTOB.

We have assumed rational (or at least quasi–rational) expectations in our model. However, to introduce them into the models we used two different variants for the inflation and the balance of payments models, (4.26–27) and (4.28–29), respectively. In the following analysis, we shall mainly concentrate on model (4.26–27), but we shall also make reference to the results of estimates from (4.28–29).

4.5.1   *Results from estimations with annual data*

We estimate our inflation and balance of payments models with annual data for the period 1956 – 85 and for subperiods 1956 – 74 and 1975 – 85 (see table 4.7). When the degrees of freedom allow us, we undertake analysis with up to four lags for all variables.

In the estimation of (4.26) for the entire period, we see that in the long run (three years), the sum of the parameters on PRISINT and PEXNONT variables is not significantly different from 1 while that on CRINTOB variables is not significantly different from 0. In the short run (one year), the sum of the parameters of PRISINT and PEXNONT is considerably lower than 1, while the CRINTOB parameter is positive even though it is not significant at the 5 per cent level. CAPACIDs parameter is significant and has the right sign. The inflation model is not significant at the 5 per cent level.

Estimation of (4.27) gives us a similar picture. While in the long run (three years) the sum of the PRISINT and PEXNONT parameters is not significantly different from 1 and that of the CRINTOB parameters is not significantly different from −1, in the short run the situation is different. During the first year, the sum of the PRISINT and PEXNONT parameters is less than 1 and that of the CRINTOB parameter is lower than −1. CAPACID is again significant and has the right sign.

Table 4.7
Results of estimations with annual data

Method: OLS   OLS
Period: 1956–85   1956–85
Dependent variable: TTPRIS   TTRESERV

Indep.var.	Coeffic.	t–value	Indep.var.	Coeffic.	t–value
CONSTANT	2.1652	0.0931	CONSTANT	− 3.0584	− 0.1720
PRISINT	0.4720	2.9657	PRISINT	0.4094	3.3660
PRISINTL1	0.2132	1.4220	PRISINTL1	0.2510	2.1910
PRISINTL2	0.1965	1.5227	PRISINTL2	0.0873	0.8856
PEXNONT	− 0.1093	− 0.2635	PEXNONT	− 0.1978	− 0.6241
PEXNONTL1	− 0.1529	− 0.4439	PEXNONTL1	0.1300	0.4936
PEXNONTL2	0.4755	1.2209	PEXNONTL2	0.6105	2.0511
CRINTOB	0.2311	1.0432	CIRNTOB	− 0.6902	− 4.0766
CRINTOBL1	− 0.0959	− 0.5506	CRINTOBL1	− 0.3735	− 2.8060
CRINTOBL2	− 0.1951	− 0.9707	CRINTOBL2	− 0.1944	− 1.2655
CAPACID	0.0527	2.0331	CAPACID	0.0559	2.8237
CAPACIDL1	− 0.0967	− 2.0144	CAPACIDL1	− 0.0972	− 2.6489
CAPACIDL2	0.592	1.6068	CAPACIDL2	0.0566	2.0113

R^2=0.6655   F=1.9898(0.1238) R^2=0.9103   F=10.1429(0.0002)
DW=1.9352   DW=2.064

Method: OLS   OLS
Period: 1956–74   1956–74
Dependent variable: TTPRIS   TTRESERV

Indep.var.	Coeffic.	t–value	Indep.var.	Coeffic.	t–value
CONSTANT	− 7.3041	− 0.5724	CONSTANT	− 4.5143	− 0.2632
PRISINT	0.2239	3.5784	PRISINT	0.1160	1.3789
PRISINTL1	0.0292	0.5756	PRISINTL1	0.0823	1.2082
PEXNONT	0.0991	0.4787	PEXNONT	0.0758	0.2724
PEXNONTL1	0.4870	2.3122	PEXNONTL1	0.1874	0.6618
CRINTOB	0.3450	2.6002	CRINTOB	− 0.5993	− 3.3600
CRINTOBL1	0.1136	0.8340	CRINTOBL1	− 0.0350	− 0.1913
CAPACID	− 0.0591	− 3.6262	CAPACID	− 0.0284	− 1.2977
CAPACIDL1	0.0554	2.9985	CAPACIDL1	0.0143	0.4600

R^2=0.94276   F=14.4114(0.0010) R^2=0.7522   F=2.6565(0.1078)
DW=2.715   DW=1.5814

88

Method: OLS
Period: 1975–85

OLS
1975–85

Dependent variable: TTPRIS

TTRESERV

Indep.var.	Coeffic.	t–value	Indep.var.	Coeffic.	t–value
CONSTANT	4.1452	0.3648	CONSTANT	23.6761	0.8047
PRISINT	− 0.0685	− 0.6770	PRISINT	− 0.1940	− 0.7409
PEXNONT	0.8999	6.0876	PEXNONT	0.7894	2.0625
CRINTOB	− 0.0734	− 0.9480	CRINTOB	0.9311	4.6419
CAPACID	− 0.0033	− 1.2852	CAPACID	− 0.0029	− 0.4314

R^2=0.9097 F=15.1033(0.0027)
DW=2.5821

R^2=0.8954 F=12.8423(0.0042)
DW=2.5173

In brief the annual estimates for the entire period show features which indicate flow disequilibrium in the money market. In the short run, there are differences between the expected and the actual growth rate in domestic credit, which have certain effects on real output.

In estimations for the subperiods, we got the following results:

During 1956–74, we got a parameter sum of PRISINT and PEXNONT in (4.26) which is considerably lower than 1 during the first year, while CRINTOBs parameters are positive and significant. CAPACID is also significant, but has the wrong sign.

We got a similar picture from the estimation of (4.27). The sum of PRISINT and PEXNONT parameters (even in two years) is considerably lower than 1, while parameters for the CRINTOB variables sum up to considerably more than −1. CAPACID is now totally insignificant.

From the estimation of (4.26), we see that the sum of the PRISINT and PEXNONT parameters is not significantly different from 1 during the first year of the period 1975–85, while CRINTOB and CAPACID are totally insignificant. In actual fact, it is only PEXNONT which is significantly different from 0 but not significantly different from 1, while PRISINT is not significantly different from 0.

We got a similar result from the estimation of (4.27).The PEXNONT parameter lies near 1 and the CRINTOB parameter near −1 already during the first year. The last–mentioned result confirms findings in the former section i.e. that openness of the economy implies an 'offset' coefficient very near 1 irrespective the flexibility of the exchange rate.

Estimation of the models with UNEMPLO instead of CAPACID did not imply great changes in the results and we do not report them.

Estimations of the other version of model (4.28–29) (see appendix in Giorgi, 1988) did not give us any important diversions.

4.5.2 Results of estimations with quarterly data

Analysis of quarterly data for the period III/67 − III/74 and IV/74 − IV/85 was carried out according to the same criteria as in the preceding section (see table 4.8). Whenever possible the inflation and balance of payments model with up to seven lags for all variables was analyzed.

Estimation of (4.26) for the entire period shows that the long term sum of parameters on PRISINT and PEXNONT variables is significantly less than 1, while their sum during the first quarter is not significantly different from 1 with high levels of significance for both parameters. CRINTOB was, for all quarters, not significant and the sum of its parameters was practically equal to 0. Nor was CAPACID significant.

Estimation of (4.27) gives us a parameter sum of PRISINT and PEXNONT variables which is very much lower than 1, while the sum of the CRINTOB parameters is not significantly different from −1.

Estimations for the entire period did not give any clear evidence regarding short term flow imbalances in the money market. On the other hand, both models, and in particular, the balance of payments model are highly significant.

Coming to subperiods, we do not get particularly good results for III/67–IV/74. Even if both the inflation and balance of payments models show high R^2 and F−values, which are significant at the 5 per cent level, the parameter signs and sizes are very difficult to interpret. On the other hand, most variables in both (4.26) and (4.27) have insignificant t−values.

Table 4.8
Results of estimations of quarterly data

Method: OLS OLS
Period: I/67 − IV/85 III/67 − IV/85

Dependent variable: TTPRIS TTRESERV

Indep.var.	Coeffic.	t−value		Indep.var.	Coeffic.	t−value
CONSTANT	8.4564	2.2117		CONSTANT	10.5020	1.4921
PRISINT	0.1073	2.6824		PRISINT	0.1395	1.8944
PRISINTL1	0.0445	1.0778		PRISINTL1	0.0361	0.4741
PRISINTL2	0.0295	0.6963		PRISINTL2	− 0.0824	− 1.0577
PRISINTL3	0.0488	1.1770		PRISINTL3	0.0419	0.5487
PRISINTL4	− 0.1091	− 2.0971		PRISINTL4	0.0272	0.2841
PRISINTL5	0.0457	0.9055		PRISINTL5	− 0.0244	− 0.2625
PEXNONT	0.8230	4.3499		PEXNONT	0.1860	0.5342
PEXNONTL1	− 0.2301	− 1.2087		PEXNONTL1	0.4062	1.1592
PEXNONTL2	− 0.0652	− 0.4064		PEXNONTL2	− 0.3144	− 1.0651
PEXNONTL3	0.2136	1.2731		PEXNONTL3	− 0.2770	− 0.8968
PEXNONTL4	− 0.2946	− 1.8696		PEXNONTL4	0.1914	0.6600
PEXNONTL5	− 0.3378	− 2.2144		PEXNONTL5	− 0.0022	− 0.0079
CRINTOB	− 0.0126	− 0.2553		CRINTOB	− 0.9372	−10.2946
CRINTOBL1	− 0.0216	− 0.3881		CRINTOBL1	0.0358	0.3497
CRINTOBL2	0.0643	1.1172		CRINTOBL2	− 0.1880	1.7739
CRINTOBL3	− 0.0146	− 0.2852		CRINTOBL3	0.1292	1.3720
CRINTOBL4	0.0173	0.3278		CRINTOBL4	0.0817	0.8410
CRINTOBL5	0.0202	0.4148		CRINTOBL5	− 0.0331	0.3691
CAPACID	0.0002	0.0572		CAPACID	0.0017	0.2436
CAPACIDL1	0.0036	0.7771		CAPACIDL1	0.0050	0.5825
CAPACIDL2	0.0056	1.1717		CAPACIDL2	0.0012	0.1393
CAPACIDL3	− 0.0036	− 0.7315		CAPACIDL3	− 0.0006	− 0.0655
CAPACIDL4	− 0.0021	− 0.4646		CAPACIDL4	− 0.0175	− 1.4073
CAPACIDL5	− 0.0053	− 1.3335		CAPACIDL5	0.0035	0.4740

R^2=0.6547 F=2.6859(0.0041) R^2=0.8935 F=11.8819(0.0000)
DW=2.4865 DW=2.0333

Method: OLS
Period: III/67 –III/74

OLS
III/67 – III/74

Dependent variable: TTPRIS

TTRESERV

Indep.var.	Coeffic.	t–value	Indep.var.	Coeffic.	t–value
CONSTANT	0.2418	0.057	CONSTANT	8.2126	1.243
PRISINT	0.0137	0.257	PRISINT	− 0.0516	− 0.617
PRISINTL1	0.0364	0.651	PRISINTL1	− 0.0398	0.455
PRISINTL2	− 0.0419	− 0.566	PRISINTL2	− 0.2550	− 2.207
PEXNONT	0.3251	1.296	PEXNONT	− 0.5530	− 1.410
PEXNONTL1	− 0.2999	− 1.646	PEXNONTL1	− 0.3106	− 1.090
PEXNONTL2	0.2749	1.357	PEXNONTL2	− 0.0030	− 0.009
CRINTOB	− 0.0754	− 0.363	CRINTOB	− 1.3349	− 4.109
CRINTOBL1	− 0.0411	− 0.212	CRINTOBL1	0.5188	1.713
CRINTOBL2	0.1272	0.807	CRINTOBL2	− 0.2799	− 1.136
CAPACID	− 0.0180	− 0.449	CAPACID	− 0.0732	− 1.166
CAPACIDL1	− 0.0116	− 0.159	CAPACIDL1	0.0452	0.398
CAPACIDL2	0.0065	0.157	CAPACIDL2	− 0.0305	− 0.471

R^2=0.8981   F=4.4068
DW=1.9823

R^2=0.8663   F=3.2397
DW=2.9059

Method: OLS
Period: IV/74 – IV/85

OLS
IV/74 – IV/85

Dependent variable: TTPRIS

TTRESERV

Indep.var.	Coeffic.	t–value	Indep.var.	Coeffic.	t–value
CONSTANT	4.0270	0.5631	CONSTANT	3.4716	0.2010
PRISINT	0.0806	1.7937	PRISINT	0.2177	2.0067
PRISINTL1	0.0684	1.4078	PRISINTL1	0.0291	0.2481
PRISINTL2	0.0081	0.1459	PRISINTL2	− 0.0111	− 0.0825
PRISINTL3	0.0344	0.5899	PRISINTL3	− 0.1151	− 0.8177
PRISINTL4	− 0.0772	− 1.5205	PRISINTL4	0.0049	0.0402
PRISINTL5	0.0078	0.1647	PRISINTL5	− 0.0070	− 0.0616
PEXNONT	0.6563	4.0854	PEXNONT	0.4353	1.1220
PEXNONTL1	0.0249	0.1778	PEXNONTL1	0.3292	1.9714
PEXNONTL2	− 0.2279	− 1.5477	PEXNONTL2	0.4737	1.3316
PEXNONTL3	0.3463	2.3276	PEXNONTL3	− 0.4388	− 1.2214
PEXNONTL4	− 0.1845	− 1.2598	PEXNONTL4	− 0.1409	− 0.3983
PEXNONTL5	− 0.1221	− 0.8983	PEXNONTL5	0.2039	0.6209
CRINTOB	− 0.0293	− 0.7387	CRINTOB	− 1.0366	−10.8131
CRINTOBL1	− 0.0166	− 0.3431	CRINTOBL1	0.0037	0.0312
CRINTOBL2	0.0107	0.2057	CRINTOBL2	− 0.1190	− 0.9500
CRINTOBL3	− 0.0034	− 0.0675	CRINTOBL3	0.1046	0.8609
CRINTOBL4	− 0.0053	− 0.0957	CRINTOBL4	0.0723	0.5399
CRINTOBL5	0.0152	0.3727	CRINTOBL5	− 0.0065	− 0.0657
CAPACID	− 0.0024	− 0.6933	CAPACID	− 0.0001	− 0.0167
CAPACIDL1	0.0055	1.3536	CAPACIDL1	0.0050	0.5013
CAPACIDL2	0.0024	0.6342	CAPACIDL2	0.0022	0.2334
CAPACIDL3	− 0.0022	− 0.5504	CAPACIDL3	0.0007	0.0705

CAPACIDL4	− 0.0012	− 0.3234	CAPACIDL4	− 0.0109	− 1.2212
CAPACIDL5	− 0.0032	− 0.9792	CAPACIDL5	0.0028	0.3566

R^2=0.8403   F=4.3864(0.0007) R^2=0.9423   F=13.6174(0.0000)
DW=1.9798   DW=1.7410

Method: OLS:
Period: IV/74 − IV/85

Dependent variable: TTRESERV

Indep.var.	Coeffic.	t− value
CONSTANT	− 7.8492	− 1.5340
PRISINT	0.3283	4.6108
PRISINTL1	0.0738	0.9974
PRISINTL2	0.0754	0.9974
PEXNONT	0.4093	1.5956
PEXNONTL1	0.5058	1.9796
PEXNONTL2	0.6747	2.8723
CRINTOB	− 1.0433	−15.7738
CRINTOBL1	− 0.0434	− 0.5578
CRINTOBL2	− 0.2052	− 3.3622
CAPACID	− 0.0064	− 1.2902
CAPACIDL1	0.0082	1.5141
CAPACIDL2	0.0001	0.1515

R^2=0.9298   F=35.3293(0.0000)   DW=1.7114

In (4.26) none of the variables was significantly different from 0, while in (4.27), both PRISINT and PEXNONT had negative parameters all the time, while the CRINTOB parameters was significantly different from 0 but not significantly different from 1. The same holds for the sum of the CRINTOB variable parameters. CAPACID was, in both models, not significant.

In the period IV/74 − IV/85, we got different results. The parameter sum of PRISINT and PEXNONT variables in the inflation model (4.26) is now not significantly different from 1, either in the short or long run. The parameter sum on CRINTOB variables, on the other hand, is not significantly different from 0. CAPACID variables are all not significant. The balance of payments model (4.27) also shows parameter sums for PRISINT and PEXNONT variables, which are near 1, in both the short and long run, while CRINTOB's sum to −1, also in the short as well as in the long run. Once again, CAPACID is not significant. On the other hand, both models show reasonable R^2− and F−values.

Even though the results from estimations with quarterly data for the whole period and the first subperiod are difficult to interpret, those from the other subperiod are clearer and correspond with the annual data analysis, as far as the existence of flow imbalances on the money market is concerned.

For this period, there are no signs whatsoever of the existence of short term flow imbalances. The disequilibrium variables do not seem to play any significant role either in the inflation or balance of payments model. Expectations of price increases on 'non−tradables' appear to have adjusted very well to the actual development and did not create any significant variations in real output.

The use of the variable UNEMPLO instead of CAPACID in models (4.26–27) has no noticeable effect on our results. It is only in the estimation of model (4.27) in the last subperiod that we get substantially more significant results for the UNEMPLO than for the CAPACID variable (see Giorgi, 1988).

Estimations of other versions of the model of real imbalances (4.28–29) (see Giorgi, 1988) did not either give us any results, which differ markedly from those shown above. Besides model (4.28–29) always appeared less significant than model (4.26–27). The F–test for the PEXNONT variables in both the inflation and balance of payments models always gave significant results, which means that inflation expectations played a special role for 'non–tradables' in all the analyzed periods and that predicted or unpredicted, variations in domestic credit have somewhat different effects on prices and output. [5]

Finally, we should say something about the results of estimations with quarterly data for periods with different exchange regimes. We estimated our inflation and balance of payments models for subperiods III/74 – IV/78, I/79 –IV/82 and I/83 – IV/85, all characterized by different exchange rate regimes. The results which we got though were mostly unstable and unreliable. This was mainly because the periods were very short and there were few degrees of freedom. Thus we do not show any estimations results for these subperiods.

4.5.3   Conclusions from the analysis of the model with real imbalances

In this section, we shall try to summarize the major results of our analysis of the model in (4.19–20). As already mentioned, the purpose of the model was to try to study the impact of short term digressions from money market flow equilibrium. These imbalances, which come about because of failure of agents to wholly predict the growth rate of domestic credit, should have real effects, which delay the impacts of stock disequilibrium on inflation and the balance of payments.

The most important results of our analysis can be summarized as follows.

1)   From our inflation model (4.26) we got high R^2– and F–values, which were significant at the 5 per cent level, except annual data estimations for the whole period. The situation was the same for estimations of the balance of payments model (4.27). When we excluded the variable PEXNONT (models 4.28–29), we got clearly poorer results in the inflation equation, with F–values which in most cases were not significant at the 5 per cent level.

2)   Whereas there was a tendency for flow imbalances in the money market to be of some importance in the period when the economy was not wholly open (1956–74), the situation was quite different after 1974 when restrictions on international capital flows were removed. Expectations concerning price increases on non–traded goods were much more flexible than before. Flow equilibrium in the monetary market seems to prevail even in the short run, and the stock equilibrium adjustment mechanism, together with the balance of payments, seems not to be significantly delayed by unpredicted variations in domestic credit.

3)   For all periods, we found out that, inflation expectations concerning non–tradables have a separate effect on both inflation and the balance of payments besides the effect of the growth rate of the domestic credit on real output. In all cases, the F–test gave significant results on the introduction of the PEXNONT variable in the model.

4)   In general, we got no clear evidence for the effects of activity level variables on inflation or the balance of payments. We got relevant results both for the sign and significance of these variables in the annual estimations for the entire period, but not in estimations for subperiods. We generally got insignificant results for quarterly data except for the UNEMPLO variable in the balance of payments equation in the second period.

To sum up, we can say that the most important result from our model (4.19–20) was the evidence that openness in the economy accelerates the money market's rate of adjustment. In our theoretical model, there are two different reasons why this should be the case. The first can be found in equations (4.11–13) of our model of real imbalances. Due to the opening up of the economy parameter a_2 becomes bigger and w^* now reflects variations in p_T^* much more than before. As a result of these two changes, the development of p_{NT}^* now follows that of p_T^* more closely. If the latter is assumed to be more stable than the former, which appears to be the case, the predictions of agents regarding the price increase of non–tradables should now be more reliable, which in terms of our model, means that parameter θ becomes smaller.

Secondly, the share of non–tradables itself decreases and with it, the gap between expected and actual price increases on these commodities. In our model, this is reflected in the direct effect of a reduction in $(1 - \lambda)$ in parameters (4.19–20).

We must, however, observe that none of these two explanations agrees very well with results of our estimations. From the period before up to that after the end of 1974, it is mainly the variable PEXNONT which is responsible for the increase of the parameter sum of variables PRISINT and PEXNONT. This should mean that it is the decrease in θ which mainly causes this sum to be equal to 1, while the parameter sum of the CRINTOB variables decreases. This would require that the inflation rate of non–tradables should now follow that of tradables closely. This does not agree with the analysis of these series for the period before and after the end of 1974. The situation is precisely the opposite.

Another aspect of our results which needs explaining is the decrease in value and significance of the PRISINT variables parameters in the second subperiod, in both (4.26) and (4.27). This ought to have been precisely the opposite due to the increase in parameter λ when the economy becomes more open.

A possible explanation for this is the increased flexibility in the exchange rate regime during this period, which could have caused parameter θ to decrease. But there are other arguments against this.

In the first place, these results conflict with those we got from model (4.24–25).

Secondly, as we explained earlier, parameter θ in the theoretical (4.19–20) model does not play the same role as in model (4.9). An increase in θ should imply a reduction in PEXNONT in (4.19–20), which, of course, is not the case.

Thirdly, when we estimated the other version of the model of real imbalances (4.28–29), we again got significant parameters for PRISINT summing up to approximately 1 in the inflation equation (see Giorgi, 1988).

A very obvious explanation to these abnormal estimation results for (4.26–27) could be the existence of high multicollinearity between PRISINT and PEXNONT, which would be the case with the opening up of the economy. However, this possibility was analyzed, using various methods, but there was no evidence of multicollinearity

Further analysis of the model and of conditions during the period in question are necessary in order to get a clear picture on this issue.

At the moment, we can conclude that the analysis of model (4.19–20) shows results, which generally agree with theory, at least as far as the relation between equilibrium variables (PRISINT and PEXNONT) and the disequilibrium ones (CRINTOB and CAPACID) is concerned, but this is not the case with regard to the interrelationships between the parameters of the equilibrium variables.

4.6 A comparison with other empirical studies using monetarist models for small open economies

In this section, we shall make a brief review of some empirical analyses of inflation and the balance of payments in monetary models for small open economies. The purpose being to compare these results with those obtained in this investigation. The results shown here should be compared, in the first place, to our analyses in section 4.4.

Here, we shall look at results from three different empirical analyses, the first by Blejer (1977), the second by Blejer and Leiderman (1981), and the third by Cervantes Islas (1985).

Blejer tested a model similar to ours (4.24–25) with annual data for Mexico, for the years 1950–73. He chose this case because, among other things, the exchange rate was for all practical purposes fixed (he introduced dummys in the model for two large devaluations, which took place during the sample period). Thus, he set $P_w^* = p_T^*$ and excluded exchange rate variations from the analysis.

Other differences, in comparison to the model in section 4, can be found in the estimation of the real demand for money and in the modeling of the lag structure. For the latter, Blejer uses a 'polynomial distributed' lag structure constructed on the basis of an λ value calculated from the empirical data. Blejer gets significant results for both the inflation and balance of payments with R^2 which lies between $0.70 - 0.75$ and $0.60 - 0.65$ respectively. Both the external factors (measured by USA inflation) and the internal imbalances in the money market are significant in the inflation model and the difference between them is significant in the balance of payments model.

In addition, Blejer finds that as explanatory variables for inflation, the external factors have the greatest weight (around 70 per cent against 30 per cent of the ex–ante excess demand for money), something he thinks agrees with monetary theory given that Mexico allowed free capital movements during the sample period. He also argues that estimates made for the balance of payments, which imply that the stock imbalance, in the money market, creates a flow of reserves which is significant for three years, are in line with the monetary approach.

If we take into consideration the country's foreign regime (fixed exchange rate and free capital movements) the adjustment process is quite slow. Besides, the coefficient for the entire distributed–lags polynomial in contrast to USA inflation and ex ante surplus demand on the money market, is about 0.50 and significantly different from 1. This result indicates not only a slow, adjustment mechanism, but also an offset coefficient which is considerably lower than 1. Under the mentioned conditions these results do not wholly agree with the monetary approach.

Blejer and Leiderman's model is the one we showed above plus an equation for the exchange rate which is a reaction function according to:

$$\epsilon_t^* = \beta \sum_{i=0}^{h} (1-\beta)^i L^i (P^* - P_w^*)_t$$

Blejer and Leiderman use the model to analyze the simultaneous determination of inflation, balance of payments and the exchange rate under a 'crawling peg' regime. They test the model with Brazilian data for the period III/68 – IV/77. To estimate the system they use the full information maximum likelihood method.

Their results indicate that inflation mainly depends on international inflation and variations in the exchange rate. From the derived reduced forms, one learns that after four quarters, less than 25 per cent of the inflation is due to imbalances on the money market. In the balance of payments equation, the reserve flow, also after four quarters, accounts for about 80 per cent of the differences between imbalances in the volume of money and the level of international inflation.

The authors are of the opinion that these results support their conclusion that 'a small open economy that indexes its exchange rate through the adoption of a purchasing power parity clause may choose its rate of inflation independently of the rest of the world' (Blejer and Leiderman, 1981, p. 147). This conclusion is not entirely supported by our estimation results. They do not suggest that it would be possible to pursue such a policy permanently without a permanent effect on the reserves. Our estimations for the period after 1974 suggest that the effect of the imbalances in the money market on reserves is not temporary nor is it eliminated by variations in the exchange rate.

Cervantes Islas' analysis takes a different course. He tries to prove that countries with fixed exchange regimes have an inflation which is more dependent on the international one, than countries with more flexible exchange rate regimes.

He uses an equation model for inflation which is similar to model (4.24), but differing on two points. Firstly, he estimates the effects of international inflation and exchange rate changes separately. Secondly, he uses, as a measure of the domestic money market activity, not the ex ante imbalance on the market but only the growth of money.

The results he gets support his hypothesis. In all countries with fixed exchange rates, the international inflation is a significant explanatory factor for domestic inflation, while the rate of growth of money at home is of little significance. In the other group of countries, the situation is reversed.

His analysis results may be criticized on two points. The choice and grouping of countries did not, with the exception of the exchange rate, take account of the regime for goods and capital transactions. Furthermore, the growth of money supply is a bad proxy for imbalances in the money market, especially in countries with a fixed exchange rate and free capital movements. For it incorporates, not only variations in domestic credit but also in the reserves. This implies a bias in favour of the significance of the money supply variables in these countries.

In his investigation, Cervantes Islas also uses another model.[6] It is a simultaneous model which can be regarded as a simplified version of the one by Blejer and Leiderman. The results of the estimations again support Cervantes Islas hypothesis, but the above objections concerning the choice of cases and the definition of the money market variable still hold.

4.7   Conclusions

The purpose of this section was to analyze the relevance of the monetarist model for a small open economy in order to explain variations in the price level and international reserves in Uruguay during 1956–85. Accordingly, we used two models based on the monetarist approach.

The first model (4.9–10) is a typical monetarist one with non–tradables and depicts a situation where stock equilibrium has not yet been reached, but where flow equilibrium exists in the money market. The relative importance of the different factors, international inflation and exchange rate changes, on the one hand, and ex ante imbalances in the money market on the other, depends on the extent to which the balance of payments adjustment mechanism influences the volume of money and how quickly stock equilibrium is reached.

The other model (4.19–20) using a less conventional approach, concentrates on the mechanisms which create flow equilibrium in the money market, that is to say, how price expectations adjust to variations in domestic credit and, consequently, ex ante stock imbalances in the money market may become totally predictable, thereby having no real effects.

For both models, we got results which, in most cases, were significant and had high explanatory power for both inflation and the balance of payments. It was only for the inflation estimations for the whole period and the balance of payments estimations for the first subperiod that our results proved to be insignificant. This was because of the changes in the regime for foreign transactions during the investigated period. These variations changed the meaning of the explanatory variables in the inflation model, thereby reducing the significance of the estimations as the latter do not take into consideration changes in policy. This also explains the low significance of the balance of payments model during the period when capital movements were limited.

We were especially interested in analyzing the fit of the model during different external regimes. Of particular interest being whether changes in the models' parameters correspond to the underlying theory.

We formulated the hypothesis that it could be the rigidity in the domestic nominal interest rate, which creates permanent differences between the international and the domestic real interest rate, that is in direct connection with variations in the exchange rate. We will take this up in the next chapter.

Results from estimation of the second model (4.19–20) were even more unreliable with regard to the relationship between variations in the model's parameter and that of economic policy. There were indications, however, showing that the flow equilibrium adjustment mechanism, i.e. the generation of expectations of non–tradables prices, appears smoother during the period of the open economy, after the end of 1974. This corresponds to the basic theory. However, these results are only of the relationship between the parameters for the equilibrium variables $((P_w^* + \epsilon^*)$ and $P_{NTe}^*)$ and the disequilibrium variables $((\gamma D^* + a^* - y^*)$ and $\ell)$, but not the mutual relationship between the first ones. The latter would require a more detailed analysis of the functioning of the model and of the empirical conditions during the sample period.

Another situation which requires detailed analysis concerns the adjustment of price expectations to the real development during 1975–1985. The nominal wage did not, during this time, depend on inflation but obviously dragged after (large reduction in real wages occurred during the period). This result, also noted in chapter 3, requires an analysis of the development of different relative price situations which do not fit within the monetarist model we applied here. We shall take up that issue in the next chapter, which shall deal with structuralist and disequilibrium approaches to inflation.

Notes

1. This can easily be calculated. The sum of the parameters on the variables $(P_w^* + \epsilon^*)$, $(P_w^* + \epsilon^*)_{-1}$, P_{NTe}^*, and $P_{NTe_{-1}}^*$ is equal to

$$\frac{\{\lambda + (1-\lambda)(a_1 b\lambda + a_2 - \theta\delta\lambda)\} + (1-\lambda)^2(a_1 b - \theta\delta)}{1 + (1-\lambda)\theta}$$

If we assume that $\theta=0$ and $b=1$ we find that the sum becomes

$$\lambda + (1-\lambda)(a_1\lambda + a_2) + (1-\lambda)^2 a_1 = \lambda + (1-\lambda)a_1 + (1-\lambda)a_2$$

which with the condition $a_1 + a_2 = 1$ also is equal to 1.

2. Due to the use of 'lagged' variables in the inflations and balance of payments model as in the expected inflations and real money demand model, we lost a number of observations at the beginning of the series. The research period, then, does not fully correspond to the periods given in the text and tables. This is true for estimations of the whole period and for the first subperiod.

3. Martin Rama even argues that the interventions were so large that this period should not be characterized as a period with a floating exchange rate.

4. Considering the type of exchange rate regime which was valid during the subperiod IV/78 − IV/82 and which could be adjusted to a fixed exchange

rate regime, we also estimated inflation and balance of payments model during IV/74 — IV/85 with a dummy variable for the given subperiod. Even if the dummy was, in some cases, significant at a 5 per cent level, there were no changes in the estimated parameters which would make us change our most important conclusions, i.e. that the exchange rate flexibility does not isolate the money market from the surroundings, even in the long run.

5.   We ought to add a reservation to this statement, since we did not test the significance of the expected growth in domestic credit against the real, but that of the expected inflation on non—tradables against the real growth of the domestic credit.

6.   This model is by A.C. Porzecanski (*Enfoque monetario de la Balanza de Pagos en la Economia Uruguaya 1970 — 1979*); and has been used in estimations for Uruguay which we unfortunately do not have access to.

5 Structuralist models of inflation

5.1 Introduction

The purpose of this chapter is to investigate to what extent structuralist models can explain the Uruguayan inflation. Here, two models based on the structuralist theory are used to analyze the inflationary process from the 1960s until 1987.

The first model incorporates structural factors such as the difference in price formation between a flexprice and a fixprice sector, the rigidity of money prices in the fixprice sector, and also the rigidity of relative prices due to indexation. This model will be estimated in a reduced form, but also in a structural version which incorporates simultaneity between inflation and nominal wage adjustments.

The second model is focused on the analysis of the short term relationship between interest rates, inflation, and the activity level of the fixprice sector, including its stagflationary implications regarding any kind of measure or exogenous factor tending to increase the activity level. This model will be estimated in a structural form.

Estimates for the models analyzed will be made for different subperiods, according to variations in economic policies and to institutional changes, which might have an impact on pricing mechanisms in any of the two sectors considered or in the labour market.

Section 5.2 presents the theory on which the models used are based including the model formulation. Section 5.3 describes the most important aspects of the economic policy applied over the period under consideration. Section 5.4 gives the results of the estimates of the the reduced form and of the simultaneous structural form of the first model considered, while section 5.5 presents the results of estimates for the second model are presented. Finally, section 5.6 summarizes the main conclusions drawn from our analysis.

5.2 Non–monetary theory of inflation

5.2.1 *General remarks*

In line with a well–known standpoint adopted by many Latin American economists with regard to inflation, we shall consider as non–monetary approaches to inflation, those which 'stress the importance of real factors as the direct causes of inflation; namely, based on the existence of non–monetary causation mechanisms which by themselves affect price levels.' (Olivera, 1960, p. 616, own translation). The starting point of this approach is its rejection of the classical dichotomy where the economy is divided into two separate spheres: the monetary sphere, where the general price level is determined, and the real sphere, where relative prices are determined.

For advocates of this approach, inflationary processes depend on imbalances in the real sphere of the economy. Insofar as these imbalances are in most cases related to specific structural features of the economies involved, this kind of analytical framework has become widely known as the structuralist approach (Kirkpatrick and Nixson, 1976).

According to this approach, all increases in the absolute price levels are due to imbalances in certain real markets, derived from the deficiencies of the pricing mechanism or simply from its inoperativeness. This is an essential difference relative to the the monetary approaches, which consider the imbalances causing inflation to operate in the monetary sphere, while the adjustments of relative prices ensure at all times the real equilibrium of the system, with the exception of temporary lags caused by general price level variations. Under these monetary approaches, all adjustments in the money market are only a requirement for the reestablishment of the general equilibrium of the system, modified by factors operating in the real sphere of the economy.

As already noted, both the variability of the relative prices and the poor operation of the money price system, which makes it incapable of reestablishing a real equilibrium without variations in the general price level, are assumed to derive from the economic structure.

There are mainly two aspects of the price system which are related to the structural features of the economies under consideration. They relate to the origin and dissemination of inflationary processes in the economy.

First, the relative inflexibility of money prices downwards is related to the origin of strictly structural inflation. Second, the inertia of the relative price system hinders its adjustment to changes in the economic structure. This element relates to the dissemination of inflationary thrusts in the economy and, consequently, to the intensity of the inflationary processes.

We shall analyze several approaches, closely related, with regard to their theoretical foundations, which, in their analysis of inflation, focus on specific features of the price system. In this sense we shall analyse the classical Latin American structuralist theory and the theory of cost–push inflation. We shall in this section, also analyze the origins of inflation focusing on the stagflationary consequences of orthodox stabilization policies, when applied in an economic context having certain specific structural characteristics. In the economic literature, these analyses are usually referred to as neostructuralist.

5.2.2 *The classical Latin American structuralist theory*

5.2.2.1 *Main theoretical assumptions.* According to the classical Latin American structurlist theory of inflation, the existence of structural inflationary pressures depends on two basic elements (Olivera, 1960, 1964, 1967; Canavese, 1982):

1) A relationship between the economic structure and the relative price system, where a certain relative price vector corresponds to a certain structure.
2) A relationship between the relative price system and the general price level, caused by the downward inflexibility of certain money prices.

Finally, the necessary condition for these inflationary pressures to lead to a continually increasing price level is the passive nature of money supply, whereby the inflationary gap caused by structural factors may be closed.

Existence of the first element implies that the price elasticity of the supply of and/or demand for certain commodities is not infinite. Consequently, if supply and demand change at different rates there will be variations in the relative prices of the commodities involved.

As already noted, the second element implies that the money prices of certain commodities are relatively inflexible downwards. In order for structural inflationary pressures to emerge, the flexibility of money prices must be smaller downwards than upwards.

Under these circumstances, and given a passive money supply, structural changes — and particularly the existence of rigidity in this process — will become the cause for an increase in the general price level. This may be shown in a general equilibrium model of the economy (Oliviera, 1960), where we have:

$$x_i(q_i,......,q_{n-2}) = 0 \qquad i = 1 \ldots n-1 \tag{5.1}$$

which states that the equilibrium conditions in the commodity markets, where x_i is the amount of commodity i and q_i is its price in terms of the numeraire $(n-1)$.

Assuming a passive money supply, which consistently equilibrates the money market, we have:

$$\sum_{i=1}^{n-1} p_i x_i = 0 \tag{5.2}$$

where p_i is the money price of commodity i.

From equation (5.2) we may infer that:

$$\sum_{j=1}^{n-2} p_j x_j = -p_{n-1} x_{n-1} \tag{5.3}$$

Given a system of $n-1$ markets where $n-2$ markets are in equilibrium, the remaining market must also be in equilibrium. Assuming the system has only one solution the system of $n-2$ equations determines relative prices. Now, if we determine any of the money prices outside the system, which is consistent with the passive nature of the money supply as stated in equation (5.2), the money price system will also be determined.

In a given structural context with a given relative price vector $(q_i)^0$, and a given money price vector $(p_i)^0$, we assume that there is a change in the economic structure.

This leads to a new relative price vector denoted $(q_i)^1$. Insofar as money prices are inflexible downwards, one of them must necessarily be determined outside the system and become a datum for the system. This will be the money price of the commodity whose relative price does not appreciate in terms of any of the others. Assuming this commodity to be k, i.e.

$$p_i^1 = p_k^1(q_i^1/q_k^1) \tag{5.4}$$

we have all money prices determined in the new equilibrium. Defining now

$$\Delta q_i = q_i^1 - q_i^0,$$

we have

$$p_i^1 = p_k^1\{(q_i^0 + \Delta q_i)/(q_k^0 + \Delta q_k)\} \qquad (5.5)$$

which, given

$$p_k^1 = p_k^0 \qquad (5.6)$$

and

$$\Delta q_i \geq \Delta q_k \qquad (5.7)$$

implies

$$p_i^1 \geq p_i^0 \qquad (5.8)$$

We thus obtain

$$(p_i)^1 \geq (p_i)^0 \qquad (5.9)$$

whereas, by definition we have

$$(q_i)^1 \neq (q_i)^0 \qquad (5.10)$$

In other words, in the new equilibrium, the absolute price level is higher than the one existing in the preceding situation.

Consequently, under the conditions we have just outlined, any change in the real equilibrium of the system causes an irreversible increase in the general price level, since any change in relative prices used to restore the system to the preceding situation will cause, by creating a new relative price vector, another increase in the price level, as may be inferred from our previous reasoning.

The impact on the price level of any changes in the real equilibrium of the system will also depend on the particular dynamics of the adjustment process of relative prices to their new equilibrium position.

Finally, it is worth noting that should money supply not adapt in a passive way to a structural inflationary gap, an adjustment will occur, within certain limits, through a variation in the velocity. Beyond such limits, the inflationary gap will cause a reduction in the activity level of the system.

5.2.2.2   *Structural imbalances in Latin American inflationary processes.* The conditions described above, which are within a structural inflationary context, have a bearing on the degree of development of the economy, while the accompanying process has an impact on the price elasticity of supply and demand, and on the rigidity of money prices.

Two aspects have been particularly analyzed in the structuralist literature (Olivera, 1960, 1964) since they are related to the development stage of the economy. On the one hand, we have the mobility of production resources, which has a direct influence on the price elasticity of supply and demand. On the other hand, we have the productive structure and its influence on the flexibility of the monetary price system.

In line with the above, it is in medium–developed or semi–industrial countries where structural inflation pressure or an inflationary process should develop. This is

102

mainly due to the relative weight of the – often oligopolistic – modern industrial and services sector. There also prevails a high degree of immobility of production factors mainly caused by conditions inherent to the economic structure of these countries, such as an insufficient infrastructure, too traditional agrarian structures, financial underdevelopment, market segmentation, etc.

Traditional Latin American literature on this subject (Sunkel, 1958; Grunwald, 1961; Pinto, 1968) has particularly emphasized two 'bottlenecks' which have an impact on the elasticity of commodities supply in Latin American economies. On the one hand, they refer to the influence of agrarian structures which curtail the output of these sectors. This means that growth in the demand for agricultural commodities which follows economic development leads to inflationary pressure. On the other, there has been a chronic external imbalance in the Latin American economies. This is an additional structural aspect, which may lead to price increases of imported commodities through devaluations.

5.2.2.3   *Basic model.* From the above sections we may infer a basic structural inflation model (Olivera, 1967; Canavese, 1982), where inflation derives from inelasticity of the supply of and/or demand for certain commodities and from the downward inflexibility of money prices.

Departing from the equilibrium condition in the agricultural commodities market, we have

$$S(p,t) = D(p, t) \qquad (5.11)$$

where S is supply, D is demand, p is the relative price P_a/P_b, where P_a is the price index for agricultural products and P_b is a price index of industrial products and where, finally, t is time. In dynamic terms we obtain

$$\frac{\delta S}{\delta p}\frac{dp}{dt} + \frac{\delta S}{\delta t} = \frac{\delta D}{\delta t}\frac{dp}{dt} + \frac{\delta D}{\delta t} \qquad (5.12)$$

or

$$\frac{1}{p}\frac{dp}{dt}(\epsilon + \eta) = \frac{1}{D}\frac{\delta D}{\delta T} - \frac{1}{S}\frac{\delta S}{\delta t} = \delta - \sigma \qquad (5.13)$$

where δ and σ are, respectively, the autonomous growth of the demand for and supply of agricultural commodities and ϵ and η are, respectively, the price elasticity of the demand for and supply of these commodities.

We thus obtain

$$\hat{P}_t = \hat{P}_{at} - \hat{P}_{bt} = \frac{\delta - \sigma}{\eta - \epsilon} \qquad (5.14)$$

where $\hat{} $ = growth rates

Assuming a general price index as a geometrical mean of both types of commodities, we have

$$\hat{\Pi}_t = \alpha \hat{P}_{at} + (1-\alpha)\hat{P}_{bt} \qquad (5.15)$$

which, through equation (5.14), gives us

$$\hat{\Pi}_t = \alpha \frac{\delta - \sigma}{\eta + \epsilon} + \hat{P}_{bt} \qquad (5.16)$$

103

Equation (5.16) gives us the general inflation rate as a function of a structural factor — the evolution of relative prices in the agricultural and industrial sectors, which depends on the evolution of agrarian supply and demand and their respective price elasticities — and of the growth rate of industrial prices.

Taking into consideration the downward rigidity of industrial prices

$$\hat{P}_{bt} \geq 0 \tag{5.17}$$

we may see that insofar as the structural element comprising the variations of relative prices is positive, the general inflation rate is also positive. From the assumptions of the model we infer that the structural element is positive, namely, that agricultural demand grows at a faster rate than supply, and that their respective price elasticities are not infinite.

Alternatively, we may incorporate into this model an internationally determined agricultural price level. In this case, the structural element in equation (5.16) must be replaced by a measure of the variability of international prices for agricultural products. We then only require an assumption of downward rigidity of industrial prices for such variability to become a source of inflationary pressures.

5.2.3   *A structuralist approach to cost–push inflation*

5.2.3.1   *Main components.* This group of theories on inflation (R.Frenkel, 1983, 1984, 1986; Taylor, 1981, 1983) starts from the same theoretical assumptions as classical structuralism and focuses on the evolution of elements which had already been incorporated into this approach. The analysis is now mainly concentrated on two issues (Heymann, 1986):

1)   A distinction between sectors having different pricing mechanisms. In particular, we refer to a distinction between a flexible price (flexprice) sector where pricing is based on market supply and demand, and a sector of rigid prices (fixprice), where pricing is based on a mark–up on production costs. This distinction develops the classical differentiation between pricing in the industrial and agricultural sectors as incorporated to the classical structuralist approach (Olivera, 1964, 1967).

2)   There are inertia aspects of inflation, mainly based on the indexation of costs in the fixprice sector. In this case, the analysis is mainly focused on the determination of pricing methods as applied to the labour market, which mainly depends, in a disequilibrium framework, on the prevailing institutional conditions.

This aspect of the approach may be considered an extension of the treatment of the structural inflation dissemination mechanisms of classical structuralist theory (Sunkel, 1958; Grunwald, 1961; Olivera, 1967).

As already noted, the first issue above refers to the existence of different pricing mechanisms in two basic sectors of the economy (Frenkel, 1986; Taylor, 1983). One of these sectors trades homogeneous commodities in competitive markets where, consequently, pricing depends on the supply and demand for the commodities involved and on agents who act as price takers. This pricing mechanism mainly applies to agricultural product and raw material markets in general. The second type of market refers to commodities having a high degree of differentiation, relatively high information costs, and prevalence of customer relations. These markets are frequently oligopolistic and with the existence of idle capacity a relatively common feature. All the factors described above explain why in this type of market prices — and output volumes — are fixed by agents, who determine a mark–up on production costs.

In general terms, there is a wide acceptance of the hypothesis of a constant mark up, as an adequate approximation to reality, with the only exception being for situations where there are shocks which deeply alter production costs (Frenkel, 1983, 1986). It is worth bearing in mind other aspects like the existence, in the fixprice sector, of prices fixed by the government or determined through international arbitration and consequently, exclusively depending on international prices and devaluation rates (Frenkel, 1986).

The second aspect refers to elements of inertia, namely those which contribute to the dissemination of inflation. To take these into account, one must analyse the reasons underlying the rigidity of certain relative price structures and their relationship to certain social and/or institutional factors.

At this stage, it is worth considering the relationship existing between this approach to the inertia elements of inflation and certain aspects of the traditional cost–push inflation theories. The latter assumed that the 'price level is governed by the levels of certain particular classes or groups of commodities' and that ' the exchange relationship existing between money and these commodities......(is) an equilibrium datum, an exogenous variable', with an amount of money endogenously determined, while 'inflation is perfectly consistent with relative prices and does not affect the stability of real equilibrium' (Olivera, 1960, p. 619, own translation). This approach is thus within the classical dichotomy and within the framework of assumptions of the monetary approach to inflation. On the contrary, according to the standpoint we are now considering, the rigidity of the relative price system is considered in terms of an imbalanced situation which prevails on certain markets where pricing depends on certain contractual and/or institutional elements. The rigidity of the relative price vector may even allow for the elongation of a disequilibrium situation. This is precisely the logic underlying the operation of the factors that disseminate structural inflation (Canavese, 1982).

As already mentioned, discussion of this type of dissemination factors, in the classical Latin American structuralist analysis of inflation mainly referred to distributive conflicts and to the relationship between salaries and inflation. This result is obtained by adding to the model comprising equations (5.11) to (5.17), the following two equations (Olivera, 1967; Canavese, 1982):

$$\hat{w}_t = \gamma \hat{\Pi}_{t-1} \qquad 0 \leq \gamma \leq 1$$

where $\hat{w}$ is the growth rate of nominal wages, and

$$\hat{P}_{bt} = \hat{w}_t \qquad (5.18)$$

This area has mainly focused on the analysis of nominal wage formation in the labour market. The basic hypothesis refers to specific features of the labour market and, consequently, to the need to take into account its pricing mechanism, as the market paradigm is unable to explain them (Frenkel, 1986). According to this standpoint real wages are determined by the growth of prices and nominal wages and implies that the labour market should be looked at from a disequilibrium standpoint, since the pricing mechanisms do not guarantee, at least during the adjustment process, the equilibrium of the market.

With regard to wage fixation, an important role is played by institutional conditions ranging from traditional customs or guidelines, to specific wage setting rules.

From this analysis we may conclude that the rule requiring indexation to past inflation is the core element behind the short term dynamics of nominal wages. Application of this kind of wage determination mechanism causes these models, at least with regard to their formulation, to be close to equilibrium models under adaptive expectations. However, the meaning behind each of the two kinds of models involved is quite different. In the case of the structuralist model, we are not dealing with the operation of expectations but rather with institutionalized mechanisms of recovery of real wages in markets ruled by implicit or explicit agreements, which derive from the relationship existing between different social groups.

To the existence of indexation methods we may add other elements which contribute to the determination of nominal wages, the most frequent being those related to conditions prevailing in the labour market or the variations in productivity.

Other relevant aspects in the determination of inflation inertia, relate to the indexation of other basic components of costs in the fixprice sector. Among them can be emphasized the indexation of the real exchange rate and/or the pressures of social groups closely related to the export sector.

5.2.3.2   *The basic model.* The model we described in the preceding section may be formalized in the following way (cfr Frenkel, 1986).

Departing from an equation similar to the one denoted as (5.16), we obtain

$$\hat{P}_t = a_1 \hat{P}_t^{flex} + a_2 \hat{P}_t^{fix} \tag{5.19}$$

where $\hat{P}$ is the growth rate of the general price index, $\hat{P}^{flex}$ is the growth rate of the price index for the flexprice sector, and $\hat{P}^{fix}$ of the price index for the fixprice sector. If we include the prices which are directly fixed by the government, the equation becomes

$$\hat{P}_t = a_1 \hat{P}_t^{flex} + a_2 \hat{P}_t^{fix} + a_3 \hat{P}_t^{gob} \tag{5.20}$$

where $\hat{P}^{gob}$ denotes an index of public tariffs.

The inflation rate of the fixprice sector is defined as

$$\hat{P}_t^{fix} = \hat{c}_t + \hat{m}_t \tag{5.21}$$

That is a result of the growth rate of production costs, $\hat{c}$, and of the mark–up. In turn, the growth rate of production costs is defined by

$$\hat{c}_t = b_n(\hat{w}_t - \hat{q}_t) + b_2 \hat{e}_t \tag{5.22}$$

namely as the growth rate of nominal wages minus the productivity rate $(\hat{w} - \hat{q})$ and the growth rate of imported commodity prices, $\hat{e}$. The latter is defined as the devaluation rate multiplied by the import price index. The existence of tradable commodities, whose prices are determined by international arbitration in the fixprice sector, implies that the import price index is construed as a general international price index rather than only as an index of import prices.

The dynamics of nominal wages are defined by

$$\hat{w}_t = \sum_{i=1}^{n} g_i \hat{P}_{t-i} + f(L)_t \tag{5.23}$$

where variable L refers to various factors related to the growth of salaries, excluding past inflation, for instance, the situation on the labour market.

The substitution of (5.23), (5.22) and (5.21) into (5.20) allows us to obtain the following inflation rate definition:

$$\hat{P}_t = a_1 \hat{P}_t^{flex} + a_3 \hat{P}_t^{gob} + a_e \hat{e}_t + a_w [\sum_{i=1}^{n} g_i \hat{P}_{t-i}$$

$$+ f(L)_t - \hat{q}_t] + \hat{m}_t \tag{5.24}$$

or, if we consider the mark–up as constant and disregard the impact of other factors, except past inflation, on the growth of nominal wages,

$$\hat{P}_t = a_1 \hat{P}_t^{flex} + a_3 \hat{P}_t^{gob} + a_e \hat{e}_t + a_w[(\sum_{i=1}^{n} g_i \hat{P}_{t-i}) - \hat{q}_t] \qquad (5.25)$$

where the sum of the coefficients of the independent variables is equal to 1.

This inflation model is the same as the one in the section devoted to the classical structuralist approach, where the growth rate of the prices of commodities in the fixprice sector has been replaced by that of its components and the growth of public tariffs has been added. Consequently, this model includes both structural and inertia factors, as origins of inflation. Thus, when relative prices in both sectors are constant, all the components of inflation tend to evolve following the rate of past inflation and inflation is then kept constant, being completely determined by inertia factors. When there is variation in the relative price of fixprice commodities, a structural component is added to the inflation rate, which then deviates from its past values.

5.2.4   A neostructuralist approach to stabilization policies

5.2.4.1   *Main issues in the approach.* The approach we use in this section is based on the same theoretical foundations as the model described in the preceding section [1], but is specifically oriented to the analysis of the effects of orthodox stabilization programs in countries with particular economic features (Bruno, 1979;Taylor, 1981, 1983; van Wijnbergen, 1983, 1986).

In general, this approach is directed at the investigation of the effects of two kinds of measures usually applied in stabilization programs advocated by international organizations in underdeveloped economies having the particular structural conditions of semi–industrial economies: devaluation of the currency and monetary contraction.   In particular, under certain assumptions inherent in the economic structure of these countries, mainly with regard to their industrial and financial sectors, these measures might, in the short term, have a stagflationary effect.

We shall focus on the relationship between the money or financial market and the rate of inflation, setting aside all considerations related to the effects of devaluations.

Semi–industrial [2] economies have, inter alia, the following characteristics (Bruno, 1979; Taylor, 1981):
1)   They are small economies and are thus price takers in international markets and depend on non–competitive imports of capital goods and raw materials for their industrial sector.
2)   Their industrial sectors have a certain degree of development, enjoy a considerable level of protection, have a highly oligopolistic structure and have started to develop an exporting capacity.
3)   Infrastructural weaknesses and other deficiencies lead to relatively long production periods and increase the need for credit for their working capital.
4)   Working capital is mainly financed by bank credits and further, given underdeveloped securities markets, banks also finance a considerable part of the fixed capital assets' transactions.
These structural characteristics give rise to forms of financial markets and, in particular, interest rates which have an impact on price and activity levels.

In the industrial sector, agents enjoy a certain monopolistic power and their maximization of profits leads them to respond to variations in demand by variations in prices and output. Furthermore, these adjustments are not instantaneous but gradual, thus giving rise to disequilibrium situations in these markets, implying variations in their inflation rate.

The inclusion of interest rates in the cost function of industrial companies, as a result of their need for working capital, implies that both output and prices are elastic with regard to interest rates.

107

Consequently, stabilization policies, via their effect on interest rates or related variables, have, in the short run, a potentially stagflationary effect since their influence on the supply of the industrial sector is negative, while they lead to higher prices.

As already noted, this model shares with the models we have analyzed above, the view of inflation rates as resulting from specific pricing mechanisms in the various sectors of the economy: in particular, pricing in the industrial sector in disequilibrium is based on production costs. Its main features comprise the so called 'working capital cost push effect', which, through specific pricing conditions in the industrial sector, establishes a positive relationship between price levels and interest rates. This fact, together with the negative effects of any increase in interest rates on the supply of this sector and, in general, on investment, causes the various factors or policies (money contraction) to have a stagflationary effect in the short run. The latter may be reversed over time, with regard to increases in the price level, by the traditional deflationary effects of increases in interest rates (van Wijnbergen, 1982, 1983).

5.2.4.2   *A working capital cost–push effect model.* We shall present a model (cfr Bruno, 1979), which includes the most outstanding aspects of the approach we have described in the preceding section, emphasizing the relationship between inflation, production and interest rates, and the supply of the industrial sector.

We start from the profit maximization conditions prevailing in the industrial sector, where producers enjoy a certain degree of monopolistic power. The production function of the firms is

$$x = f(k)F(\ell,n)^{1/a} \qquad (5.26)$$

where F is linearly homogeneous in labour ℓ and in imported inputs n, with a>1, x is production and k the capital stock, which is assumed to be fixed in the short term.

Given both the capital stock and output level, the minimization of variable costs gives the following cost function

$$c = x^a f(k)^{-a} v(w,P_n) \qquad (5.27)$$

where $v(w,P_n)$ is minimum variable costs per unit of output when $x/f = 1$. The function v is linearly homogeneous in w and P_n, and its elasticities, λ and $(1-\lambda)$ represent the share of variable factors (labour force and imported inputs) in costs. From equation (5.27) we obtain the following marginal costs:

$$MC = ac/x \qquad (5.28)$$

which, expressed in terms of growth rates and given a constant capital stock, allows us to derive

$$\hat{MC} = (a-1)\hat{x} + \hat{v} = (a-1)\hat{x} + \lambda\hat{w} + (1-\lambda)\hat{P}_n \qquad (5.29)$$

If we now turn to the financial costs corresponding to the working capital hypothesis that was advanced, we may see that profit maximization implies

$$MR = MC(1+r) \qquad (5.30)$$

where r is the nominal bank interest rate. In terms of growth rates, we consequently have:

108

$$\hat{MR} = \hat{MC} + \hat{\rho} \qquad \hat{\rho} = (1\hat{+r}) = (1+r)^{-1}\hat{rr} \qquad (5.31)$$

Companies are assumed to face a demand function of the following type

$$X^d = \mu(P/P^e)^{-\sigma} \qquad (5.32)$$

where price–elasticity $\sigma < 1$ and μ and P^e represent the relative expectations regarding the level of demand and the general price level. From the equation (5.32) we obtain

$$\hat{MR} = \hat{P} = \hat{P}^e + \sigma^{-1}\hat{\mu} - \sigma^{-1}\hat{X} \qquad (5.33)$$

Finally, through equations (5.28) to (5.33), we obtain the adjustment equations required for prices and output

$$\hat{P} = \frac{\beta}{1+\beta}\hat{P}^e + \frac{1}{1+\beta}\hat{v} + \frac{1}{1+\beta}\hat{\rho} + \frac{\beta}{\sigma(1+\beta)}\hat{\mu} \qquad (5.34)$$

$$\hat{X} = \frac{1}{\sigma}[(1+\beta)\hat{P}^e - (1+\beta)\hat{v} - (1+\beta)\hat{\rho} + \frac{1+\beta}{\sigma}\hat{\mu}] \qquad (5.35)$$

where $\beta = \alpha(\alpha-1)$.

These equations show the stagflationary effects of cost elements ($\hat{v}$ and $\hat{\rho}$) which contribute to increasing prices and reduced output, while expected variations in the price level and in the aggregate demand level tend to increase both prices and output.

The derivation of the aggregate price and output adjustment equations for the whole industrial sector requires a more detailed specification of the relationships involved. (This issue was carefully analyzed by Bruno, 1977). In this paper we shall limit ourselves to assuming the existence of the following aggregate adjustment equations for the fixed price sector:

$$\hat{P}^{fix} = a_0\hat{w} + a_1\hat{P}_m + a_2\hat{\rho} + a_3\hat{P}^e + a_4\Omega(Y^d)_{-1} \qquad (5.36)$$

$$\hat{Y}^{fix} = -b_0\hat{w} - b_1\hat{P}_m - b_2\hat{\rho} + b_3\hat{P}^e - b_4\Omega(Y^d)_{-1} \qquad (5.37)$$

where P_m are import prices and Y^d is aggregate demand.

The growth rate of wages is determined by

$$\hat{w} = d_0 + \hat{P}^e \qquad (5.38)$$

as a function of expected inflation.

Nominal interest rates are determined as a function of the international rates and internal factors related to the demand for financial credit to be allocated to working capital, and to the expected level of inflation, as follows:

$$\hat{\rho} = f(\hat{\rho}_{in}, \hat{\rho}_m, \hat{\rho}_w, \hat{\rho}_{Yfix}, \hat{\rho}_{pe}) \qquad (5.39)$$

where $\hat{\rho}_{in}$ is the growth rate of $(1+r_i)$, r_i represents international interest rates, $\hat{\rho}_m$ is the growth of $(1+\hat{P}_m)$, $\hat{\rho}_w$ is the growth rate of $(1+\hat{w})$, $\hat{\rho}_{Yfix}$ is the growth rate of $(1+Y_{fix})$ and $\hat{\rho}_{pe}$ is the growth rate of $(1+\hat{P}^e)$.[3]

Finally, the aggregate inflation rate is determined as the geometrical mean of the inflation rates of the industrial sector and the competitive sector, where prices may be considered to be determined by international prices. Thus, we have:

$$\hat{P} = \alpha \hat{P}^{fix} + (1-\alpha)\hat{P}^{int} \qquad (5.40)$$

where $\hat{P}^{int}$ is the growth rate of the international price index.

5.3   Institutional framework and pricing policies

As already pointed out in our introduction, the purpose of this paper is to analyze the relevance of a series of non—monetary models in explaining the inflationary process which Uruguay has undergone in the last twenty—five years. Over these years, there were profound changes in the general institutional environment as well as in the pricing procedures in the key markets of the economy.

Given the inherent importance of particular pricing mechanisms in the various markets for the approaches we are considering, it is important for our analysis to consider the changes both in the institutional situation of the economy, for instance, implementation of price controls and in other areas which are more specifically economic, e.g. the opening of the economy to external competition, which may have an impact on the operation of markets.

As regards pricing mechanisms in the commodity markets and given their assumed influence on structural inflation, it is essential to consider agricultural and industrial markets.

Until the 1970s, the traditional policy towards agriculture involved the intervention of the government in pricing. This system was used, in general terms, even in the period when the liberalization of the economy was being implemented. In fact, by June 1978, 60 per cent of agricultural prices were still administratively determined. In August 1978, the liberalization of the agricultural product markets was implemented, and there was a notable change in the operation of this market. By the end of 1978, 22.2 per cent of agricultural prices were still administratively controlled, but by late 1982, the system was only applied to 3.5 per cent of agricultural products (Notaro,1984).

Regarding the prices of non—agricultural products, an administrative control system was applied in 1968 within the framework of a general price freeze, which was more or less in force until early 1972. From the first half of 1974, there was a process of price liberalization which was implemented gradually, with significant acceleration in the second half of 1978. Thus, the share of controlled prices in the household budget decreased from 49 per cent in June 1978, to 27.8 per cent in late 1982 (Notaro, 1984).

Another aspect relevant to pricing in the various commodity markets, is the system of external transactions in force in the economy. While this fact, which is quite evident with regard to commercial policies, must be extended to the consideration of the system applicable to capital, given its influence on the short term relationship between prices of tradable and non—tradable products.

The policy of external openness began in the second half of 1974, implied from the start an almost full liberalization of international capital transactions. It was applied more gradually in the commercial area (Astori, 1981; Notaro, 1984). Although in 1975 practically all quantitative restraints to foreign trade were eliminated, protective tariffs underwent, during the first years of the policy change, only a minor reduction. It was only from the second half of 1978 that the reduction of commercial tariffs was

It was only from the second half of 1978 that the reduction of commercial tariffs was implemented, within the framework of a program oriented to reducing tariff protection to a common 35 per cent level (Notaro, 1984).

There is another very important aspect in the evaluation of the models we are analyzing. This refers to nominal wage fixation mechanisms. The traditional way of determining wages, involving tripartite negotiations with representatives for workers, employers and the government was abandoned when the state created Prices and Income Control Administration (COPRIN) in June 1968. Under various institutional frameworks, this system was used to determine wages until 1985, when Uruguay went back to tripartite wage negotiations. In 1974, the membership of COPRIN was modified, and in June 1978, the entity was replaced by DINACOPRIN (National Trade, Prices and Income Department). Between 1974 and 1981, DINACOPRIN only decided the level of minimum wages. From July 1981, this restriction regarding the transfer of wages to prices was eliminated. From then onwards, the State limited itself to determining minimum wages.

However, another relevant aspect of the real wage fixation mechanisms, in the period under consideration, concerns the restrictions imposed on the economic organization of workers. In fact during the whole period of military rule (1973–1985) not only was the role of labour unions in wage fixation eliminated, but also their mere existence was in most cases forbidden by the government. During the period of fixed nominal wages and mainly during the time of severe restrictions on labour union activities shows a serious deterioration; in 1985 wages were only about two thirds of their value in 1968.

To take into account the main aspects of the evolution we shall in our empirical analysis divide the data into different periods. Regarding pricing in commodity markets, we pay special attention to the economic policy measures implemented in the second half of 1978. Although these measures refer to price liberalization, especially to that of agricultural prices, and reduction in the level of tariff protection, they imply a stronger role for market forces, and particularly international markets, on internal pricing. The effect of this policy change on the structural components of inflation is worth analyzing. We shall also take into consideration 1968–1971, the period when a generalized price control was in force. Another change which had a large impact on relative prices was the liberalization of international capital transactions in the second half of 1974.

Concerning the methods used to determine nominal wages, we shall compare the period when wages were set in collaboration with parties on the labour market (before 1968 and since 1985) with the period when wages were fixed by the state. With a view to determining the impact of the general institutional and political conditions, including labour union restrictions, on the mechanisms used to index wages to previous inflation rates, we shall especially analyze the period of military rule.

5.4 Analysis of a structural inflation model

5.4.1 *Reduced form estimates*

5.4.1.1 *Some general observations.* In this section we shall give the results of the reduced form estimates of the model shown in section 5.2.3.2. The estimated model is an empirical version of (5.24).

$$\hat{P}_t = a_0 + \sum_{i=0}^{n} v_i \hat{P}_{t-i}^{flex} + \sum_{i=1}^{n} s_i \hat{e}_{t-1} + \sum_{i=1}^{n} g_i \hat{P}_{t-i} + \mu_t \qquad (5.41)$$

The mark–up is considered to be constant over the period in question and we disregard the influence on nominal wages of labour market demand.

The estimates based on annual data and the period 1963–1987 do not include lags

111

in the independent variables, while those for quarterly data, from the fourth quarter of 1968 until the fourth quarter in 1987, have up to three lags. The variables used are specified in the respective sections devoted to annual and quarterly estimates. Before discussing the results obtained, it is necessary to look at some aspects related to the interpretation of such results.

Estimation of model (5.41) implies regressing the growth rate of the price index on all its components. The rationale underlying the model is that the various components of the price index evolve in an independent way, at least in the short to medium term. This implies the existence of variations in relative prices, which are associated to the growth rate of the absolute price level. This may be shown in the following way.

Substituting (5.16.) and (5.14) into (5.18), we obtain

$$\hat{\Pi}_t = \alpha[(\frac{\delta-\sigma}{\eta+\epsilon}) + \hat{P}_{bt}] + (1-\alpha)\hat{P}_{bt} \qquad (5.42)$$

which is simply another way of stating that the rate of inflation is a geometrical average of the growth rate of the prices of two kinds of commodities.

From equation (5.42) it is clear that there will be a perfect correlation between the first and the second terms, unless in the first one, the term $\frac{\delta-\sigma}{\eta+\epsilon}$ is different from 0; namely, if the numerator is different from 0 (which implies that there are differences between the growth of the demand for and supply of agricultural products) and the denominator is not infinite (which implies that neither supply nor demand have an infinite elasticity). Otherwise, i.e., if the assumptions adopted by the structuralist approach regarding the variation of relative prices are relevant, we should find that the two goods prices do not evolve in a parallel way. The inflation rate would thus deviate from the growth rate of the sectorial prices which comprise the index.

However, in order for the growth rate of the components in the index to be mutually independent, another condition is required: industrial prices must be relatively inflexible downwards. As we have already shown, this is the second condition for the existence of structural inflation. In fact, admitting that structural imbalances determine growth in the relative price of agricultural commodities need not imply acknowledgement of its effect on the general price level. This is precisely the neoclassical and monetarist approach regarding the independence of the evolution of relative prices from that of absolute price level. Insofar as such increases are off–set by a reduction in the price of industrial products, the increase of agricultural prices does not imply that there is an increase in the general price level. Under these conditions, we have:

$$\alpha(\frac{\delta-\sigma}{\eta+\epsilon}) = -\hat{P}_{bt} \qquad (5.43)$$

and also, once again, any variations in the growth rate of the components of the general price index are mutually interrelated. Monetarists assume that this growth rate depends on the rate of growth of money supply.

The preceding reasoning implies that fulfillment of the conditions necessary for the presence of structural inflation implies, not only the existence of a positive correlation between the variations in the general price index and its components, but also, more precisely, the lack of correlation among the latter.

In the absence of these conditions, we would have to accept the two hypotheses presented above which, respectively, imply that the variations in the components of the general price index are either positively or negatively correlated with each other. From both hypotheses we would conclude that when estimating equation (5.41) we would be using explanatory variables which are highly correlated to each other the resulting problems of multicolinearity would, in turn, imply very imprecise estimates of the coefficients.

All this makes us very cautious with regard, not only to the forecasting power or overall significance of the model, but also to that of the individual variables. In particular, we look at the significance of the variable which represents the growth rate of the price index of the flexprice commodities since this is, according to the hypothesis of absence of structural inflation, a linear combination of the remaining variables in the model.

5.4.1.2   *Estimates using annual data.* In the estimations based on annual data for model (5.41), the average growth rate of the consumer price index (PREC) was used as a dependent variable. The independent variables are the growth rate of the agricultural price index (FLEXPREC), the sum of the growth rate of import prices in US dollars plus the growth rate of the commercial rate for the US Dollar (IMPOPR), and the lagged average growth rate of the CPI (PREC (−N)).

The model was estimated for 1963–1987 and the results obtained are shown in table 5.1.

Table 5.1
Estimates based on annual data − 1963–87

Estimation method: OLS
Dependent variable: PREC

Independent variables	Coefficient	t–ratio
CONSTANT	2.0058	0.2747
FLEXPREC	0.4015	3.3013
IMPOPR	0.1996	2.1722
PREC(−1)	0.3586	3.5871

$R^2=0.7793$ Adj.$R^2= 0.7492$ F–value=25.8982   DW=2.2470 [4]

The results show the model to be highly significant. All the explanatory variables proved to be significant at a 5 per cent level, which suggests the presence of structural inflation. The size of the estimated parameters also proved to be consistent with the theoretical assumptions of the model, while their sum is not significantly different from 1 at the 5 per cent level.

In the analysis with annual data no estimates for subperiods were made. To determine the effects of variations in economic policy, on the behaviour of the model. This analysis was done for estimates based on quarterly data, and the results are described in the following section.

5.4.1.3   *Estimates based on quarterly data.* Different versions of the model under investigation were used. Thus, together with model (5.41) estimates were obtained for a version of the model which distinguishes between costs of different industrial inputs, namely those which indirectly depend on import prices and those whose prices are influenced by price control and/or on the intervention of the state. Thus we obtain:

$$\hat{P}_t = a_0 + \sum_{i=0}^{1} v_i \hat{P}_{t-i}^{flex} + \sum_{i=0}^{n} m_i \hat{e}'_{t-i} + \sum_{i=0}^{n} n_i \hat{P}_{t-i}^{tar}$$

$$+ \sum_{i=1}^{n} g_i \hat{P}_{t-i} + \mu_t \qquad (5.44)$$

where $\hat{e}'$ is the devaluation rate plus the growth rate of import prices, excluding the

113

price of fuel which is set by the state, and where $\hat{P}^{tar}$ is the growth rate of an index of the main industrial inputs, fuel and electricity, whose prices are controlled.

Finally, another version of the model was estimated for IV/1979–IV/1987, where prices managed by the state were taken into consideration, disregarding their impact on industrial costs but including their direct influence on the general price index. We consequently have:

$$\hat{P}_t = a_0 + \sum_{i=0}^{n} v_i \hat{P}_{t-i}^{flex} + \sum_{i=0}^{n} s_i \hat{e}_{t-i} + \sum_{i=0}^{n} \ell_i \hat{P}_{t-i}^{gob}$$

$$+ \sum_{i=0}^{n} g_i \hat{P}_{t-i} + \mu_t \qquad (5.45)$$

where $\hat{P}^{gob}$ represents the growth rate of an index of public tariffs.

The following variables were used in the specification of the empirical models: The average growth rate of the consumer price index (PREC) was used as a dependent variable in model (5.41), while the following independent variables were used: the growth rate of the wholesale agricultural price index (FLEXPR) and the sum of the growth rate of import prices in US dollars plus the rate of change in the commercial rate for the US Dollar (IMPOPR).[5]

In the estimation of (5.44), IMPOPR was replaced by IMP2PR which is the growth rate of the local currency import price index, which excludes the price of fuels, as the latter is fixed by the state. Finally, we include as a variable GOBPRE, which is the growth rate of a composite index of fuels and electricity prices, inputs whose prices are managed by the government, weighted by their shares in the wholesale price index of industrial products.

Finally, in the estimation of (5.45) we used the local currency import price index (IMP1PR) and a public tariff index (GOBPRE) obtained by taking the weight of a series of services covered by the state in the consumer price index.

We did not get any significant results in the models where the growth rate of industrial productivity was included as a dependent variable.

Depending on the available data, estimates were made for IV/1968–IV/1987, III/1972–IV/1987 and IV/1979–IV/1987.

Estimates were also made for several subperiods taking into consideration variations in economic policy and institutional context, as mentioned in section 3.[6] Thus, regarding the conditions prevailing in the pricing of commodities, the following were considered: the price freeze period (III/1968 – I/1972), the liberalization and external openness period from the third quarter of 1974, and the acceleration of this policy from the last quarter of 1978.

Concerning the determination of nominal wages, the various systems used in the period under analysis are considered, particularly the period when wages were determined by the state and/or when there were restrictions on labour unions, and the period when wages were determined in concert with organizations on the labour market.

As already stated, and provided the degrees of freedom allow it, estimates are done with up to three lags on the independent variables.

Estimates of (5.41) and (5.45) (tables 5.2 and 5.3) for the full period were highly significant (F–values significant at the 1 per cent level, R^2 lying between 0.70 and 0.80 in the lagged cases).

The high significance of the parameters of all independent variables is probably the reflection of a low degree of correlation among these variables. This supports, as we have already stated, the relevance of the structural model of inflation. Both the variables which represent the growth rate of prices in the flexprice sector and those which refer to the components of costs in the fixprice sector gave positive coefficients, which were significant at the 5 per cent level. This held, in particular, for the growth

114

rate of fixprice sector prices in the current quarter, as well as for the growth rate of import prices and of those managed by the government, in the first quarter. For the lagged values of the inflation rate, which show the degree of indexation of wages and inflationary inertia, we obtained significant coefficients in the first lag of both models (5.41) and (5.45), and in the third lag of model (5.45). The quantitative importance of the structural element, measured as the size of the parameter of FLEXPR, is notable, reaching about 0.15–0.20.

Finally, in all cases, the sum of the parameters estimated was not significantly different from 1, which is also consistent with the theoretical model.

Following the outline in section 3, we find support for the relevance of structural factors in the inflationary process in the analysis of all but one subperiod (tables 5.2 and 5.3). Structural factors do not seem to influence inflation in the period between the last quarter of 1974 and the third quarter of 1978. In both the years before that period and in those after, the F– and R^2–values and the high t–ratios of the coefficients show that the basic assumptions of the model used are relevant. This is particularly evident, with regard the mutual independence of the explanatory variables, in the period after 1978, with particularly high t–values.

As we have already observed, the outcome is different for the period IV/1974 – III/1978, which was an intermediate period in the process of liberalization and opening up. In this subperiod, not only is the significance of the model and its explanatory value lower than in the other cases, but the explanatory variables included in the model are also in general not significant at the 5 per cent level and do frequently have the wrong sign. This is particularly the case with regard to the variable representing the rate of inflation in the flexprice sector, which was not significant, at the 5 per cent level, in any of the equations and frequently had a negative coefficient.

Regarding elements with an influence on the degree of inflationary inertia (table 5.4), we find that it is important to differentiate between the period characterized by governmental control of wages and/or labour union activities and those when parties on the labour market were involved in the determination of nominal wages. Although, in all subperiods analyzed, we found a significant degree of inertia in the inflationary process, i.e. parameters for variables representing the lagged inflation rate were significant. They were lower in the period 1968–1985 when the state intervened and directly determined wages and/or severely restricted the activities of the labour unions. Thus we found that the sum of the parameters of the lagged values of the inflation rate is, over the period, significantly below 1 at the 5 per cent level, while in the period after the recovery from the first half of 1985, it is above 1. This is fully consistent with the deterioration of real wages since the early 1970s and their recovery from the second half of 1985.

Finally, the estimation of the model in table 5.5 does not enable us to draw conclusions which are different from the ones arrived at in the other versions.

Table 5.2
Reduced form estimates based on quarterly data

Estimation metod: OLS   OLS
Period: III/69–IV/87   III/69 – III/74

Dependent variable:PREC   PREC

Ind.var.	Coeffic.	t–ratio	Ind.var.	Coeffic.	t–ratio
CONSTANT	1.3174	1.1076	CONSTANT	2.4954	1.6376
FLEXPREC	0.2323	4.8623	FLEXPREC	0.2216	2.3034
FLEXPR(–1)	– 0.0087	– 0.1478	FLEXPR(–1)	0.2623	1.5385
FLEXPR(–2)	0.0091	– 0.1569	IMPOPR	0.1908	2.7038
IMPOPR	0.1969	5.0725	IMPOPR(–1)	0.0102	0.1261
IMPOPR(–1)	– 0.0432	– 1.0199	PREC(–1)	– 0.4514	– 1.8464
IMPOPR(–2)	0.0513	1.2357	PREC(–2)	0.2755	2.1470
PREC(–1)	0.0994	0.8608	PREC(–3)	0.2624	1.8718
PREC(–2)	0.0994	0.8608			
PREC(–3)	0.2754	3.1675			

R^2= 0.6609   F–value=13.8597 R^2= 0.8897   F–value= 14.9858

Adj.R^2= 0.6132   DW= 0.4067   Adj.R^2= 0.8303   DW= 2.1495

Estimation method: OLS   OLS
Period: IV/74–III/78   IV/78 – IV/87

Dep. variable:PREC   PREC

Ind. var.	Coeffic.	t–ratio	Ind.var.	Coeffic.	t–ratio
CONSTANT	7.1255	0.9564	CONSTANT	– 0.7733	– 0.4133
FLEXPREC	– 0.0146	– 0.0629	FLEXPREC	0.2444	4.8811
FLEXPR(–1)	– 0.2148	– 0.8191	FLEXPR(–1)–	0.0935	– 1.5126
IMPOPR	0.5524	2.2677	IMPOPR	0.1301	2.9897
IMPOPR(–1)	– 0.0218	– 0.0905	IMPOPR(–1)	0.0291	0.6120
PREC(–1)	– 0.1225	– 0.3276	PREC(–1)	0.4426	2.5417
PREC(–2)	– 0.2485	– 0.7557	PREC(–2)	0.0545	0.4059
PREC(–3)	0.4504	1.5333	PREC(–3)	0.2618	2.2041

R^2= 0.6296   F–value=1.9425 R^2= 0.6971   F–value= 9.5346

Adj.R^2= 0.3054   DW= 1.7157   Adj.R^2= 0.6240

Table 5.3
Reduced form estimates based on quarterly data

Estimation method: OLS
Period: I/73 – IV/87

Dependent variable: PREC

Ind.var.	Coeffic.	t–ratio
CONSTANT	1.4444	1.0337
FLEXPREC	0.1795	3.3850
FLEXPR(−1)	− 0.0952	− 1.6858
FLEXPR(−2)	0.0575	1.0720
IMP2PR	0.1257	2.5463
IMP2PR(−1)	0.0284	0.5698
IMP2PR(−2)	− 0.0031	− 0.0649
GOBPRE	0.1215	4.8841
GOBPRE(−1)	− 0.0715	− 2.3855
GOBPRE(−2)	0.0689	2.1300
PREC(−1)	0.2852	2.2744
PREC(−2)	− 0.0533	− 0.4452
PREC(−3)	0.1228	2.7686

R^2= 0.7687   F–value=13.0165   Adj.R^2= 0.7096

Estimation method: OLS
Period: IV/74–III/78

Dep variable: PREC

Ind.var.	Coeffic.	t–ratio
CONSTANT	9.6161	1.2972
FLEXPREC	0.0930	0.5105
FLEXPR(−1)	− 0.3429	− 1.4215
IMP2PR	− 0.0999	− 0.2756
IMP2PR(−1)	0.4367	1.8764
GOBPRE	0.2588	1.7611
GOBPRE(−1)	− 0.2156	− 1.7160
PREC(−1)	0.0878	0.2947
PREC(−2)	− 0.0716	− 0.2735
PREC(−3)	0.0442	0.1259

R^2= 0.8109   F–value= 2.8593
Adj.R^2= 0.5273   DW= 1.8636

OLS
IV/78 – IV/87

PREC

Ind.var.	Coeffic.	t–ratio
CONSTANT	− 0.8327	− 0.6637
FLEXPREC	0.1754	4.2894
FLEXPR(−1)	− 0.0673	− 1.4408
IMP2PR	0.1348	3.3572
IMP2PR(−1)	− 0.0501	− 1.1270
GOBPRE	0.1953	4.2743
GOBPRE(−1)	− 0.0669	− 1.1446
PREC(−1)	0.5007	2.8878
PREC(−2)	0.1183	1.2210
PREC(−3)	0.1267	1.4038

R^2= 0.8612   F–value= 18.6115
Adj.R^2= 0.8149

Table 5.4
Reduced form estimates based on quarterly data

Est. method: Cochrane Orcutt
Period: III/69 − IV/87

OLS
III/69 − III/74

Dependent variable: PREC

PREC

Ind. var.	Coeffic.	t−ratio	Ind.var.	Coeffic.	t−ratio
CONSTANT	1.6393	0.9739	CONSTANT	12.5227	− 2.3071
FLEXPREC	0.1750	2.8614	FLEXPREC	0.1644	2.9517
IMP2PR	0.1046	2.1335	IMP2PR	0.1329	0.7721
GOBPRE	0.1468	8.0662	GOBPRE	0.2400	5.6043
PREC(−1)	− 0.2082	− 2.5373	PREC(−1)	0.5020	2.9217
PREC(−2)	0.2233	2.9726	PREC(−2)	0.3041	1.6026
PREC(−3)	0.3774	4.8745	PREC(−3)	0.5585	3.5290
AR(1)	0.5578	3.5969			
AR(2)	− 0.4891	− 3.2129			

R^2= 0.7730   F−value=17.4519

Adj.R^2= 0.7287

R^2= 0.9239   F−value= 8.0984

Adj.R^2= 0.8099   DW= 2.2445

AR(n): nth order autocorrelation coefficient

Table 5.5
Reduced form estimates based on quarterly data

Estimation method: OLS
Period: III/79 − IV/87

Dependent variable: PREC

Ind.var.	Coeffic.	t−ratio
CONSTANT	− 0.9419	− 0.7683
FLEXPREC	0.1714	4.6017
FLEXPR(−1)	− 0.0854	− 1.8569
IMP1PR	0.0823	2.4203
IMP1PR(−1)	− 0.0360	− 1.0088
GOBPR1	0.2852	4.9839
GOBPR1(−1)	− 0.0943	− 1.2619
PREC(−1)	0.5427	3.1288
PREC(−2)	0.0771	0.8092
PREC(−3)	0.1209	1.4036

R^2= 0.8855   F−value= 20.63179   Adj.R^2= 0.8426

5.4.1.4   *Some conclusions on the reduced structural inflation model.* From the analysis the reduced form of the model, in section 5.2.2, we may draw several conclusions:

The model we used, which combines structural and inertia elements, and for which we obtained very significant results, seems to be relevant in the explanation of inflation during the period under consideration. The size and precision of the coefficients of the explanatory variables and, in particular, those corresponding to FLEXPR, comprising the growth of prices for agricultural products, point to structural factors in the period under consideration which had considerable impact on the inflation rate. The demonstrable influence of past inflation on the present rate of inflation suggests, in the period under consideration, that there exists inertia in the inflationary process.

The analysis of subperiods seems to indicate that the model used is relevant both for the period of a controlled and closed economy and the subsequent period, from the mid 1970s, of an open and liberalized economy. However, in the latter, the higher significance of the estimates obtained for the coefficients of the model seems to indicate a higher degree of independence in the variation of the various prices considered and, consequently, a potentially stronger presence of structural factors.

This does, however, not hold when we consider the period between IV/1974 and III/1978. As already noted not only do the models considered have a lower explanatory power in this period, but the precision of the estimated coefficients falls sharply, showing the lack of independence of the changes in the various components of the price index.

Several explanations might be used to account for the similarity in the evolution of the prices of the flexprice and the fixprice sectors during this period. This might, for instance, be due to the presence of exogenous factors having impacts on the evolution of prices. Yet, this phenomenon might also, hypothetically, relate to the economic policy applied during the period.

To some extent, this period may be considered as intermediate in the process of economic reform. The liberalization and financial openness reached a high level, while commercial openness and price liberalization advanced at a slower pace. It is particularly noteworthy that control of all agricultural products was maintained.

We may hypothetically posit that financial openness, since it accelerates the monetary adjustment of the economy, tends to approximate the evolution of the prices of tradable and non–tradable commodities, while the reduction in protective barriers and the enhancement of price liberalization tends to approximate their evolution to international levels. On the other hand, the persistence of strict controls for prices of agricultural products may have reduced, to some extent, transfers to internal prices of any sudden changes in the prices of goods with shares in international markets.

Finally, it is worth noting that the adjustment of nominal wages to past inflation, and its influence on the inertia of inflation, seem to be a more or less permanent characteristic during the whole period under analysis. Yet this element seems to have a lower incidence in the years characterized by the state control of nominal wages and labour unions − a period when real wages fall drastically − while its weight increases in the period following the first half of 1985.

5.4.2   *Simultaneous structural model estimates*

In this section, we present the results obtained in the estimation of a simultaneous version of the structural model set out in section 2.3.2. The main difference compared to the model we considered in that section is that the growth rate of wages depends not only on lagged values but also on the present rate of inflation. Because of this, they are simultaneously determined in the model. The model comprises the following basic equations:

119

$$\hat{P}_t^{fix} = \sum_{i=0}^{n} v_i \hat{P}_{t-i}^{flex} + \sum_{i=0}^{n} o_i \hat{P}_{t-i}^{fix} + \mu_{1t} \qquad (5.46)$$

$$\hat{P}_t^{fix} = \sum_{i=0}^{n} s_i \hat{e}_{t-i} + \sum_{i=0}^{n} h_i \hat{c}_{t-i} + \mu_{2t} \qquad (5.47)$$

$$\hat{w}_t = \sum_{i=0}^{n} k_i \hat{P}_{t-i} + \sum_{i=0}^{n} r_i \hat{L}_{t-i} + \mu_{2t} \qquad (5.48)$$

and the following identity:

$$\hat{c}_t = \hat{w}_t - \hat{q}_t \qquad (5.49)$$

In the latter, $\hat{c}$ represents the growth rate of the wage costs and $\hat{q}$, the growth rate of labour productivity in the sector. Variable L in equation (5.48) is a measure of the excess demand in the economy.

We considered the inclusion of a price equation for the flexprice sector commodities in the structural model. Given possible dependence on the evolution of domestic demand, we assumed that such pricing might be simultaneous in nature. The result from the incorporation of an equation for the growth rate of agricultural prices, whose explanatory variables were the growth rates of import prices and real wages, was that only the first explanatory variable had a significant influence. For this model, therefore, we may consider the pricing of agricultural products to be exogenous, so that no equation representing it is necessary in the model.

Estimates were done with annual and quarterly data. As in the analysis of the reduced forms, and for the case of estimates based on quarterly data, together with the model shown above (model 1), we estimated another version (model 2) in which the price of industrial inputs is broken down into import prices and tariffs. Thus, (5.47) is replaced by

$$\hat{P}_t^{fix} = \sum_{i=0}^{1} m_i \hat{e}_{t-i}' + \sum_{i=0}^{n} \hat{P}_{t-i}^{tar} + \sum_{i=0}^{n} \hat{c}_{t-i} + \mu_{2t}' \qquad (5.47')$$

The variables used are the same as in the estimation of the reduced forms, to which we added the growth rate of the wholesale price index of industrial products (FIXPR), the growth rate of the index of average nominal wages (SALNOM), the growth rate of industrial labour productivity measured as the ratio of the physical output volume index and the hours worked per week. In the estimates included in this chapter, use is made of the average rate of productivity growth (TPROD), rather than the current rate. This was because when the former was used, the model was more significant than when current productivity growth was used. By subtracting the average productivity growth rate from the growth rate of the average wage index we obtained the wage cost index (SALCOS).

As mentioned above, we have included a variable which represents the evolution of the level of excess demand (EXDEM) in the equation for nominal wages. It is built using the logarithmic difference between current aggregate demand — assumed to represent GDP — and potential aggregate supply, obtained on the basis of the exponential growth of GDP between business cycle peaks.

In estimates with annual data, we only consider the present value of the variables, while with quarterly data variables included in the system were lagged up to three periods to form predetermined variables.

Estimates were made for the full period with both types of data, while quarterly data were used to prepare estimates for the subperiods.

Given the simultaneous nature of the model used, we used the full information maximum likelihood procedure which takes into account all restrictions incorporated in the model in the course of estimation of parameters.

5.4.2.1   *Estimates with annual data.* The model comprising equations (5.46) to (5.47) is estimated with annual data for the period 1962–87 (table 5.6).

The χ^2–statistic, which represents the degree to which the model is consistent with the data, was significant at the 2.5 per cent level. Moreover, t–values were significant at the 5 per cent level for all the explanatory variables included in the model.

The results obtained from the estimation of the annual structural model were in conformity with those obtained in the reduced form. The model was able to explain the evolution of the endogenous variables over the sample period. In particular, the variable representing the growth rate of flexprice sector prices – which indicates the influence of structural factors – had a significant positive coefficient in the inflation equation, although its size was somewhat lower than in the reduced form of the model. Finally, in the case of estimates with annual data, coefficients on the inflation rate of the nominal wage equation and on the wage costs of the fixprice sector price equation were close to 1 and highly significant, indicating the existence of a high degree of simultaneity in the relationship between the inflation rate and the growth rate of nominal wages.

Table 5.6
Structural model estimates based on annual data

Estimation method: FIML
Period: 1962–1987

Equation 1 for PREC

Equation 2 for FIXPR

Variable.	Coeffic.	t–ratio	Variable	Coeffic.	t–ratio
FLEXPREC	0.2532	1.901	IMPOPR	0.1435	2.586
FIXPR	0.6588	4.580	SALCOST	1.0777	11.393

Equation 3 for SALNOM

PREC	0.8740	18.419
EXDEM	0.1263	0.675

Definition of SALCOST = SALNOM – TPROD

$\chi^2(6) = 16.751$

5.4.2.2   *Estimates with quarterly data.* Estimates based on quarterly data allow us to analyze in greater detail the behaviour of the model and its ability to explain inflation over the period under consideration.

As already stated, the model is estimated in both its versions (models 1 and 2), with up to three lags in the explanatory variables. Estimates are made for the period for which data were available, as well as for several subperiods differentiated by variations in economic policy and in institutional conditions which had an impact on the pricing of commodities or labour. Estimates for the full period cover the IV/69–IV/87 period in model 1 and II/72–IV/87 in model 2.

In all cases the χ^2 values are highly significant at the 1 per cent level indicating that the models are consistent with the data (tables 5.7 and 5.8). Explanatory variables, are significant at the 5 per cent level, either the current or some of the lagged values. The only exception being EXDEM.

In the estimates for model 1, we find that in equation 1, the parameter of FLEXPR is always positive and significant at the 5 per cent level. When lagged values are incorporated, the results are not significant with no major changes in the significance or value of the FLEXPR parameter, which is about 0.15–0.20. On the other hand, FIXPR was significant, both the current and when the lagged values were incorporated, the parameters adding up to 0.75–0.80.

In equation 2, both IMPOPR and SALCOS have positive and significant parameters at the 5 per cent level. Yet this only refers to their current values, which suggests that increases in industrial costs might have all their effect on prices in the first quarter. It is also worth noting that compared to that of SALCOS the weight of IMPOPR is extremely small. This applies to all estimates of the model and may suggest the existence of multicolinearity between the two variables.

Finally, in equation 3, which represents the growth rate of nominal wages, the inflation rate (PREC) is significant at the 5 per cent level, with a positive parameter of around 0.90 on the current value. The lagged values of this variable are not significant. EXDEM, on the other hand, shows an irregular behaviour, having proved to be significant only on its current value in the two–lagged equation. Further, in this case, it has a negative parameter, which is contrary to all theoretical forecasts. However, the method we have used to calculate EXDEM (with GDP representing aggregate demand) means that classical unemployment is ruled out. This may explain the lack of significance.

Table 5.7
Structural model estimates based on quarterly data

Estimation method: FIML
Period: II/1970 – IV/1987

Equation 1 for PREC

Variable	Coeff.	t–ratio
FLEXPREC	0.1768	4.156
FLEXPR(−1)	0.0284	0.841
FLEXPR(−2)	− 0.0255	− 0.760
FIXPR	0.4543	5.534
FIXPR(−1)	0.1055	2.237
FIXPR(−2)	0.1966	4.020

Equation 2 for FIXPR

Variable	Coeff.	t–ratio
IMPOPR	0.1224	4.497
IMPOPR(−1)	0.0008	0.032
IMP0PR(−2)	− 0.0180	− 0.745
SALCOS	1.1874	11.078
SALCOS(−1)	− 0.0869	− 1.875
SALCOS(−2)	− 0.0013	− 0.031

Equation 3 for SALNOM

Variable	Coeff.	t–ratio
PREC	0.8911	9.104
PREC(−2)	0.0233	0.408
PREC(−3)	− 0.0133	− 0.202
EXDEM	− 0.0786	− 2.257
EXDEM(−1)	0.0402	0.959
EXDEM(−2)	0.0122	0.326

Identity for SALCOS = SALNOM − TPROD (TPROD = 0.007657)

$\chi^2(30) = 99.332$

Table 5.8
Structural model estimates based on quarterly data

Estimation method: FIML
Period: IV/1972 − IV/1987

Equation 1 for PREC   Equation 2 for FIXPR

Variable	Coeff.	t−ratio	Variable	Coeff.	t−ratio
FLEXPR	0.1281	3.241	IMP2PR	0.1530	3.906
FLEXPR(−1)	− 0.0016	− 0.048	IMP2PR(−1)	0.0209	0.712
FLEXPR(−2)	− 0.0084	− 0.266	IMP2PR(−2)	− 0.0064	− 0.243
FIXPR	0.5627	8.720	GOBPRE	0.1009	4.289
FIXPR(−1)	0.0940	2.030	GOBPRE(−1)	− 0.0566	− 2.996
FIXPR(−2)	0.1639	3.397	GOBPRE(−2)	− 0.0001	− 0.005
			SALCOS	0.8936	6.919
			SALCOS(−1)	0.0322	0.660
			SALCOS(−2)	− 0.0121	− 0.263

Equation 3 for SALNOM

Variable	Coeff.	t−ratio
PREC	0.9141	8.730
PREC(−1)	0.0257	0.384
PREC(−2)	0.0317	0.417
EXDEM	− 0.0207	− 0.537
EXDEM(−1)	0.0187	0.404
EXDEM(−2)	0.0043	0.104

Identity for SALCOS = SALNOM − TPROD (TPROD = 0.007657)
$\chi^2 = 114.390$

The sum of the parameters corresponding to the explanatory variables is, in all three equations, near unity, which seems to indicate homogeneity.[7] It is worth noting, however, that the sum of the parameters tends to be above 1 in equation 2 and below 1 in equation 3. This might be indicative, over the period, of a higher growth of industrial prices than of industrial costs and a lower growth of wages than of inflation (the latter due to the fact that the effect of excess demand appears to be neutral in the estimations).

The analysis of model 2 for the full period gives results which are similar, both in terms of the general significance of the model and in terms of the individual variables included, to the ones described above. It is worth pointing out that GOBPRE is significant when incorporated as a variable in equation 2, while it implies a reduction in the parameter of SALCOS, as compared to its value in model 1.

Regarding the homogeneity condition of the equations of the model, the comments made regarding model 1 are still valid, although the sum of the parameters is now even closer to unity.

The results we have described, both in terms of the annual and of the quarterly models, point to the relevance of structural factors in the explanation of the inflationary process. Thus, the results obtained do not, compared to the reduced form model, show a qualitative difference.

As for the mutual relationship between inflation and the growth of nominal wages, we must emphasize the importance of its simultaneous aspects, while the lagged effects are not significant. Insofar as the simultaneity may be explained by the quarterly periodicity of the data used or by the specification of the model, this does not imply, by itself, a small influence of inertia factors or the applicability of rational expectations in the determination of wages. An enhanced analysis of the institutional mechanisms used in wage determination, together with a consistent specification of the model, as well as the use of shorter time series, would be required to determine the influence of inertia factors of inflation.

As stated above, quarterly data were also used to make estimates for the subperiods, taking into account those which, according to the analysis of the reduced forms of the model, were relevant to performance. We here comment briefly on the results. Regarding pricing mechanisms in commodity markets, the subperiods considered were: the period prior to the last quarter of 1974, that beginning in the last quarter of 1974 and ending in the third quarter of 1978, and finally, the period after the third quarter of 1978. Regarding the mechanisms used in the determination of nominal wages, three periods were considered: the period when there was direct intervention of the state in wage determination and/or in the activities of the entities involved in the labour market (III/68–1/85), and the period immediately before and after that period, when there was an active role of the above described bodies.

For all the subperiods analyzed, we obtained models with χ^2–values which are significant at the 1 per cent level, except for the IV/74–III/78 for which models are not significant at the 5 per cent level. Homogeneity holds for the various subperiods as it does for estimates for the full period.

Regarding the behaviour of the parameters in the model, we find that FLEXPR in equation 1, a key factor in determining the relevance of structural factors in inflation, was in general positive and significant but its lagged values were not. Once again, the only exception was the period from IV/74 to III/78 in which, the introduction of lags in the variables of equation 1, gave insignificant results for the FLEXPR parameter at the 5 per cent level or has negatively signed parameters in the lagged values of the variable.

Results obtained for the subperiods determined by the system prevailing in the labour market (only model 1 was used) point to a lower degree of interdependence in the relationship between the adjustment of wages and inflation in the period when there was government control in the labour market. In fact, the main difference between II/72–I/85 and the subsequent period lies in the size of the coefficient of the unlagged PREC variable, which fluctuates between 0.75 and 0.80 in the former and is somewhat higher than 1 in the latter. The total sum of the parameters of PREC is also higher in the second period.

5.4.2.3   *Some conclusions from the analysis of the simultaneous structural model.* From the results described in the preceding section, we may draw certain conclusions about the applicability of the model used and about its behaviour under various economic and income policy systems.

First, it is worth noting that the results obtained with the reduced form, regarding the relevance of the structural model in explaining inflation in the period under consideration, are validated. In fact, except for one of the subperiods considered, the estimated models were always highly significant.

In particular, we found that the growth rate of prices in the flexprice sector was, in general terms, a significant variable in the explanation of inflation. Although its impact is somewhat lower than that obtained in the reduced forms, the effect of structural factors operating through variations in relative prices is also evident in the estimation of the simultaneous structural models. Coinciding with the results from the reduced forms, we also found that this effect seems to be smaller in the period from late 1974 to late 1978. As already stated, this period can be seen as an intermediate period in the process of liberalization and external openness of the economy: financial liberalization was consistently developed while commercial openness and price liberalization for commodities was still going on, particularly for agricultural products.

Finally, regarding the mutual relationship between inflation and wage growth, we found a high degree of simultaneity. In fact, estimates of the simultaneous model suggest that most of the effects of inflation on wages appear during the first quarter, while the effect of lagged inflation is lower. As already stated, this kind of result does not necessarily imply the validity of rational expectations or the lack of inertia factors in inflation. The simultaneity obtained from our estimations may derive from the specification of the model and/or the use of quarterly data which does not allow us to properly account for the periodicity of wage adjustment mechanisms. This points to the need of making a more detailed analysis of wage determination mechanisms, applied over the period under consideration.

Another outstanding aspect of the results obtained is the marked increase of simultaneity in the relationship between inflation and wages, in the period after March 1985, characterized by the participation in wage determination of the organizations involved in the labour market. This might be an indication of a quicker adjustment of wages to inflation under the new prevailing institutional conditions.

5.5   Analysis of a neostructuralist model

5.5.1   *Model applied*

In the analysis described below we use the basic model presented earlier, which, as already stated, is a modification of a model developed by Bruno for a financially repressed economy (Bruno, 1979). It is in line with the conditions of an open economy with a credit market which is relatively integrated with external markets. The model was estimated in its structural form, and comprises the following equations

$$\hat{P}_t = \sum_{i=0}^{n} \hat{P}_{t-i}^{int} + \sum_{i=0}^{n} \hat{P}_{t-i}^{fix} + v_{1t} \tag{5.50}$$

$$\hat{P}_t^{fix} = \sum_{i=0}^{n} m_i \hat{P}_{t-i} + \sum_{i=0}^{n} n_i \hat{w}_{t-i} + \sum_{i=0}^{1} r_i \hat{e}_{t-i}$$
$$+ \sum_{i=0}^{n} o_i Y_{t-i}^{d} + b\hat{P}_t^{e} + v_{2t} \tag{5.51}$$

$$\hat{Y}_t^{fix} = \sum_{i=0}^{n} r_i \hat{P}_{t-i} + \sum_{i=0}^{n} s_i \hat{w}_{t-i} + \sum_{i=0}^{n} v_i \hat{e}_{t-i} + \sum_{i=0}^{n} z_i Y_{t-i}^{d}$$
$$+ c\hat{P}_{t-i}^{e} + v_{3t} \tag{5.52}$$

$$\hat{P}_t = \sum_{i=0}^{n} \lambda_i \hat{P}_{t-i}^{int} + \sum_{i=0}^{n} \delta_i \hat{P}_{wt-i} + \sum_{i=0}^{n} \tau_i \hat{P}_{mt-i}$$
$$+ \sum_{i=0}^{n} g_i \hat{P}_{Y_{fixt-i}} + d\hat{P}_p^{e}{}_t + v_{4t} \tag{5.53}$$

and

$$\hat{w}_t = \sum_{i=0}^{n} g_i \hat{P}_{t-i} + v_{st} \tag{5.54}$$

In the specification of the model, we assume the existence of (quasi–)rational

125

expectations on the part of businessmen. The expected inflation rate is consequently obtained from an estimation using the ordinary least squares method, in which the inflation rate is regressed on lagged values of the growth rate of import and export prices, the devaluation rate, the growth rate of nominal wages, active banking interest rates and the gross domestic product.

We also assume a mechanism for the adjustment of nominal wages based on past inflation, in line with the application of institutional regulations or agreements, implying a degree of indexation of nominal wages. Based on these definitions, we replaced equation (5.38) by equation (5.54).

Apart from the variables used in previous models, the following were also used: the growth rate of an international commodity price index plus the rate of devaluation of the US Dollar (PRISIN); the growth rate of internal financial costs (COSFIN) in terms of the factor $(1 + r)$ where r is the active interest rate of up to three month bank loans; the expected inflation rate (PRECEX), computed as above; the real gross domestic product (PBIRT); the growth rate of international financial costs (COSINT) in terms of $(1 + r_{in})$, where r_{in} is the LIBOR rate on three month deposits; the growth rate of factor $(1 + \hat{w})$ (TSALNO) where w is the growth rate of nominal wages; the growth rate of factor $(1 + \hat{e})$ (TIMIPR), where e is the growth rate of factor $(1 + \hat{y}_{fix})$, where $\hat{y}_{fix}$ is the growth rate of industrial output, and finally, the growth rate of factor $(1 + \hat{p}^e)$ (TPRECEX), where $\hat{p}^e$ is the expected inflation rate.

Estimates were done with quarterly data for the period from II/77 to IV/87, for which information, related to all the variables included in the model, was available. Estimations considered one lag in all variables except in PREC, for which up to three lags were used.

5.5.2   Estimation results

Estimates of the model (table 5.9) were made using the three stage least squares method, which takes into account the set of relations in the system.

The χ^2 statistic is significant at the 1 per cent level. Regarding the interrelationships in the model, it may be concluded that the basic ingredients at the core of the underlying theoretical model, expressed before as a working capital cost push effect, is, in general, valuated by our estimations. In fact, a detailed analysis of the estimates for the various equations in the system may be summarized as follows.

Equation 1 shows on the one hand that the growth rate of prices in the fixprice sector (FIXPRI) is highly significant and close to unity. On the contrary, the growth rate of international prices behaves in an irregular way, with a negative parameter, and significance at the 5 per cent level.

From equation 5 we see that lagged inflation rates are, in general, significant in the explanation of the variations in the growth rate of wages. In particular, the sum of the parameters of these values was very close to 1. As already analyzed in prior sections, these results show that wage determination mechanisms imply adjustment to past inflation and, consequently, to a high degree of inertia in the inflationary process.

Yet, the three remaining equations, which form the core of the model and show the relationship between interest rates and the variations in price (the working capital cost push effect) and activity levels, are the ones which give the most interesting results.

Equation 2 shows that the key variables have the expected sign and a high level of significance. Thus the variable which represents the rate of change of financial costs (COSFIN) has a parameter which is positive, sizeable and significant at the 5 per cent level. The lags were not significant. The remaining components of industrial

126

costs had also a positive effect on inflation, their parameters being significant at the 5 per cent level for the growth rate of nominal wages (SALNOM) and at the 10 per cent level for that of imported commodity prices (IMPIPR). On the other hand, expected inflation (PRECEX) had, in line with our forecasts, a positive and highly significant parameter. Finally, the level of aggregate demand in preceding periods measured by GDP (PBIRT) does not have the expected sign and is not significant.

Table 5.9
Estimations of the neostructuralist model (quarterly data)

Estimation Method: 3SLS
Period: III/1977 – IV/1987

Equation 1 for PREC

Variable	Coeff.	t–ratio
PRISIN	− 0.1696	− 4.561
FIXPR	1.1173	22.086

Equation 2 for FIXPR

Variable	Coeff.	t–ratio
COSFIN	0.3987	2.064
COSFIN(−1)	− 0.0910	− 0.633
SALNOM	0.3268	3.206
SALNOM(−1)	− 0.1384	− 1.623
IMP1PR	0.0781	1.412
IMP1PR(−1)	0.0579	1.380
PRECEX	0.6399	5.080
PBIRT(−1)	− 0.0002	− 0.304
PBIRT(−2)	0.0002	0.413

Equation 3 for PRIND

Variable	Coeff.	t–ratio
COSFIN	− 0.0877	− 1.889
SALNOM	− 0.0635	− 0.306
IMP1PR	− 0.0409	− 0.336
PRECEX	0.7051	2.280
PBIRT(−1)	− 0.0006	− 2.416

Equation No 4 for COSFIN

Variable	Coeff.	t–ratio
COSINT	− 0.4915	− 1.689
COSINT(−1)	0.2163	0.719
TSALNO	0.1500	1.423
TSALNO(−1)	0.2153	2.172
TIMP1PR	0.1458	2.737
TIMP1PR−1)	0.1500	3.804
TPRIND	− 0.0705	− 1.568
TPRIND(−1)	− 0.0305	− 0.687
TPRECEX	0.1530	1.053

Equation 5 for SALNOM

Variable	Coeff.	t–ratio
PREC(−1)	0.2755	1.826
PREC(−2)	0.4995	3.105
PREC(−3)	0.2317	1.536

$\chi^2(72) = 450.240$

Equation 3 shows, once again, that all variables other than PBIRT have the expected sign. Among them, both the expected inflation rate (PRECEX) and COSFIN, showing the influence of financial costs on activity levels, are significant at the 5 per cent level. PBIRT was significant, but with the incorrect sign.

In equation 4, it is worth noting the importance of factors associated with the local demand for credit. Thus, the variables related to wage growth (TSALNO) and import price growth (TIMP1PR) are the ones with a positive sign and significance at the 5 per cent level. The influence of TPRIND, associated with the variations in the level of industrial activity, is opposite to the one expected, and surprisingly, the same is true for the variable related to the evolution of international interest rates (COSINT). Finally, the expected inflation variable (TPRECEX) has an insignificant effect, although with the correct sign.

5.5.3   *Some conclusions from the results obtained*

It may be concluded that the results contribute to the short term analysis of variations in price and activity levels and their relationship to corporate financial costs. Of particular interest is the positive effect of financial cost variations, measured by changes in bank interest rates, on inflation, and their negative effect on industrial output. These relationships form the basic structural explanation for the tendency of economic policy measures, such as monetary contraction via increasing interest rates, to cause stagflationary effects in the short run.

In the case of the model used here, no aspects related to economic policies were included, but rather the specification of equation 4 is directed to the analysis of the effects of inflation on the variations in the domestic demand for credit. In this sense, the results obtained emphasize the relevance of another channel through which industrial costs influence inflation: the effect derives from an increase in interest rates caused by an increase in the price of inputs or in wages which in turn raise the price of inputs or wages, leading to an increase in the total demand for credit to finance working capital.

This channel, which shows the influence of costs on the inflation rate, also implies a new source for inflationary inertia. In fact, taking into consideration the characteristics inherent in the determination of nominal wages, which in line with equation 5 are highly dependent on past inflation, an increase in nominal wages has an impact on interest rates, which tend to increase inflation which in turn has a renewed effect on wages, and so on and so forth. The same rationale applies to the price of imported inputs, if real exchange rates are indexed, and consequently import prices depend on inflation. From this standpoint, a new channel is open not only for the direct influence of costs on inflation through demand for credit and interest rates, but also for the role of inertia aspects in the inflationary process.

5.6   Conclusions

This final section summarizes the main conclusions drawn from this chapter.

First, it is worth pointing out that the models estimated in this chapter, can contribute to the explanation of Uruguayan inflation over the period under consideration and over several subperiods characterized by differences in economic policy, and with implications on the pricing mechanisms in the various markets involved.

These models had a level of significance and explanatory power which at least equalled that of several versions of the monetary models applied to the same period (chapters 3 and 4).

In particular, it is interesting to note the special relevance of structural inflation factors, expressed as the variability of relative prices in all estimations. These factors appear to have an impact on the inflationary process, both in the period prior to the liberalization and opening up measures and, in the most recent period, when these policies were implemented.

As stated in the theoretical discussion of the structuralist model, there are three conditions for the existence of structural inflation: 1) inelasticity of the supply of and/or demand for commodities, 2) downward rigidity of some money prices, and 3) a passive money supply. The influence of liberalization and external openness on these conditions may be analysed in a number of ways.

In short, we may assume that supply inelasticities and money price rigidities, the latter associated with the structure of the industrial sector, are particularly important in the context of a closed economy. Regarding the third condition, the passive nature of money supply may be understood differently in a closed economy, such as being caused by distributive conflicts and the pressures they exert on the authorities, the latters' attempt to keep a certain real level of public expenditures, etc.

Although the inelasticity of the supply of certain commodities decreases, it is difficult in the context of an open economy to assert that the downward rigidity of domestic prices, a characteristic of the industrial sector and of the modern services sector, would be substantially altered. Insofar as the international price system itself suffers from such deficiencies, the stronger impact of international prices may fail to correct deficiencies in the price system. This is particularly evident in the volatility of international agricultural price and their incidence on relative prices. Regarding the third condition, the passive nature of money supply, the financial openness of the economy, under conditions associated with the exchange system and the operation of financial markets as those prevailing after the mid 1970s, implies a high degree of endogeneity (chapter 4), which favours the development of structural inflationary tendencies.

Our estimations show that the incidence of these inflationary factors does not seem to have decreased through the extension of the liberalization of domestic markets and openness to international ones. We showed through the various models used, that the influence of structural inflation factors seems to have decreased in the period which, with regard to the economic policy pursued, may be considered intermediate. In fact, in the period from late 1974 to late 1978, when financial liberalization had taken a significant step forward while the openness of the economy and commercial liberalization were still incipient, structural inflation seems to have been lower than in other periods. One possible relationship between the decrease of structural pressures and economic policy might be that while financial openness might imply, through the operation of monetary mechanisms, a parallel evolution of prices of tradables and non–tradables, the control of a high percentage of agricultural prices might prevent internalization of violent fluctuations of international agricultural prices. The result obtained under those circumstances might be a lower variability of relative prices and a weaker indication of the presence of structural inflation factors.

Another interesting aspect of the models used is that of inflationary inertia, which derives from the existence of a mutual relationship between inflation and the growth rate of production costs, derived, in turn, from pricing mechanisms applied to labour and to industrial costs, based in turn on past inflation. There are mainly two cost elements through which the inertia nature of inflation is generated: wages and imported input prices. Through wages via indexation to past inflation and imported input prices via indexation to exchange rates. In the models analyzed in this paper, we only looked at the first of the above aspects. The results obtained from the reduced forms of the structural model and the neostructuralist model indicate a strong inertia component, which reflects the indexation of wages to past inflation.

Although these inertia elements seem to be relevant over the whole period under consideration, their incidence seems to increase in the period after the first quarter of 1985, marking a return to a system where the organizations on the labour market, once again, participate in wage determination, and when there is a change in the general politics of the country. This period, 1985–87, saw a real wage recovery.

A structural model incorporating a simultaneity element in the determination of inflation and the growth rate of nominal wages offered, however, a result which is somewhat different from the one we described in the previous paragraphs. Here, the relationship between wages and inflation is essentially simultaneous, while the relationship of wages to past inflation seems to be lower. This result may be related to the existence of rational expectations among employers, in the context of equilibrium on the labour market. However, this result may also relate to the existence of indexation mechanisms to past inflation, which are sufficiently quick so as not to be captured in quarterly data estimations, and also to deficiencies in the ability of the model to capture the periodization of wage adjustments. Settlement of this point would require a reformulation of some aspects of the model.

Finally, regarding the neostructuralist model, the main conclusion refers to the existence of a positive supply side link between the evolution of financial costs and inflation, the latter operating through the influence of financial costs on the fixprice sector's working capital costs (working capital cost—push effect). Also from a supply side, the evolution of financial costs seems to have had a negative effect on the activity level of this sector.

Another interesting aspect associated with the above is that the financial costs equation of the model, allows us to see the existence of a positive influence on interest rates of wages and imported inputs prices, through the incidence of the former on the internal demand for credit.

This relationship between industrial costs and interest rates is, together with the working capital cost—push effect, another channel through which inertia elements may appear in the inflationary process. In fact, while industrial costs are indexed, their effect on interest rates and consequently on inflation, is once again via the price of inputs.

In debates on inflation, and particularly on the inflationary process of Latin America, the presence of structural and inertia elements in such processes as already noted is particularly important in the design of stabilization policies. In fact, current orthodox anti—inflationary measures, comprising a reduction of fiscal deficits and a contraction of money aggregates, lose, when faced with these elements, parts of their efficiency as stabilization policy. It is worth noting three particular aspects:

1) The existence of structural inflationary pressures, due to the variability of relative prices, leads in the long run to the inefficiency of contractive monetary measures, if they are not complemented by measures destined to correct the structural causes of the deficiencies of the price system. In the short run, this may imply that orthodox stabilization programs, as they fail to deal with structural pressures, will lead to a contraction of the activity level of the system.

2) This last point is particularly dependent on the existence of inertia elements in inflation, which are due to the indexation mechanisms prevailing in the economy. This implies that monetary adjustments would tend to have a large impact on the activity level, unless measures to reduce indexation are taken.

3) Finally, from the standpoint of the working capital cost—push effect model, monetary restriction measures would not only be unable to reduce the inflationary pressure without leading to a large reduction in the activity level, but would also, in the short run, have an inflationary effect, which would operate through an increase in corporate financial costs.

Notes

1. All the approaches we consider share a basic assumption, namely that the general price level depends on particular features of pricing in the various sectors and on the relationships existing among them. This is an essential difference in comparison to the monetary approach, which isolates the determination of the absolute price level from the particular conditions of the various markets, the latter only having an impact on relative prices.

2. In this paper we restrict the analysis of the features of semi—industrial

economies to those which we consider central to the origin of inflationary effects and with a specific significance to the case under analysis. Bruno (1979) and Taylor (1981, 1983) undertake a more general analysis of these features and their consequences on the short term macro economic equilibrium.

3. This financial costs function implies an open economy where money supply is endogenous and there does not exist, at least in the short term, a perfect substitution between local and external credit.

4. In the models using the dependent lagged variable as an explanatory variable, the Durbin–Watson test results are asymptotically biased towards the acceptance of the non–autocorrelation hypothesis. An alternative test, which performs better in large samples, is the Durbin–H test whose form is

$$h = \hat{p}\sqrt{\frac{T}{1+Tv}}$$

where $\hat{p}$ is the estimated first order autocorrelation coefficient, T is the total number of observations and v is the variance of the ordinary least squares estimator of the parameter of the lagged dependent variable. Given that this test performs best in large samples, it is calculated in estimations made for over twenty–five observations, insofar as that is possible (namely, when $Tv(1)$). In estimations using smaller samples, the Durbin–Watson test is more reliable.

5. When creating the IMPOPR variable, we were forced to quarterize the annual series of the imported commodities US Dollar price index for the period II/1972.

6. This model was also estimated using, instead of this variable, the growth rate of imported inputs local currency price index for the period II/1972, for which this series is available.

7. With a view to determine the homogeneity property of the equations comprised in this model in a systematic way, we may apply a likelihood ratio test to each of them. It was not possible to calculate these tests and consequently, all considerations regarding the homogeneity of the equations were made on a purely intuitive basis in line with the value of the addition of their parameters.

131

6 Conclusions

We have in this study analysed the causes of inflation in Uruguay. Major questions that have been raised in the Latin American debate on inflation, and which have guided us in our work, concern the endogeneity vs exogeneity of money supply, the degree of flexibility in the price structure, and the balance between supply and demand policies to fight inflation. We have used monetarist, structuralist and neostructuralist approaches to analyse these issues, and we have paid particular attention to the effect of different systems of external economic relations.

The main approach used was to deduce from theoretical models reduced forms for the rate of inflation and then to estimate these relations for different external regimes.

The first model applied was a monetarist one with exogenous money supply, that is a model that was originally developed for a closed economy. Within this model we first investigated the stability of the velocity of money. We found that it was constant in the long term, but that it became unstable in the short term after the mid 1970s, when the economy was opened up. Then the public could induce changes in money supply by altering their foreign reserves. Money supply thus became endogenous after the mid 1970s. We find for this period, however, a stable relationship between M3, which includes foreign reserves, and inflation.

Application of Friedman's model with adaptive expectations gave relatively poor results, especially for the period after 1975. No significant results with regard to the short term effects of unpredicted monetary growth were obtained.

We also tested the Natural Rate of Unemployment Hypothesis and found some support for this, namely that the activity level is independent of monetary measures once expectations of agents are realized. Tests of Lucas' model suggested that most of nominal demand variations transfer to inflation already during the first year. These two tests suggests that inflation and output are not only independent in the long run, but that their short term relationship is also weak.

There was some evidence on real wage changes, which suggested that the monetarist model might not be applicable during the period. When we interpreted the data in terms of a disequilibrium model, we got results that suggested that due to excess supply of labour effective demand changes did have an impact on output.

The results we have reported so far come from analyses with models of an essentially closed economy character, and for the period after the mid 1970s this did not fit the facts. Therefore, we instead applied models for an open economy, which distinguish between tradables and non–tradables.

The standard model for an open economy with non–tradables generally gave significant explanations of inflation. We found that in the relatively closed economy period up to 1974 it is the ex ante domestic credit market imbalance which is the most important determinant of inflation, while the importance of external inflation and changes in the exchange rate increased in importance when the economy was opened. The balance of payments model was more significant after the mid 70s, as one would expect, when the balance of payments became more sensitive to domestic ex ante imbalances in the money market.

However, the theory also predicts that with a floating exchange rate the economy can be insulated from external monetary disturbances, and thereby monetary policy would again be effective. We found, however, no evidence that the shift towards more flexible exchange rates led to a greater scope for monetary policy. The failure of the model, in this respect may be due to differences between our assumptions and reality. It is, for example, assumed that prices are equalized internationally, but this was obviously not the case, for example, for the real interest rate. This credit market may explain why the exchange rate did not adjust smoothly enough to changes in domestic credit to eliminate the effect on foreign reserves.

In the alternative model, where we allowed for the possibility of real imbalances, we found that flow imbalances in the money market had some effects until the mid 1970s, when the restrictions on international capital transfers were removed. Expectations about non–tradables prices then adjusted more rapidly, and flow equilibrium seems to have prevailed even in the short run. We found that expectations about non–tradables prices had a separate effect on both inflation and the balance of payments apart from the effect of the growth rate of domestic credit on real output. The major result was that the openness of the economy accelerated the rate of adjustment in the money market.

Some results obtained, suggested a need for an analysis of relative price changes, which could not be undertaken in our monetarist models. Therefore, a few structuralist and disequilibrium approaches were tried. In the estimates of the basic structural model we got a highly significant coefficient for the growth of the price of agricultural products, which suggests that structural factors may have had a considerable impact on inflation. We also estimated a simultaneous structural model, where also the present rate of inflation affects the growth of wages. The results were similar to those obtained from the reduced form.

We finally estimated a neostructuralist or working capital cost push model. It was here shown that higher interest rates had a positive effect on inflation and a negative one on output. Monetary contraction, leading to higher interest rates may thus lead to stagflation.

We conclude that the structuralist models have a good explanatory power and suggest that also relative price shifts had an effect on inflation both before and after the liberalization. It seems as if the structural factors were less important between 1974 and 1978, because the increased openness was combined with control of agricultural prices.

Another result was that there seemed to be considerable inertia in inflation due to indexation of wages to past inflation. This was particularly pronounced after 1985 when a conscious real wage recovery policy was pursued.

The conclusion from the analysis of the structuralist models is that failure to deal with supply side imperfections may mean that orthodox stabilization measures may cause economic contraction. This is particularly likely where there exist indexation mechanisms in the economy. It is even possible that prices may increase due to the working capital cost–push effect.

As we have seen in our analyses all three approaches pursued do seem to explain to some extent, the process of inflation in Uruguay. Ideally one would have liked to test explicitly the different models against each others, but this has not been possible. The results with regard to their relative explanatory power are not clearcut. The models, to some extent, fit different periods more or less well, but it is impossible to say that one model clearly dominates the others.

Can we then come up with a synthesis of the different models? It seems as if all of them do contribute something to the explanation of inflation in Uruguay and some model elements of course appear in several models. It does not seem possible to reject outright either the neoclassically oriented approaches or the structuralist approach. The main question is rather where it is most fruitful to put the emphasis. We do not believe that it is possible to give a final answer to this question here. We have to be content with having identified some interesting regularities in the process of inflation in Uruguay.

Bibliography

Anichini, J. et al. (1978), La politica comercial y la protección en el Uruguay, Banco Central del Uruguay, Montevideo.

Astori, D. (1981), Tendencias recientes de la economía uruguaya, Fondo de Cultura Economica – CIEDUR, Montevideo.

Astori, D. et al. (1982), Cuatro respuestas a la crisis, Ediciones de la Banca Oriental, Montevideo.

Aukrust, O. (1977), 'Inflation in the Open Economy; A Norwegian Model', in Worldwide inflation. Theory and recent experience, The Brooking Institution, Washington D.C.

Banco Central del Uruguay (1984), Aranceles, moneda y precios, Banco Central del Uruguay, Montevideo.

Barro, R.J. (1977), 'Unanticipated money growth and unemployment in the United States', Journal of Political Economy, 62(4).

Barro, R.J. (1978), 'Unanticipated money, output, and the price level in the United States', Journal of Political Economy, 86(4).

Barro, R.J. and Grossman, H. (1971), 'A general disequilibrium model for income and unemployment', American Economic Review, 61.

Barro, R.J. and Grossman, H. (1976), Money, employment and inflation, Cambridge University Press, Cambridge.

Bension, A. and Caumont, J. (1979), Politica económica y distribución del ingreso en el Uruguay, 1970–1976, Acali Editorial, Montevideo.

Blejer, M. (1977), 'The short run dynamics of price and the balance of payments', American Economic Review, 67(3).

Blejer, M. and Leiderman, L. (1981); 'A monetary approach to the crawling–peg system: theory and evidence', Journal of Political Economy, 89(1)

Blinder, A.J. and Solow, R.M. (1974), 'Analytical foundations of fiscal policy'. in Economics of Public Finance, Brookings Institution, Washington DC.

Branson, W.H.(1975), 'Monetarist and Kenynesian Models of the Transmission of Inflation', American Economic Review, 65(2).

Brunner, K. and Meltzer, A.H. (1972), 'Friedman's monetary theory', Journal of

Political Economy, 80(5).

Bruno, M. (1977), 'Price and Adjustment. Micro Foundations and Macro Theory', Harvard Institute of Economic Research, Discussion Paper no 534, Cambridge, Mass.

Bruno, M. (1979), 'Stabilization and Stagflation in a Semi–Industrialized Economy', in Dornbusch and Frenkel (eds).

Bruno, M. and Sussman, Z. (1979), 'Exchange–rate flexibility, inflation, and structural change. Israel under alternative regimes', Journal of Development Economics, 6(4).

Buffie, E.F. (1984), 'Financial Repression, the New Structuralists, and Stabilization Policy in Semi–Industrializaed Economies', Journal of Development Economics,14.

Calmfors, L. (1977), 'Inflation in Sweden', in Krause , Salant (eds)

Canavese, A.J. (1982), 'The Structuralist Explanation in the Theory of Inflation', World Development, 10(7).

Cancela, W., Alberti, J.P. (1987), 'Inflación y estabilidad', seminario "Uruguay 88", Instituto de Economía – FESUR – CEPAL – Banco Central, Montevideo.

Castel, P., Forteza, A. and Vaillant, M. (1989), 'Relaciones entre el nivel de actividad y el comercio exterior', mimeo., Universidad de la República, Montevideo

Cervantes Islas, J. (1985), 'La inflación en dos marcos cambiarios: el caso de seis países latinoamericanos en el período 1960–1980', Centro de Estudios Monetarios Latinoamericanos, Nr. 2, Mexico D.F.

CIEDUR (1980), 'La inflación uruguaya. Consecuencia necesaria, proceso incontrolable o instrumento deliberado?', seminario "El Uruguay en los 70", CIEDUR, Montevideo.

Claassen, E. Salin, P. (eds) (1976), Recent issues in international monetary economics, North Holland, Amsterdam

Cline, W.R. Weintraub, S. (eds) (1981), Economic Stabilization in Developing Countries, The Brookings Institution, Washington, D.C.

Corbo, V. (1985), 'International prices, wages and inflation in an open economy: a chilean model', Review of Economics and Statistics, 67(4).

Diaz, R.(1987), 'Inflación y políticas de estabilización en 1987–88', seminario "Uruguay 88", Instituto de Economía – FESUR – CEPAL – Banco Central, Montevideo.

Dornbusch, R. (1973), 'Devaluation, money and non–traded good', American Economic Review, 63(5).

Dornbusch, R. (1976), 'Capital mobility, flexible exchange rates and macroeconomic equilibrium', in Claassen, Salin (eds.).

Dornbusch, R. (1980), Open macroeconomics, Basic Books, New York.

Dornbusch, R. (1981), 'Exchange rate rules and macoreconomic stability', in Exchange rate rules. The theory, performance and prospects of the crawling peg, Macmillan, London and Basingstoke.

Dornbusch, R. (1982), 'PPP exchange–rate rules and macroeconomic stability', Journal of Political Economy, 90(1).

Dornbusch. R. Frenkel, J.A. (eds) (1979), International Economic Policy. Theory and Evidence, Johns Hopkins University Press, Baltimore.

Edgren, G. et al. (1970), Lönebildning och samhällsekonomi, Raben & Sjögren, Stockholm.

Facultad de Ciencias Económicas y Administración (1977), Plan nacional de desarrollo, Montevideo.

Faroppa, L et al. (1974), Cuatro tesis sobre la situacion económica nacional, Colegio de Doctores en Ciencias Económicas y Contadores del Uruguay – Fundacíon de Cultura Universitaria, Montevideo.

Fernandez, R.B. (1979), 'Dinero y precios: su interrelación en el corto plazo', Ensayos Económicos, Banco Central de la República Argentina, No.12.

Fernandez Vaccaro, P. (1978), La economía uruguaya en el quinquenio 1973–78, Alcali Editorial, Montevideo.

Ffrench–Davis, R. (1983), 'El experimento monetarista en Chile: una sintesis crítica', Desarrollo Económico, 23 (90).

Fomby, T.B., Carter Hill, R., Johnson, S.R. (1984), Advanced Econometric Methods, Springer Verlag New York Inc, New York.

Foxley, A. (1981), 'Southern Cone Stability', in Cline, Weintraub (eds).

Frenkel, J. (1976), 'Adjustment mechanisms and the monetary approach to the balance of payments: a doctrinal perspective', in Claassen, Salin (eds).

Frenkel, R. (1979), 'Decisiones de precio en alta inflación', Estudios CEDES, 2(3), Buenos Aires.

Frenkel, R. (1981), 'Mercado financiero, expectativas cambiarias y movimientos de capital', Estudios CEDES, 4(3), Buenos Aires.

Frenkel, R. (1983), 'La Dinamica de los Precios Industriales en la Argentina 1966–1982. Un Estudio Econométrico', Estudios CEDES, Buenos Aires.

Frenkel, R. (1984), Inflación y Salario Real. Capitulo 2: La Dinámica de los Salarios Nominales 1975–1982, mimeo., CEDES, Buenos Aires.

Frenkel, R. (1986), 'Salarios e inflación en América Latina. Resultados de investigaciones recientes en la Argentina, Brasil, Colombia, Costa Rica y Chile', Desarrollo Economico, 25(100).

Frenkel, J. et al. (1980), 'A synthesis of monetary and keynesian approaches to short–run balance–of–payments theory', Economic Journal, 90.

Frenkel, J. and Johnson, H.(eds.), (1976), The Monetary Approach to the Balance of Payments, George Allen & Unwin, London.

Frenkel, J. and Mussa, M. (1985), 'Asset Makets, Exchange Rates, and the Balance of Payments', in Jones and Kenen (eds).

Frenkel, R. and Fanelli, J.M. (1987), El plan Austral: un año y medio despues, mimeo., CEDES, Buenos Aires.

Friedman, M. (1968), 'The role of monetary policy', American Economic Review, 58(1).

Friedman, M. (1970), 'A theoretical framework for monetary analysis', Journal of Political Economy, 78(2).

Friedman, M. (1971), 'A monetary theory of national income', Journal of Political Economy, 79(2).

Friedman, M. (1972), 'Comments on the critics', Journal of Political Economy, 80(5).

Frisch, H. (1977), 'Inflation theory 1963–1975: a second generation's survey', Journal of Economic Literature, 15(4).

Frischknecht, F. (1979), PLANEC XVII. Modelo dinámico estructural de planeamiento económico, Facultad de Ciencias Económicas de la Universidad de Buenos Aires, Buenos Aires.

Giorgi, E. (1987), 'Uruguays inflationsprocess: En empirisk analys av dess orsaker i en monetaristisk inflationsmodell med exogent penningutbud', mimeo., Economics Department, Gothenburg University.

Giorgi, E. (1988), 'Inflation och betalningsbalans i en monetaristisk modell för en liten öppen ekonomi. Fallet Uruguay 1956–1985', mimeo., Economics Department, Gothenburg Unviersity.

Giorgi, E. (1989), 'La inflación uruguaya en una perspectiva no monetaria. Un estudio empírico del período 1963–1987', in Uruguay '89. La coyuntura económica nacional regional e internactional. Tomo II, Instituto de Economia, FESUR, Montevideo

Gordon, R.J. (1976), 'Recent developments in the theory of inflation and unemployment', Journal of Monetary Economics, April.

Gordon, R.J. (1981), 'Output fluctuations and gradual price adjustment', Journal of Economic Literature, 19(2).

Graziani, C. (1985), Producto, inflación y política monetaria: algunas estimaciones para el caso de Uruguay, Seleccion de Temas, Nr. 25, Banco Central del Uruguay, Montevideo.

Griffin, K. (ed) (1971), Financing development in Latin America, Macmillan & San Martin's Press.

Grunwald, J. (1963), 'La escuela estructuralista. Estabilizacion de precios y desarrollo económico. El caso chileno', in Hirschman (ed).

Hanson, J.A. (1980), 'The short–run relation between growth and inflation in Latin America: a quasi–rational or consistent expectations approach', American Economic Review, 70(5).

Harberger, A.C. (1979), Una visión moderna del fenomeno inflacionario, Selección de Temas, Nr. 6, Banco Central del Uruguay, Montevideo.

Heymann, D. (1986), 'Inflación y Políticas de Estabilizacion', Revista de la CEPAL, no 28.

Hirschman, A.O. (ed) (1963), Controversia sobre Latinoamerica, Ediciones del Instituto, Buenos Aires.

Instituto de Economía, (1971), El proceso económico del Uruguay. Contribución al estudio de su evolución y perspectivas, Departamento de Publicaciones de la Universidad de la Republica, Montevideo.

Instituto de Economía, (1971), 'El fin de la estabilización', Estudios y Coyuntura, nr.2, Fundación de Cultura Universitaria, Montevideo.

Instituto de Economía, (1973), 'Un reajuste conservador', Estudios y Coyuntura, Nr.3, Fundación de Cultura Universitaria.

Johnson, H.G., (1972), Inflation and the monetarist controversy, North Holland, Amsterdam–London.

Johnson, H.G. (1972), Further essays in monetary economics, George Allen & Unwin Ltd., London.

Jones, R.W. Kenen, P.B. (eds) (1985), Handbook of international economics, Vol. 2, North–Holland, Amsterdam.

Kamas, L. (1986), 'The balance of payments offset to monetary policy: monetarist, portfolio balance and Keynesian estimates for Mexico and Venezuela', Journal of Money, Credit, and Banking, 18(4).

Kenen, P.B. (1985), 'Macroeconomic theory and policy: how the closed economy was opened' in Jones, Kenen (eds).

Kierzkowski, H. (1976), 'Theoretical foundations of the Scandinavian models of inflation', Manchester School, September 1976.

Kirkpatrick, C.H. and Nixson, F.I. (1976), 'The origins of inflation in less developed countries: a selective review', in Livingstone (ed).

Kmenta, J. (1971), Elements of Econometrics, Macmillan, New York.

Krause, L., Salant, W.S. (eds), (1977), Woldwide inflation. Theory and recent experience, Brookings Institution, Washington D.C.

Laidler, D.E.W. (1975), Essays on money and inflation, University of Chicago Press, Chicago.

Leiderman, L. (1979), 'Expectations and output–inflation trade–off in a fixed–exchange–rate economy', Journal of Political Economy, 87(6).

Levich, R.M. (1985), 'Empirical studies of exchange rates: price behavior, rate determination and market efficiency', in Jones, Kenen (eds).

Licandro, O. (1987), 'Uruguay: un modele de déséquilibre du marché du travail', mimeo.,Université Catholique de Louvain, August.

Little, I.M.D. (1982), Economic development. Theory, policy and international relations, Basic Books, New York.

Livingstone, I. (ed), Development Economics and Policy: Readings, George Allen & Unwin, London.

Lopes, F.L. Bacha, E. (1983), 'Inflation, Growth and Wage Policy. A Brazilian Perxpective', Journal of Development Economics, 13.

Lucas, R.E. Jr. (1972), 'Expectations and the neutrality of money', Journal of Economic Theory, 4(2).

Lucas, R.E. Jr. (1973), 'Some international evidence on output–inflation trade off', American Economic Review, 63(3).

Lucas, R.E. Jr. (1975), 'An equilibrium model of the business cycle', Journal of Political Economy, 83(6).

Lybeck, J. (1978), Konjunkturer och svensk ekonomisk politik, Raben & Sjögren,

Nacka.

Macadar, L. (1982), 'Uruguay 1974–1980: un nuevo ensayo de reajuste económico?', CINVE, Ediciones de la Banda Oriental, Montevideo.

Marston, R.C. (1985), 'Stabilization policies in open economies' in Jones, Kenen (eds.).

Modigliani, F. (1977), 'The monetarist controversy or, should we forsake stabilization policies', American Economic Review, March 1977.

Noguez, R.E. (1979), 'Bases tentativas para la preparación de un modelo explicativo del proceso inflacionario uruguayo (periodo 1968–1977)', Seleccion de Temas, Nr.8, Banco Central del Uruguay, Montevideo.

Notaro, J. (1984), La politica económica en el Uruguay 1968–1984, CIEDUR–Ediciones de la Banda Oriental, Montevideo.

Obstfeld, M. (1985), 'Exchange–rate dynamics', in Jones, Kenen (eds).

Olivera, J. (1960), 'La teoria no monetaria de la inflación', El Trimestre Economico, 27(4).

Olivera, J. (1964), 'On structural inflation and American "structuralism"' Oxford Economic Papers, 16.

Olivera, J. (1967), 'Aspects Dinámicos de la Inflación Estructural', Desarrollo Economico, 7(27).

Olivera, J. (1979), 'On structural stagflation', Journal of Development Economics, 6.

Phelps, E.S. (1979), Studies in macroeconomic theory. Volume 1. Employment and inflation, Academic Press, New York.

Pinto, A. (1960), 'Estabilidad y desarrollo: metas incompatibles o complementarias', El Trimestre Economico, April–Juny 1960.

Pinto, A. (1963), 'El analisis de la inflación: estructuralistas y monetaristas; un recuento', Revista de Economia Latinoamericana, 2nd semester of 1963.

Pinto, A. (1968), 'Raices estructurales de la inflación en America Latina', El Trimestre Economico, 35(1).

Porter, R.C., Ranney, S.I. (1982), 'An Eclectic Model of Recent LDC Macroeconomic Policy Analysis, World Development, 10(9)

Prebisch, R. (1961), 'El falso dilema entre desarrollo económico y estabilidad monetaria', Boletín Económico de America Latina, 6(1).

Protasi, J.C. and Graziani, C. (1984), 'Determinantes de la demanda de dinero en el Uruguay', in Premio Banco Central de economía, año 1981, tema: determinantes de la demanda de dinero en el Uruguay, Banco Central del Uruguay, Montevideo.

Rama, M. (1986), 'Recesión y reactivación: problemas de oferta o insuficiencia de demanda?', Suma, 1(1), pp. 97–128, CINVE, Montevideo, October.

Rama, M. (1987), La regla cambiaria, la regla salarial y el comportamiento inflacionario de la economia uruguaya, seminario "Uruguay 88", Instituto de Economia – FESUR – CEPAL – Banco Central, Montevideo.

Rana, P.B. and Dowling, J.M. Jr. (1985), 'Inflationary effects of small but continuous changes in effective exchange rates: nine Asian LDCs', Review of Economics and Statistics, 67(3).

Rodriguez, O. (1981), La teoría del subdesarrollo de la CEPAL, Siglo Veintiuno Editores S.A., Mexico D.C.

Sagari Suarez, S. and Ramos Carbajales, A. (1984), 'La demanda de dinero: el caso uruguayo', in Premio Banco Central de economía, año 1981, tema: determinantes de la demanda de dinero en el Uruguay, Banco Central del Uruguay, Montevideo.

Santomero, A.M. and Seater, J.J. (1978), 'The inflation–unemployment trade–off: a critique of the literature', Journal of Economic Literature, 16(2).

Sargent, T.J. (1986), Rational expectations and inflation, Harper & Row, London.

Sargent, T.J. and Wallace, N. (1973), 'Rational expectations and the dynamics of hyperinflation', International Economic Review, 14.

Sargent, T.J., Wallace, N. (1976), 'Rational Expectations and the Theory of Economic Policy', Journal of Monetary Economics, April.

Seers, D. (1962), 'A Theory of Inflation and Growth in Underdeveloped Economies Based on the Experience of Latin America', Oxford Economic Papers, 16.

Seers, D., (1963), 'La teoria de la inflación y el crecimiento en las economías subdesarrolladas: la experiencia latinoamericana', El Trimestre Economico, July–September

Sheeney, E.J., (1984), 'Money and Output in Latin America. Some Tests of a Rational Expectations Approach', Journal of Development Economics, 14.

Steigum, E. Jr (1980), 'Keynesian and classical unemployment in an open economy', Scandinavian Journal of Economics.

Sunkel, O. (1958), 'La inflación Chilena un Enfoque Heterodoxo', El Trimestre Economico, 25(4).

Swoboda, A.K. (1976), 'Monetary Approaches to Balance–of–Payments Theory', in Claasen, Salin (eds).

Taylor, L. (1981), 'IS/LM in the Tropics: Diagrammatics of the New Structuralist Macro Critique', in Cline, Weintraub (eds).

Taylor, L. (1983), Structuralist Macroeconomics. Applicable Models for the Third World, Basic Books, New York

Thorp, R., 'Inflation and the Financing of Economic Development', in Griffin (ed).

Torres, G. (1979), 'Politicas antiinflacionarias en el Uruguay (1955–1977)', Investigaciones, (7), CLAEH, Montevideo.

van Wijnbergen, S. (1982), 'Stagflationary Effects of Monetary Stabilization Policies. A Quantitative Analysis of South Korea', Journal of Development Economics, 10.

van Wijnbergen, S. (1983), 'Credit Policy, Inflation and Growth in a Financially Repressed Economy', Journal of Development Economics, 13.

van Wijnbergen, S. (1986), 'Exchange Rate Management and Stabilization Policies in Developing Countries', Journal of Development Economics, 23.

Whitman, M. (1975), Global Monetarism and the Monetary Approach to the Balance of Payments, Brookings Paper on Economic Activity, 3.